Ravi Mendis

KU-685-090

WebObjects®
Developer's
Guide

SAMS

201 West 103rd Street, Indianapolis, Indiana 46290

WebObjects Developer's Guide

Copyright © 2002 by Sams Publishing

All rights reserved. No part of this book shall be reproduced, stored in a retrieval system, or transmitted by any means, electronic, mechanical, photocopying, recording, or otherwise, without written permission from the publisher. No patent liability is assumed with respect to the use of the information contained herein. Although every precaution has been taken in the preparation of this book, the publisher and author assume no responsibility for errors or omissions. Nor is any liability assumed for damages resulting from the use of the information contained herein.

International Standard Book Number: 0-672-32326-5

Library of Congress Catalog Card Number: 2001096693

Printed in the United States of America

First Printing: June 2002

05   04   03   02   4   3   2   1

Trademarks

All terms mentioned in this book that are known to be trademarks or service marks have been appropriately capitalized. Sams Publishing cannot attest to the accuracy of this information. Use of a term in this book should not be regarded as affecting the validity of any trademark or service mark.

WebObjects is a trademark of Apple Computer, Inc. in the U.S. and other countries.

Warning and Disclaimer

Every effort has been made to make this book as complete and as accurate as possible, but no warranty or fitness is implied. The information provided is on an "as is" basis.

Acquisitions Editors
Patricia Barnes
Betsy Brown

Development Editor
Damon E. Jordan

Managing Editor
Charlotte Clapp

Project Editor
George E. Nedeff

Copy Editor
Chip Gardner

Indexer
Sandy Henselmeier

Proofreader
Jody Larsen

Technical Editor
Bill Bumgarner

Team Coordinator
Amy Patton

Multimedia Developer
Dan Scherf

Interior Designer
Gary Adair

Cover Designer
Alan Clements

Page Layout
Michelle Mitchell

Contents at a Glance

Table of Contents

About the Author

Ravi Mendis is an international consultant based in the United Kingdom who specializes in WebObjects application development. He has worked in the UK, Switzerland, the Netherlands, Malaysia, and New Zealand for companies such as Apple Computer, American Management Systems, AIG, and IBM.

He is the principle architect and developer of SVGObjects, a framework for delivering data-driven graphics for WebObjects. Mendis also authors a series of articles on how to use WebObjects to implement new interfaces, interactivity, graphics, and print with Trapeze and SVG on www.svgobjects.com.

Most notably in the past, Mendis has been instrumental in delivering a content management system for www.btcellnet.net working aside Traffic Interactive, in the UK—a London-based new media company.

A graduate of Oxford University in Mathematics, Mendis is currently pursuing an MSc in Mathematical Logic and Computation at the University of Manchester in the UK.

He can be contacted at http://www.svgobjects.com or rmendis@mac.com.

Dedication

To Keith, Ian, and my father.

Acknowledgments

First and foremost I would like to thank my friends and family in Sri Lanka and England for putting up with my antisocial behavior during the writing of this book. Special mention goes to Ronnie for his understanding and for giving me the time and space I needed to write this book. I love you.

Next, I would like to thank those people who have been a true inspiration and encouragement in my life. I am eternally indebted to the Masters of Rugby School for their faith, understanding, and friendship. It has truly shaped my life. In particular I would like to thank Rev. Keith Lanyon-Jones and my housemaster Mr. Ian Graham to whom I dedicate the book.

Last and by no means least, I would like to thank the team at Sams Publishing for making this a really remarkable experience. Writing this book has been a labor of love. It's been exhilarating and exhausting at the same time. I cannot thank you more. Patricia, Betsy, Damon, Chip, George, Carol, Amy, and the tech editors Max and Bill have been an excellent team to work with. There has been a clear demonstration of intelligence, patience, good manner, and great teamwork. Thank you.

We Want to Hear from You!

As the reader of this book, *you* are our most important critic and commentator. We value your opinion and want to know what we're doing right, what we could do better, what areas you'd like to see us publish in, and any other words of wisdom you're willing to pass our way.

You can email or write me directly to let me know what you did or didn't like about this book—as well as what we can do to make our books stronger.

Please note that I cannot help you with technical problems related to the topic of this book, and that due to the high volume of mail I receive, I might not be able to reply to every message.

When you write, please be sure to include this book's title and author as well as your name and phone or email address. I will carefully review your comments and share them with the author and editors who worked on the book.

Email: webdev@samspublishing.com

Mail: Mark Taber
            Associate Publisher
            Sams Publishing
            201 West 103rd Street
            Indianapolis, IN 46290 USA

Reader Services

For more information about this book or others from Sams Publishing, visit our Web site at www.samspublishing.com. Type the ISBN (excluding hyphens) or the title of the book in the Search box to find the book you're looking for.

Introduction

As recently as a year or two ago, Web publishers and New Media shops typically charged with developing and maintaining (static) content for the Web have been challenged with producing database-driven, dynamic content—from questionnaires and forms to online stores.

The contracts for these projects were no longer being exclusively awarded to IT services companies such as EDS, IBM, and Cap Gemini.

As the Internet became more pervasive, demand for dynamic, data-driven Web sites increased. Larger publishing outfits were beginning to win the bids for these contracts.

As a result, we have seen New Media developers—HTML "coders" start to learn technologies such as Perl and PHP, even though many of these techniques and languages are complex and difficult to use.

New Media and Publishing shops were in dire need of solutions that were simple yet powerful enough to challenge those offered by the IT services companies.

To those developers, many of whom are Mac users, WebObjects, another product of Apple Computer, offers itself as a solution to this problem. It provides an opportunity to make developing dynamic or database-driven sites easy (or easier at the very least).

I hope to demonstrate with this book that WebObjects really is a toolkit "for the rest of us."

What Is WebObjects?

WebObjects is a best-of-breed, object-oriented platform for developing Web applications. Nowadays it is often compared to PHP, JSP (Java Server Pages), and ASP (Active Server Pages). However, more appropriate comparisons ought to be made to IBM's WebSphere, Oracle's Application Server, and BEA Systems' WebLogic.

It is an enterprise-class solution, therefore its clientele includes Fortune 500 companies such as Disney, Adobe, BBC, and AIG to name a few.

WebObjects 5 is an overhaul of the Objective-C WebObjects legacy—a rewrite in 100% Pure Java.

Apart from other things, this is the first version to run on a Mac OS client.

Who Is This Book For?

The book is primarily intended for the Web Developer with knowledge of HTML, Java, and some SQL (very little, though). Knowledge of object-oriented techniques will help greatly.

Developers who have been introduced to WebObjects should benefit the most from the book. However, this is not a prerequisite.

It is my intention that those just beginning with WebObjects will be able to follow through the material as well.

How to Use This Book

The book requires active participation; it is not bedtime reading, but very much hands-on.

If you are new to WebObjects, you will get the most out of the book by following the tasks and examples along with the text. If, on the other hand, you are familiar with WebObjects, be selective about the chapters and sections you pursue.

The focus of the first few chapters is on WebObjects, its concepts and paradigm. The final chapters serve as an introduction to Enterprise Objects and focuses on object modeling and designing database-driven sites.

As a guide to readers new and experienced alike, I'd recommend following Part I as far as possible. If and when you feel like a change of direction, move onto Part II.

Aim of the Book

I hope this book will demystify WebObjects and help to dispel the misconception that WebObjects is an obscure and sometimes difficult technology to use.

1

A WebObjects Primer

"How many times have I said use the right tool for the right job!"

—*Scotty from Star Trek V: Final Frontier*

This chapter is a gentle introduction to WebObjects and its tools. We are going to lay the groundwork for subsequent chapters by creating the fabled "Hello World" application.

Developers who are already familiar with WebObjects, or who have already created their first application (or two) can proceed onto the next chapter.

Throughout this chapter, you might find ideas and concepts on which you would like a more thorough explanation. For more resources, please visit Apple's WebObjects Developer's site at `http://developer.apple.com/techpubs/webobjects/`.

Creating A New Project

Launch `ProjectBuilder.app` from */Developer/Applications/*.

This is WebObjects main IDE tool. As you will soon discover, this is where you'll edit your code, organize your project, and build, debug, and run your application.

FIGURE 1.1   Launch Project Builder.

Setting Up a New Project with the Assistant

Choose *File, New Project...*, from the Project Builder's menu bar.

> **NOTE**
>
> The very first time you run Project Builder you will see its Setup Assistant. If you do, accept the default options it presents and move on to the next step. You might reconfigure these later, when you become more familiar with the tool.

You should now see the New Project Assistant, as in Figure 1.2.

1. Choose the *WebObjects Application* project type.

2. Click *Next* to proceed to the panel in Figure 1.3.

3. Enter Hello in the *Project Name* field.

4. Choose or enter a location for the project in the *Location* field. You can choose a suitable location to navigate to a folder or place by using the *Set...* button.

5. Click *Finish* to create the new project.

> **NOTE**
>
> If in doubt, locate the project in your Documents folder, *~/Documents/*

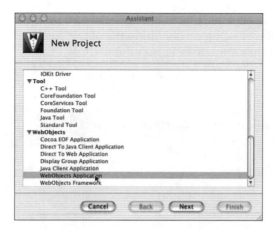

FIGURE 1.2   Choose WebObjects Application from the New Project Assistant.

FIGURE 1.3   Enter a project name.

Finally, the project window for the Hello application should appear, as shown in Figure 1.1.

Editing Component Source in Project Builder

In the *Groups & Files* panel, navigate to the Main.wo component located under the *Web Components, Main* group.

Instead of Double-clicking Main.wo to open it in WebObjects Builder, click the triangle to the left of it to view its contents in Project Builder.

You will see the two files: Main.html and Main.wod. Main.html is the HTML template and Main.wod is the WebObjects definition file of the component. Select the Main.html to edit the template in Project Builder:

```
<!DOCTYPE HTML PUBLIC "-//W3C//DTD HTML 3.2//EN">
<HTML>
    <HEAD>
        <META NAME="generator" CONTENT="WebObjects 5">
        <TITLE>Untitled</TITLE>
    </HEAD>
    <BODY BGCOLOR=#FFFFFF>
    </BODY>
</HTML>
```

Within the <BODY...> and </BODY> tags type the text Hello. In addition, replace the Untitled document title to Hello World.

So far, we have made simple textual changes to the HTML template. There is nothing dynamic about it just yet. However, when we build and run the application we'll start looking at making some dynamic enhancements to the component.

Choose *File, Save* to save the changes, and then build and run the application.

Build and Run an Application

1. To build an application, click the icon labeled *Build* in the project toolbar. Alternatively, choose *Build, Build* from the Project Builder's menu.

NOTE

When building you will notice scrolls of output in the build panel. Errors will be displayed in the top half of the panel. On this occasion, however, there should not to be any errors, therefore you can continue running the application.

2. Running an application is similar. Click the icon labeled *Run,* or, *Debug, Run Executable* from the Project Builder menu.

NOTE

Running a WebObjects application will automatically launch a client in your default Web browser. This might take a few minutes.

3. Finally, you should see something similar to Figure 1.4.

FIGURE 1.4   Hello World.

Marking Up HTML in WebObjects Builder

In this section, we are going to experiment with making the Main component dynamic.

Using WOString

Double-click `Main.wo` in *Web Components, Main* in the Project Builder's *Groups & Files* panel. This will open it in the WebObjects Builder, the visual HTML component editor.

Select the *Hello* text and replace it with a WOString. You do this by choosing *WebObjects, WOString* from the WebObjects Builder menu. Alternatively, click the WOString icon in the toolbar, as shown in Figure 1.5.

In the WebObjects Builder Inspector, (the second panel; toward the bottom of the screen in Figure 1.5) double-click the *Binding* column of the *Attribute* value. Enter `"Hello"` (within double quotation marks) and hit return.

If your application is still running, there is no need to restart it. Just save your changes as before and hit the refresh button on your browser. You are witnessing what is known as developing in *Rapid Turnaround* mode.

You should now see the same results as before: a blank page with `Hello`, as shown in Figure 1.4.

TIP

To keep development moving along at a swift pace, take advantage of WebObjects' Rapid Turnaround Mode. If you have only made changes to WebObjects components, and not to any code, then it isn't necessary to rebuild and rerun your application. Just refresh your browser to see the results of your changes.

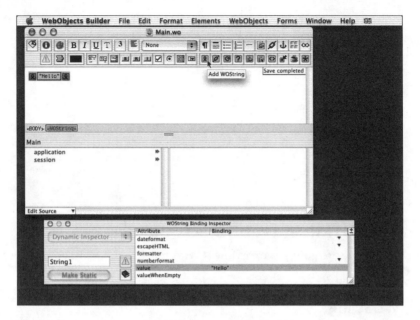

FIGURE 1.5   Use WebObjects Builder to layout your page.

Now take a look at the Main.html and compare it to what you had before. Choose *Edit, Source View* and you should see the WebObjects Builder in source view mode, as shown in Figure 1.6.

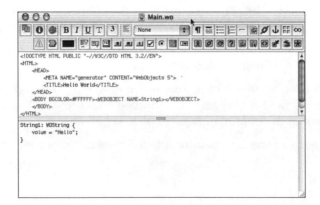

FIGURE 1.6   Choose Edit, Source View to see the WebObjects Builder in Source View Mode.

Notice how the text "Hello" within the <BODY> tags has been replaced with a dynamic element:

```
<!DOCTYPE HTML PUBLIC "-//W3C//DTD HTML 3.2//EN">
<HTML>
    <HEAD>
        <META NAME="generator" CONTENT="WebObjects 5">
        <TITLE>Hello World</TITLE>
    </HEAD>
    <BODY BGCOLOR=#FFFFFF><WEBOBJECT NAME=String1></WEBOBJECT>
    </BODY>
</HTML>
```

Now the WebObjects definition file is relevant. It defines the bindings for the WOString in the HTML template file:

```
String1: WOString {
    value = "Hello";
}
```

In this case, the value is bound to a constant "Hello". Therefore, it has the same results as a nondynamic component. In the next section, we'll add a key to Main.wo and look at some dynamic results.

Adding a Key To a Component

At the bottom left-hand corner of the screen there is a drop-down menu labeled *Edit Source*. Click it and select *Add key...* from the drop-down menu. An *Add Key* panel will appear, as in Figure 1.7.

FIGURE 1.7   Select Add Key... from the drop-down menu labeled Edit Source, and the Add Key panel will appear.

Enter msg for its *Name and* keep the type as *String*. Make sure that only the *Generate source code for instance variable* is checked. The other two check box options are for adding accessor methods to your component controller class. Finally, click *Add* to add the variable to Main.java.

In Project Builder, go to *Web Components, Main* and select Main.java.

Change the line

```
protected String msg;
```

to

```
protected String msg = "Hello Again";
```

save your changes.

Binding a Value to a WebObjects Element

In the WebObjects Builder, click and drag the key msg, which appears in the bottom half of the window, to the WOString in the top half of the window, as pictured in Figure 1.8.

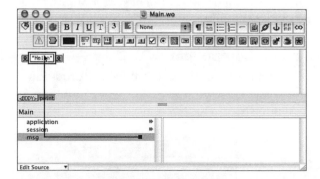

FIGURE 1.8   Binding elements in WebObjects Builder.

If the value of the WOString has been bound correctly, you should see "msg" in the WOString instead of "Hello". Save your changes: *File, Save.*

As you have made a change to the code, you can't use Rapid Turnaround to refresh the changes. Instead you will have to build and run.

TIP

A shortcut for building and running is to choose *Build, Build & Run* from the Project Builder menu. This performs both steps in one. The keyboard shortcut Command+R works even better. If your application is still running make sure to stop it first.

You should again get results similar to Figure 1.4.

Using Inputs and Dynamic Form Elements

In this section, we are going to add a form with a text field from which we are going to enter in the msg text.

In WebObjects Builder, move the cursor to the top-left corner. Click the icon to add a horizontal rule, or choose *Elements, Horizontal Rule* from the WebObjects Builder menu.

Again position the cursor before the horizontal rule and add a WOForm. Click the icon representing a WOForm, or choose *Forms, WOForm*. In place of the text "Form", add a WOTextField by choosing *Forms, WOTextField*. Then choose *Forms, WOSubmitButton*.

If the Inspector window isn't already up, select *Window, Inspector* to open it. With the WOSubmitButton highlighted, click the button labeled *Make Static* in the Inspector. This changes the dynamic element to a static HTML element.

Bind the Main key msg to the WOTextField. Unlike when binding a WOString, you should get a drop-down menu. Choose the *value* attribute to bind to. Your screen should look like Figure 1.9.

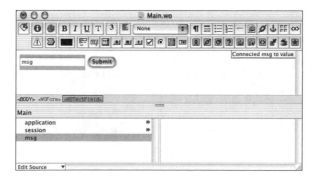

FIGURE 1.9 Form elements.

Adding an Action

When a user submits a form by clicking on the submit button the event is referred to as the *action* of clicking a submit button. Similarly, if a user clicks on a hyperlink it is referred to as the *action* of clicking a link. So, for every submit button and hyperlink in an application there is an action.

We are now going to add an action for the user submitting text in the msg field. To add an action, choose *Add Action …* from the *Edit Source* drop-down menu on the WebObjects Builder window. In the panel that pops up, enter submit for the name of the action, and then click *Add*. Notice how the action submit has appeared in the WebObjects Builder window. It is separated from the component keys to identify it as an action.

Bind the submit action to the WOForm as follows: Select the submit button, and then proceed to bind the submit action as normal, except click and drag to the <*WOForm*>, as shown in Figure 1.10.

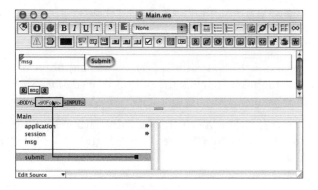

FIGURE 1.10   Binding an action to a WOForm.

In the drop-down menu that appears, select to bind submit to the *action* attribute, and then build and run. Now you should get an HTML form as in Figure 1.11.

FIGURE 1.11   The Hello World page.

Type some text, then click submit. Notice how the text under the horizontal rule gets dynamically updated to match the text you typed. Now let's take a quick look at the HTML being generated.

```
<!DOCTYPE HTML PUBLIC "-//W3C//DTD HTML 3.2//EN">
<HTML>
   <HEAD>
      <META NAME="generator" CONTENT="WebObjects 5">
      <TITLE>Hello World</TITLE>
   </HEAD>
   <BODY BGCOLOR=#FFFFFF>
      <form method="post"
➥action="/cgi-bin/WebObjects/Hello.woa/wo/jdtenl52oLCwoV7PeTZ0t0/7.1">
         <input type=text value="Hello World" name="1.1">
         <input type=SUBMIT>
      </form>
      <HR>Hello World
   </BODY>
</HTML>
```

Highlighted are bits of HTML that get generated dynamically. In particular, the msg key of the Main component provides the string for the form's text field, as well as the text after the horizontal rule. I'm sure you will notice the unusual URL for the form action.

The page vended in response to the form action must also be generated dynamically. Hence, a WebObjects URL for the form action.

WebObjects Component State

In this section, we'll take our first look at component state, or *memory*. At the same time we might get a better understanding of WebObjects' application architecture, and then be able to dissect and explain the components of a WebObjects URL.

Adding a Second Page to the Application

We are going to add a second page to the Hello application. When the user submits some text, we will display it on a new page.

Go back to the Hello project in Project Builder.

1. Highlight the *Web Components* group, and then choose *File, New File …* from the menu. This will open the New Component Assistant.

2. Enter Greeting for the *File Name* of the component.

3. Select *Application Server* as the *Target* (and only target) for the new file.

4. Click *Finish* to create and add the new component to the project.

FIGURE 1.12   Creating a new page with the New Component Assistant.

Passing Values Between Pages

Open up the Greetings.wo component in WebObjects Builder and add the following key:

Name: username

Type: String (java.lang.String)

As Variable: YES

Accessors: NO

Type the text "Hello", and then a nonbreaking space (Shift+space). Add a WOString, binding username to its *value* attribute, and then save your changes. Now open up Main.wo in WebObjects Builder.

Delete everything after the form: namely the horizontal rule and the WOString. To do this select everything after the form and press the *Delete* key.

To pass the msg from the Main page to the greeting page, we need to edit the submit action. So, select Main.java in the Project Builder.

TIP

To make more room for the edit window in the Project Builder, click the blue tabs to collapse the top and left sections as required.

Edit the submit action to look like this:

```
public WOComponent submit() {
    WOComponent nextPage = pageWithName("Greeting");

    // set values
    nextPage.takeValueForKey(msg, "username");

    return nextPage;
}
```

The pageWithName("Greeting") identifies and returns a new page for the component named Greeting. We set the name of the Greeting page using the takeValueForKey(msg, "username"), which sets the username key in the Greeting page with the value of msg.

> **NOTE**
>
> takeValueForKey() along with valueForKey()are part of the EOKeyValueCoding API. This is a very useful protocol, with which you can get and set values. We will take a more in depth look at key value coding in the next subsection.

Finally, the action is instructed to return the nextPage in response. Build and run, and then after clicking *Submit*, you will be directed to a new page displaying what you typed. If you want to return the Main page, click the browser *back* button. Later we'll add in a link back to the Main page.

Now, let's take a break from the Hello application and take a look at the key value–coding interface.

Introduction to Key Value Coding

Getting and setting values via the key value –coding interface is a particularly useful method of accessing variables of other WebObjects components, or even objects. You will find that the key value coding APIs, and similar methods, permeate much of WebObjects and its foundation.

When valueForKey() is called on an object, first the accessor methods are called. If there are no accessor methods then the variable of the same name is retrieved. This might seem slow, but the WebObjects runtime has optimizations that don't necessarily take a performance hit.

The convenience of using the valueForKey() and takeValueForKey() methods are

- Leaner code: You don't have to write custom accessors for variables.

- A strong Design Pattern: Use of key value coding consistently will result in more transparent and expressive code.

- Adherence to the Object-Oriented Principle of not accessing an object's variables directly.

- Flexibility: Allows the filtering and sorting of variables by means of accessors.

As a general principle, throughout this book we'll stick to using the key value coding interfaces as a preference over using accessor methods. This is design pattern #1.

Component State

Let's add that much needed back link from the Greetings page in the Hello application.

Open `Greetings.wo` in WebObjects Builder. Position the cursor at the end of the WOString and press return. Then choose WOHyperlink from the WebObjects menu to add a WOHyperlink to the page.

In the WebObjects Builder Inspector (*Window, Inspector*), with the WOHyperlink selected, scroll down to the *pageName* attribute. Click the triangle to see a drop-down menu and select *"Main"*, as in Figure 1.13.

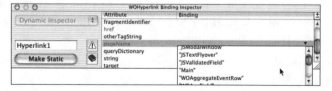

FIGURE 1.13   Set the WOHyperlink pageName from the Inspector drop down.

> **NOTE**
>
> Because there is no need to pass values from the Greeting page to the Main page, we don't have to add a trivial action to return the Main page programmatically. We can bind the WOHyperlink's *pageName* attribute, which will conveniently perform the action of creating the page and returning it.

Highlight the bit of text within the WOHyperlink `Hyperlink` and replace it with `Back`. Save changes and refresh.

NOTE

Remember, if the Hello application is still running you don't need to rebuild and rerun to see your changes because we didn't add or change any code to add the back button.

The Greeting page will now display a *Back* link. Notice, however, the difference between clicking the browser back button and the *Back* link.

When the browser back button is clicked you get the Main page with whatever you typed, whereas clicking the *Back* link gives you a fresh Main page. A Fresh Main component will have an empty msg string when it is initialized, whereas the older Main component will still *remember* the msg you typed.

Using Session Variables

There is another way for WebObjects pages to share values. That is, to use Session variables instead of Component variables.

This way we might not get the discrepancy we observed between clicking the browser back button and clicking the *Back* hyperlink in the last exercise.

Introduction to WebObjects Application Architecture

Run the Hello application again.

This time when the browser window appears, before you type anything and hit submit; open a new identical window to the Hello application.

Now, type your name and submit in the first window and a friend's name in the second. Notice how the two greeting pages will display the two different names. What you are witnessing is two open *Sessions* to the Hello application.

The WebObjects application is maintaining a *Session* per user. In one session the username is yours and in the other session it's your friend's.

In this exercise, we are emulating two users accessing the only instance of the Hello application running from Project Builder.

So, in other words, one application spawns several different *Sessions*—one for each user.

Moving Component State into the Session

Let's return to the Hello application and put some of this theory to work. Currently, the msg and username are Component variables. So they need to be passed from one component to the next.

However, as discussed in the previous section, a username seems more naturally scoped by the *Session*. In other words, we could move the username into the *Session*.

In Project Builder, edit `Main.java` and copy and cut the line:

```
protected String msg;
```

Paste it into `Session.java` and rename the key username.

Now we need to edit `Main.wo` and `Greeting.wo` to use the session key username. Open `Main.wo` in WebObjects Builder, and then select the `session` key from the WebObjects Builder window. Notice how username will appear in the second column, as shown in Figure 1.14.

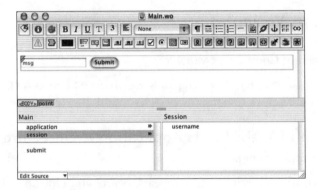

FIGURE 1.14   Session keys.

Select username and bind it to the *value* of the WOTextField. Edit the `Main.java` class by removing the line

```
nextPage.takeValueForKey(msg, "username");
```

Now, open `Greeting.wo` and bind `session.username` to the WOString. Delete the username key local to the Greeting component by right-clicking it in the WebObjects Builder. From the drop-down menu, select *Delete username*. Save your changes to both components and their Java classes, and then build and run.

As a quick exercise, try noticing the difference between clicking the *Back* hyperlink and the back button on the browser.

Application State

Just as you can *scope* variables beyond a component and into the session, you can share variables between sessions by placing them in the application.

Before we embark on the next exercise, make a duplicate of the project. The changes we make to it are purely for the purpose of the exercise and, therefore, are going to be discarded.

Duplicating the Project

1. Duplicate the *Hello* project directory.

2. Rename the *Hello copy* directory *HelloTest*.

3. Locate the `Hello.pbproj` file inside the new directory and rename it `HelloTest.pbproj`.

4. Open the HelloTest project. Double-click the file `HelloTest.pbproj` or drag the entire folder into the Project Builder icon on your *Desktop* or *Dock*.

5. Select the *Targets* tab and highlight the *Hello* target. Then choose *Project, Rename* from Project Builder's menu to rename `"Hello"` to `"HelloTest"`.

6. Click the *Clean All* icon to clean the project.

NOTE

The Project Builder maintains a subdirectory called *build* for every project. It keeps compiler files, executables, and other intermediate files it needs to optimize building, here. From time to time it is necessary to *Clean* the project.

Using Project Find and Replace

This subsection is mostly an exercise: We are going to test using an *Application* variable `username` instead of the *Session* variable.

Using the duplicated *HelloTest* project, try moving the `username` key from the *Session* into the *Application*, just as before.

This time, however, instead of editing `Main.wo` and `Greeting.wo` in WebObjects Builder, we are going to use a *Find and Replace* in the Project Builder to change those bindings.

1. Open the *HelloTest* project in Project Builder.

2. Click the *Find* tab.

3. Enter `session.username` in the *Find* text field, and then click the *Find* button.

4. Now select the two entries in the Find Panel as in Figure 1.6.

5. Enter `application.username` in the *Replace* text field and press the *Replace* button. In the drop-down panel that appears select *Replace* to replace the `session.username` with `application.username` in the two locations.

6. Save changes.

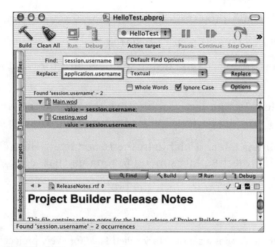

FIGURE 1.15   Project find and replace.

You should build and run the application. Now, open a second browser window to the Hello application as we did once before. Try typing in two different names in the two windows. You will notice that one window's input will override the other!

Using Images and Fonts in WebObjects

Revert to using the Hello project because we are going to discard the changes made in the last exercise.

In this section, we are going to add the finishing touches to the Hello application by adding images, a background, and a custom component.

Adding Images

1. We are going to add an image to the Hello application. Take an image from the HelloWorld example that ships with WebObjects.

2. Highlight the *Web Server Resources* group in the Hello project's *Groups & Files* panel.

3. Choose *Project, Add Files* ... then navigate to the */Developer/Examples/JavaWebobjects/HelloWorld* directory and open `hello_world_title.gif`.

4. In the drop-down panel that appears, check the Copy items into the destination folder (if necessary), and make sure that only the *Web Server* target is selected, as shown in Figure 1.16.

5. Click *Add* to complete the task.

FIGURE 1.16   Adding an image to the Web Server target.

Now open up `Main.wo` in WebObjects Builder.

Position the cursor before the WOForm and choose *WebObjects*, *WOImage*, and then press *return*. This will separate the image from the form using a paragraph.

With the WOImage selected, open the Inspector and select the *filename* attribute. Scroll and select `hello_world_title.gif` from the binding drop down. WebObjects Builder should then show the graphic, as seen in Figure 1.17.

Run the application to see the changes.

Adding a Framework to a Project

This is similar to adding an image to a project.

1. Highlight the *Frameworks* group in the *Groups & Files* panel.

2. Choose *Project, Add Frameworks...* from the menu. In this case navigate to and add `WOExamplesHarness.framework` from */Library/Frameworks/*.

3. In the drop-down panel make sure only *Application* is the selected target, and then click *Add*.

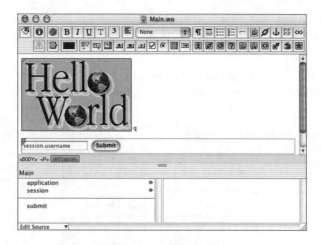

FIGURE 1.17   Displaying graphics in the WebObjects Builder.

Setting the Background Imagew

To set the background image of the two pages, open the components in WebObjects Builder.

> **NOTE**
>
> You might have to close and reopen the components in WebObjects Builder for it to pick up the newly added framework.

In WebObjects Builder, select <BODY> in the Main.wo window.

Click *Make Dynamic* in the Inspector panel, which will convert it to a WOBody element. Set the *framework* attribute to *WOExamplesHarness* and the *filename* to aqua_bg.jpg respectively from the binding drop down menus. Repeat this for the Greetings page, then build and run.

This time you will indeed have to build and run because you've added a framework to the application. Finally, you should have an application that looks similar to the HelloWorld example: */Developer/Examples/JavaWebObjects/HelloWorld*.

> **NOTE**
>
> To run an example, make a local copy of it in your home directory and run it from Project Builder.

Summary

In this chapter, you built a Hello World application with the aim of learning how to use the WebObjects tools and dynamic elements. You also learned a little about the WebObjects Application architecture and had an introduction to Component and Session State.

2

DHTML and WebObjects

A manager went to the Master Programmer and showed him the requirements document for a new application.

The manager asked the Master: "How long will it take to design this system if I assign five programmers to it?"

"It will take one year," said the Master promptly.

"But we need this system immediately or even sooner! How long will it take if I assign ten programmers to it?"

The Master Programmer frowned. "In that case, it will take two years."

"And what if I assign a hundred programmers to it?"

The Master Programmer shrugged. "Then the design will never be completed," he said.

—The Tao of Programming, Book 3.4.

In this chapter we are going to look at using DHTML with WebObjects. At the same time this chapter is an introduction to WebObjects components and how to create and use them.

Introduction to JavaScript and WebObjects

First, let's revisit the *Hello* application created in Chapter 1, "A Web Objects Primer." We are going to return the greeting in the form of a JavaScript pop-up window instead of a second page.

Dynamically Vended JavaScript Alert Panel

Duplicate the *Hello* project and rename it *DynamicHello* by following the instructions in Chapter 1.

Open Main.wo in WebObjects Builder. We are going to use an *onLoad* script to perform the JavaScript alert.

Add the following key to the Main page:

> **Name:** onLoad
>
> **Type:** String (java.lang.String)
>
> **As Variable:** NO
>
> **Accessors**: Only the Method returning the value

Now bind the onLoad key to the *WOBody* element. Because *onLoad* isn't a defined binding for *WOBody* (that is, you wouldn't see it listed in the *WOBody* Inspector) we need to add it to a new binding.

From the binding drop down, select *Connect to new Binding* .... Enter onLoad into the Attribute field in the Inspector. This will bind the onLoad key to the *custom binding onLoad* of the <BODY> element.

Copy the following lines into the onLoad() accessor:

```
public String onLoad() {
  String username = (String) valueForKeyPath("session.username");
  String onLoad = "javascript: alert('Hello " + username + "!');";

  return (username != null) ? onLoad:null;
}
```

The first line uses the utility Key Value Coding method to get the username key from the *Session*. Instead of having to write valueForKey("session").valueForKey ("username"), you can use valueForKeyPath("session.username") to access the session.username.

In the second line we generate a JavaScript string with the session.username. It will display the greeting Hello *username*!. Finally, we return the *onLoad* string if a username has been submitted.

If this last statement seems unfamiliar, it is equivalent to the following:

```
If (username != null) return onLoad;
else return null;
```

Change the submit action by replacing the lines:

```
  WOComponent nextPage = pageWithName("Greeting");
  return nextPage;
```

With:

```
return this;
```

By returning this instead of a new or different page, we are returning the same instance of the Main component. Select Build and Run.

Now you should get a pop-up window greeting on *submit*.

Creating A Basic WebObjects Component

Let's take a break from the *Hello* application and take a look at the *ThinkMovies* example application that comes with WebObjects 5. Notice how every page has the same navigation bar component. We are going to create a dynamic navigation bar with rollover buttons that we will plug into the *ThinkMovies* example.

Prototyping A Toolbar Component

We are going to build the component in isolation. That is, develop it in an application of its own, strictly for the purposes of development and testing. When it is completed it can be incorporated into the *ThinkMovies* application.

Create a new WebObjects Application project, and call it *ToolbarComponentTest*.

Add the images from the Web site (see companion Web site at www. samspublishing.com) to the project. Remember to select the *Copy items...* check box and to select *Web Server* as the *Target*.

Open Main.wo in WebObjects Builder. For now use *WOImage* and *WOHyperlink* in place of a rollover link element to define the Toolbar Component.

So, click the *WOHyperlink* icon to add a link. Then click the *WOImage* icon to add an image inside the link, as shown in Figure 2.1.

NOTE

Note that we would have used *WOActiveImage* instead of a *WOImage* embedded in a *WOHyperlink*, if it allowed us to bind to *direct actions*. These are special WebObjects actions that we'll discuss later.

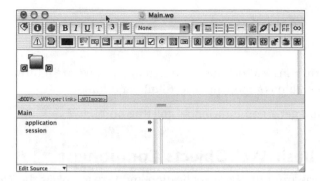

FIGURE 2.1   A WOImage embedded in a WOHyperlink.

Highlight the *WOImage* element and open its Inspector.

In the *filename* attribute, select home.gif, and set its border to 0. Temporarily set the *pageName* to Main. Later we will have to bind the links to *directActions* in the *ThinkMovies* application.

Do the same for similar image links for search.gif, index.gif, add.gif, and help.gif. You can cut and paste the components to make duplicates. Separate the image links with a nonbreaking space.

TIP

To add nonbreaking spaces in the WebObjects Builder press *Shift+Space*. If you're editing the HTML template in Source Mode, type   for a nonbreaking space.

Your Main.wo component should look similar to Figure 2.2. Select Build and Run.

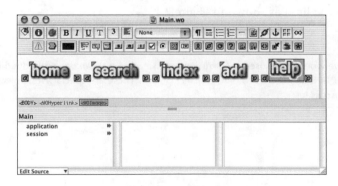

FIGURE 2.2   Navigation.

Factoring Out a Component

Now we are going to factor out these WebObjects elements into a reusable *ToolbarComponent*. This is necessary so we can simply plug in the component on any page for navigation.

1. Create a New Component called `ToolbarComponent`.

2. Open it up in WebObjects Builder and click the Inspector. Choose *Partial Document* from the Page Inspector pop-up, as shown in Figure 2.3. Click *Continue* in the *Convert Document* panel that appears to grant the change to the component.

3. Cut and paste the entire contents of the Main component into the `ToolbarComponent`.

NOTE

A component set to *Partial Document* is a reusable component that can only be used inside other components. Components such as `Main`, which are *Full Documents*, should only be used as *pages*.

In terms of HTML, a *Partial Document* will lack the document declaration, the <HTML> and <BODY> tags of a *Full Document*.

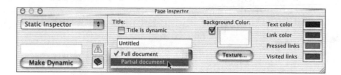

FIGURE 2.3   Setting a component as a Partial Document.

Embedding Components in a Page

Now in `Main.wo`, click the *WOCustomComponent* icon. In the *Custom Component* panel that appears type `ToolbarComponent` in the *WebObjects class to use* field. Save the changes and refresh the browser window.

There should not be a change in what is vended to the browser. If you find that there is indeed a change then move onto incorporating it into the *ThinkMovies* example.

Make a duplicate of the *ThinkMovies* example application: */Developer/Examples/JavaWebObjects/ThinkMovies*. Call the copy *DynamicMovies* and, from the Project Builder, copy the contents of the `ToolbarComponent.html` and `ToolbarComponent.wod` files from the *ToolbarComponentTest* into the *DynamicMovies* equivalent.

Remember to copy in the images into the *DynamicMovies* project. We must now hook up the navigation links to the appropriate *directActions*.

To do so open *ToolbarComponent* from the *DynamicMovies* project in WebObjects Builder.

To remove the *pageName* binding from the *WOHyperlinks*, select the binding in the Inspector and press the Delete key. Notice how some attributes will appear in red. These indicate a mandatory binding: one of which must be set.

Now, bind the *directActionName* attribute to Home (for the home link). Similarly, bind the other links to Search, MasterIndex, AddMovie, and Help. Select Save and Run.

Now you will be able to click the links in the navigation bar of the *DynamicMovies* application. However, pretty as it might look, we still haven't added any DHTML.

Designing WebObjects Components

In this section we will prototype and develop a *WORollover* component. One that is essentially an active link with a rollover image.

Prototyping WORollover

Before we dive into developing the component, let's think about what is required.

In terms of generating HTML, we're looking at producing something along the lines of the following:

```
<a href="/index.html" onMouseOver="image.src='/imageH.gif'"
                       onMouseOut="image.src='/imageH.gif'">
       <img src="/image.gif" name="image">
</a>
```

The differences will be that the link *href* will be a WebObjects URL. The image *src* will also point to a WebObjects Resource.

> **NOTE**
>
> Images in WebObjects are vended differently from those in WebObjects pages because of performance and efficiency. We shall take a more reasoned look into WebObjects Resource actions later.

To begin, just as before, create a development or test project for *WORollover,* call it *WORolloverTest*. Again, we'll develop it first in the Main component. So open Main.wo in WebObjects Builder. Setup a link and an image as before and copy in the images home.gif and homeH.gif into the project.

Now, bind the *filename* attribute of the image to a key `unhighlightedImage` (without the quotation marks to indicate a key binding). Add the `unhighlightedImage` key as a variable.

While still on the image, click the *plus/minus* icon in the Inspector window to *add a binding* to an attribute called *name*. Set the *name* attribute to a new variable key `imageName`.

NOTE

To perform the rollover, we need to identify the image by name, therefore, give it a *name* binding.

Bind the *directActionName* of the hyperlink to *default* for now. As before, add two bindings *onMouseOver* and *onMouseOut* to the hyperlink. For the *onMouseOver* attribute, type `onMouseOver`. When prompted by the *Add Key* panel, choose to add it as an accessor method only. Do the same for *onMouseOut*.

Now, add a third variable key, `highlightedImage`, to the code, this time manually to `Main.java`:

```
protected String unhighlightedImage = "home.gif";
protected String highlightedImage = "homeH.gif";
protected String imageName = "home";
```

For the purposes of development, use the defaults of `home.gif`, `homeH.gif` and `home` for the filenames and the name of the image.

When the mouse rolls over the image link, the image should change to the highlighted image:

```
public String onMouseOver() {
        WOResourceManager resourceManager = application().resourceManager();
        String url = resourceManager.urlForResourceNamed(highlightedImage,
null, null, context().request());

        return imageName + ".src='" + url + "';";
}
```

The *WOResourceManager* is responsible for the vending, caching, and locating the resources of an application.

To get the WebObjects Resource URL for a particular image, use the `urlForResourceNamed()` method. I will refer you to the documentation for a more detailed look at this particular method.

TIP

A quick way to search the documentation is to choose *Help, Developer Help Center*. Click the *WebObjects* link to get to more specific help. Type a text or phrase to search for, and the *Help Viewer* application will open a list of suitable matches.

When the mouse rolls off the image, the image should revert back to the original:

```
public String onMouseOut() {
        WOResourceManager resourceManager = application().resourceManager();
        String url = resourceManager.urlForResourceNamed(unhighlightedImage,
➥null, null, context().request());

        return imageName + ".src='" + url + "';";
}
```

Now you're ready to build and run.

Defining the Component API

In this section we'll extract the WebObjects elements and functionality that make up the *WORollover* component. At the same time, we'll get our first introduction to Variable Synchronization between WebObjects components.

Making the Component Reusable

To make a component reusable we need to make it generic. But before we start to discuss this any further, factor out the WebObjects elements that comprise a *WORollover* component.

Create a new component called *WORollover*. From the WebObjects Builder cut the WebObjects elements that make up the rollover from the Main component and paste it into the *WORollover* component. Remember to set the component as a *Partial Document*.

In addition, copy over the three variable keys highlightedImage, unhighlightedImage, and imageName from Main.java into WORollover.java. Do the same for the accessor keys onMouseOver() and onMouseOut(). Now embed, or place, a *WORollover* component in Main.wo, and select Build and Run.

Notice, however, that we've effectively hard coded the image to use and the image name. But we want to make it similar to *WOImage* or *WOHyperlink*, so that we can set which images to use and what action to perform on clicking. Only then would it be truly *reusable*.

To do that we're going to define the API of the *WORollover* component.

Defining the Component API

Select the *WORollover.wo* window in WebObjects Builder.

Choose API from the Window menu to open the *API Editor*. This is where you define which bindings are of a component and which ones are optional or mandatory. Click *Add Keys From Class*.

The *API Editor* will automatically pick up all the keys it can find from the components' controller class. In this case, WORollover.java. Refer to Figure 2.4.

FIGURE 2.4   API Editor.

For the *highlightedImage* binding, select *Resources* from the *Value Set* column pop up. Click *Required* to ensure that the binding is set.

Do the same for *unhighlightedImage* and remove the bindings for onMouseOut and onMouseOver. Select the binding and press *Delete*. Then, make the *imageName* binding mandatory.

Add one more key, *directActionName*, as a binding. Select *Direct Actions* as the *Value Set*. When you've finished with the API Editor, add a key directActionName to *WORollover*. Be sure to bind the *WOHyperlink directActionName* to the key of the same name directActionName.

Finally, remove the constants from the variable keys in WORollover.java. In other words, remove the constants home.gif, homeH.gif and home:

```
protected String unhighlightedImage;
protected String highlightedImage;
protected String imageName;
protected String directActionName;
```

Save your changes and select the window for Main.wo. Clicking the *WORollover* component should reveal the bindings as we just defined, as shown in Figure 2.5.

FIGURE 2.5   WORollover bindings appearing in the Inspector.

Now you can set the values for the bindings in the Inspector. Notice how you can set the *highlightedImage* and *unhighlightedImage* from the pop-up in the binding column. Set the *directActionName* to default for now. Also give it a suitable *imageName,* that is, bind the *imageName* attribute to rollover1, for example.

To observe the reusability of the newly created *WORollover* component, go back to the Main component in WebObjects Builder and change the images to search.gif and searchH.gif from the inspector pop-up list.

Save and refresh the browser to see a rollover with the search images.

Review of Component Variable Synchronization

You have already been introduced to variable synchronization in WebObjects as you just applied it to the *WORollover* example in the previous exercise.

However, it might be worth taking some time to look at how variable synchronization works in WebObjects.

As in the previous example, when we set the images to the constants home.gif and homeH.gif, these constants get passed onto the *WORollover* component.

Here the Main component is referred to as the *parent* component, whereas the *WORollover* placed on the Main page is referred to as the *child*. As in real life, values get passed on from *parent* to *child*.

So, the constants home.gif and homeH.gif of the Main component were passed to the child component as values for the keys *highlightedImage* and *unhighlightedImage*.

Optimizing WebObjects Generated DHTML

You might have noticed that the DHTML we generated was not optimal. In particular, it didn't employ image preloading, which helps to improve the first impression of the rollovers.

In this section we'll look at adding image preloading to *WORollover* and then incorporate it into *DynamicMovies*.

Using WOJavaScript

Let's return to WORollover. Open the component in WebObjects Builder.

What we want to achieve in terms of HTML and JavaScript is something along the lines of the following:

```
<script language=JavaScript>
        image_U = new Image();
        image_U.src = '/image.gif';
        image_H = new Image();
        image_H.src = '/imageH.gif';
</script>
<a href="/index.html" onMouseOver="image.src=image_H.src;"
                      onMouseOut="image.src=image_U.src;">
    <img name="image" src="image.gif">
</a>
```

The image preloading in the previous example is done in the embedded JavaScript. The mouse over and mouse out events simply swap the images instead of reloading them.

To add a dynamic JavaScript component, position the cursor before the active image link and choose *WebObjects, WOJavaScript*. Bind its *scriptString* to a new accessor key of the same name scriptString.

```
public String scriptString() {
        WOResourceManager resourceManager = application().resourceManager();
        String unhighlightedImageURL = resourceManager.urlForResourceNamed(
[ic.ccc]unhighlightedImage, null, null, context().request());
        String highlightedImageURL = resourceManager.urlForResourceNamed(
➡highlightedImage, null, null, context().request());
        String scriptString = imageName + "_U = new Image();\n" +
            ➡imageName + "_U.src='" +unhighlightedImageURL + "';\n" +
            ➡imageName + "_H = new Image();\n" +
            ➡imageName + "_H.src='" + highlightedImageURL + "';\n";

        return scriptString;
}
```

The scriptString absorbs the complexity of the onMouseOver and onMouseOut events and accessors. Now they are much simpler:

```
public String onMouseOver() {
        return imageName + ".src=" + imageName + "_H.src;";
}
```

```
public String onMouseOut() {
        return imageName + ".src=" + imageName + "_U.src;";
}
```

Select Build and Run.

When you are certain that *WORollover* works satisfactorily, then you can proceed to plug it into *DynamicMovies*. By this I mean copy the *WORollover* component from its test project into *DyanmicMovies*.

Copying Components into a Project

Copying a WebObjects component and its class from one project to another is almost identical to copying resources into a project.

1. Select the *Web Components* group from the *Groups & Files* panel. Choose *Project, Add Files...* from the Project Builder menu.

2. Navigate to and highlight the files that comprise the WebObjects component: .api, .java, and .wo files. Click *Open*.

3. Check the *Copy items into the destination* box. This time however, choose the *Create Folder References for any added folders* radio.

This ensures that the .wo file isn't interpreted as a *Group Folder* and is copied in correctly. The .wo component folder should appear as blue, not yellow.

1. Make sure that the *Application* target is highlighted, and then click *Add*.

2. Finally, choose *Project, New Group*, to collect the component files together in a project folder. Give the group the same name as the WebObjects component (in this case WORollover).

3. Then drag the files of the component into the group, as shown in Figure 2.6.

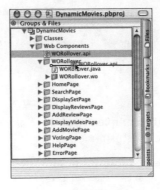

FIGURE 2.6   Moving a file into a Group Folder.

Using Tables to Position Elements of a Component

You might have noticed by now that the help image link in the *DynamicMovies* application was misaligned with the others. Now we'll use a table to position and align the icons correctly.

Choose Table from the Elements menu to add a table to the *ToolbarComponent,* as shown in Figure 2.7.

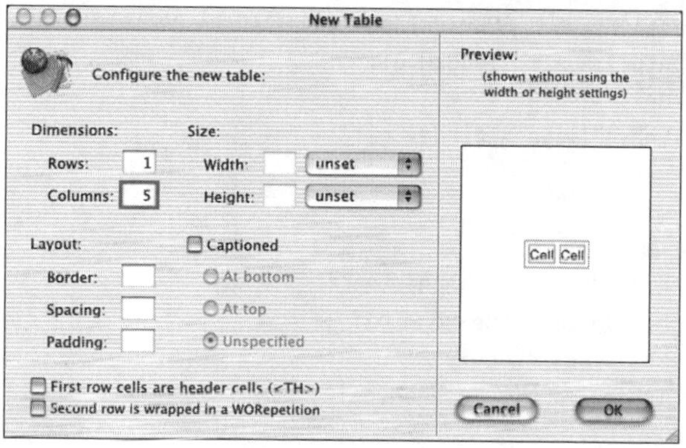

FIGURE 2.7   Adding a Table.

Insert a table of one row and five columns for each of the rollovers. Remove the image links because they are to be replaced by rollovers. Also, remember to remove the redundant nonbreaking spaces.

In each cell insert a *WORollover* component. Set their attributes as follows:

```
Add: WORollover {
        directActionName = "AddMovie";
        highlightedImage = "addH.gif";
        imageName = "add";
        unhighlightedImage = "add.gif";
}

Help: WORollover {
        directActionName = "Help";
        highlightedImage = "helpH.gif";
        imageName = "help";
        unhighlightedImage = "help.gif";
}
```

```
Home: WORollover {
        directActionName = "Home";
        highlightedImage = "homeH.gif";
        imageName = "home";
        unhighlightedImage = "home.gif";
}

Index: WORollover {
        directActionName = "MasterIndex";
        highlightedImage = "indexH.gif";
        imageName = "index";
        unhighlightedImage = "index.gif";
}

Search: WORollover {
        directActionName = "Search";
        highlightedImage = "searchH.gif";
        imageName = "searchMovies";
        unhighlightedImage = "search.gif";
}
```

You might want to set the alignment of the table row to the top so that the images are aligned properly.

You can do this using the Table Inspector in WebObjects Builder, or by adding the attribute *valign="top"* to the <TR> tag in the component template.

> **NOTE**
>
> You might notice that the Search link wasn't named search. This is because search is a reserved word in the JavaScript Document Object Model.

Select Save and Run and your search screen should look similar to Figure 2.8.

Further Exercise

In addition to *onMouseOver* and *onMouseOut* there is a third event that can be used in the *WORollover* to add a little more responsiveness: *onMouseDown*.

As an additional exercise, you might want to add another set of icons to represent the rollovers when they are clicked.

FIGURE 2.8   Dynamic menu bar.

Summary

In this chapter we looked at vending WebObjects generated DHTML. While at the same time, learning how to develop reusable WebObjects components.

3

Optimizing WebObjects Components

"It's not what you put on, it's what you put in."

—evian

In this chapter we continue our introduction to developing WebObjects Components that we started in Chapter 2, "DHTML and WebObjects."

In particular, we look at developing nonsynchronized and stateless components and see how they improve and optimize WebObjects applications. We start however, by adding a splash page to *DynamicMovies*.

Adding a Splash Page

First impressions do count, whatever people say. In particular, any good WebObjects application or site needs to have a good starting point. Having a great home page is more than a bonus.

In this section we look at making a dynamic splash page using an image map and rollovers.

Using Image Maps in WebObjects

Let's start by creating another test project: *WOMappedRolloverTest*.

Locate the graphics for this exercise in the file download for the chapter on the book companion Web site (www.samspublishing.com). Copy the images into the *Web Server Resources group*, selecting the Web Server target and Copy files options when doing so.

Open Main.wo in the WebObjects Builder. This time, to add the image, click and drag splash.gif from Project Builder into the Main component window. The image will instantly display itself as a *WOImage* in the Main component.

To use a map, you must add the *usemap* attribute to the image. Add the non-API attribute to the WOImage and set its value to #splashmap. Remember that you do this by choosing a new binding and naming it usemap.

When in source mode, copy the following HTML into the Main component template, just before the WOImage.

```
<map name="splashmap">
        <area shape=rect coords="191,137,259,174" href="http://www.dell.com">
        <area shape=rect coords="0,80,215,159" href="http://www.apple.com">
        <area shape=rect coords="146,52,253,97" href="http://www.ibm.com">
        <area shape=rect coords="204,89,265,128" href="http://www.sun.com">
</map>
```

When that's completed, build and run.

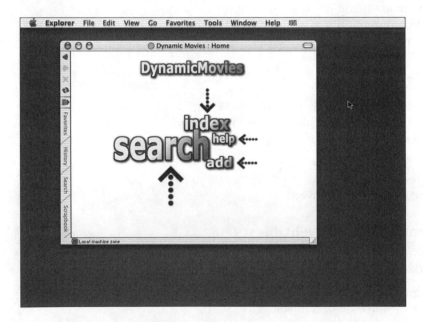

FIGURE 3.1   Creating a Splash Page.

Using WOGenericElement to Markup the Image Map

It is fairly trivial to add a static image map to an image in WebObjects. But the splash page for DynamicMovies should have actions into the application itself. So next, we will look at producing an image map with WebObjects URLs.

To do this, create a new component called WOArea. Make it a partial document to indicate that it is a reusable component. Add the following keys as variables only:

directActionName (String)--Generates the href for the <AREA>.

coords (String)--The coordinates of the area in the map.

shape (String)--The shape of the area in the map.

Also add the href accessor key:

```
public String href() {
        return context().directActionURLForActionNamed(directActionName, null);
}
```

Use the API Editor to add the three variable keys to the WOArea component API.

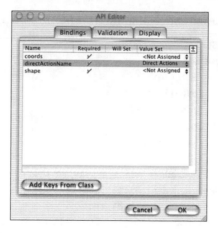

FIGURE 3.2   Setting the WOArea API.

Finally, add a WOGenericElement from the WebObjects menu to the WOArea component. Set its *elementName* attribute to area, as shown in Figure 3.3.

FIGURE 3.3   Set the elementName attribute in the Generic WebObjects Inspector.

Add bindings for *href* and *coords*. Then *shape* and bind them to the respective keys in WOArea.

Now in the Main component, replace each of the image map area elements with WOArea dynamic elements. For now bind the *directActionName* to the *default* action, and Build and Run.

Optimizing Components Using Nonsynchronized Variables

Our next task is to add rollovers to the image map. That is when a link becomes highlighted when the mouse rolls over it. We'll prototype the component using image preloading right from the start. Otherwise, you can't expect the rollovers to be smooth for larger images.

Hence, we'd produce a DHTML along the lines of

```
<script language=JavaScript>
        image_U = new Image();
        image_U.src = '/image.gif';
        image_H1 = new Image();
        image_H1.src = '/imageH1.gif';
        image_H2 = new Image();
        image_H2.src = '/imageH2.gif';
</script>
<Map Name="splashmap" onMouseOut="image.src=image_U.src">
        <Area Shape=Rect Coords="191,137,259,174" Href="/page1.html"
        onMouseOver="image.src=image_H1.src">
        <Area Shape=Rect Coords="191,137,259,174" Href="/page1.html"
        onMouseOver="image.src=image_H2.src">
</Map>
<img name="image" src="/image.gif" usemap="#map">
```

Before we do this we'll attempt to make what we've got a little more generic. So let's factor out the image map and the image into a WOMappedRollover component. For now we won't give it an API; that'll be added later.

So create a new component called WOMappedRollover. Cut and paste the elements for the image map (that is the script, the image map itself, and the image) into the WOMappedRollover component. Finally, place a WOMappedRollover where the image map originally was.

Remember to incorporate the custom component back into the Main page, then build and run.

Finally we get to the crux of this chapter, converting WOArea into a nonsynchronized component. Before that, let's have a quick introduction to nonsynchronization and optimization of WebObjects Components.

Introduction to Optimizing WebObjects Components

There are two ways to optimize reusable WebObjects Components; that is, from a functional point of view. Optimizing components is no remedy for a badly designed application or a poor implementation of one. It can however, give a good application design the performance edge it deserves.

The most significant performance throttle is not so much CPU cycles as people often think. These days, microprocessors are chugging along at hundreds of millions of instructions per second, or even billions of instructions per second. A few hundred extra here and there won't impact the performance of a Web application server much if at all. The real performance choke is memory.

Look at a WebObjects application. The more users logged onto a particular server, the more sessions the application has to maintain. The more sessions an application has, the more memory it consumes. Quickly, it can consume the hardware's physical memory, at least broadly speaking.

So, instead of trying to flatten loops and avoiding expressive code, think of how to conserve memory. In WebObjects, one way to do this is to make your components *stateless*. This topic will be discussed later in the chapter.

Good WebObjects design has a tendency to produce pages with substantial amounts of reusable components. Normally, this would have the unfortunate side effect of increasing the memory of an application. Roughly, more components imply more memory. Making components stateless is a mechanism used to reduce this trade off.

Here, we trade off CPU time for Memory space, for an explanation in informal computational complexity.

A second way to improve performance of WebObjects components is to make them nonsynchronizing.

A nonsynchronized component doesn't have to keep local instances of variables. Instead, it can fetch them as needed from its parent. In fact, this is how it achieves its performance edge.

Disabling Component Variable Synchronization

Disabling variable synchronization requires setting a switch in every component that uses it. Place the following in WOArea.java:

```
public boolean synchronizesVariablesWithBindings() {
        return false;
}
```

Now remove *all* the variable keys defined for WOArea so that WOArea has only the accessor key href, which we alter

```
public String href() {
        String directActionName = (String) valueForBinding("directActionName");
        return context().directActionURLForActionNamed(directActionName, null);
}
```

The way nonsynchronized components pull their values from their parents is by using valueForBinding(). This method along with takeValueForBinding() are comparable to the key value coding APIs.

Now open up WOArea.wo in WebObjects Builder. You might have to edit the component in Source View. For each of the WOGenericElement attributes that were bound to a variable key, append a ^ to the key. This is a convenience in WebObjects that enables the component to take its value from its parent. So, instead of setting the value for that binding from one of its own keys, it uses its parent's key values instead. WOArea.wod should look like

```
Area: WOGenericElement {
        coords = ^coords;
        elementName = "area";
        href = href;
        shape = ^shape;
}
```

After this step is completed build and run.

Congratulations! You should have constructed your first nonsynchronized component.

Using Plists

In this next subsection, we're going to make our WebObjects component WOMappedRollover more generic.

So far, we've hard coded the image and the image map into the reusable component. In order for it to be reusable, we should be able to set the image and it's image map as attributes.

To abstract the information in an image map, we are going to use a Plist or property list version of the image map.

Under the *Resources* group, add a new empty file called `ImageMap.plist`. Make sure it is added to the *Application Server* target only. Copy in the following into `ImageMap.plist`:

```
{
    "name" = "splashmap";
    "areas" = ({
        "shape" = "rect";
        "coords" = "221,151,209,188";
        "directActionName" = "default";
    "imageOnMouseOver" = "splash_addH.gif";
    }, {
        "shape" = "rect";
        "coords" = "30,94,245,173";
        "directActionName" = "default";
    "imageOnMouseOver" = "splash_searchH.gif";
    }, {
        "shape" = "rect";
        "coords" = "176,66,283,111";
        "directActionName" = "default";
    "imageOnMouseOver" = "splash_indexH.gif";
    }, {
        "shape" = "rect";
        "coords" = "234,103,295,142";
        "directActionName" = "default";
    "imageOnMouseOver" = "splash_helpH.gif";
    });
}
```

Note its similarities and differences to an HTML image map. The main difference, apart from the format, is that instead of an *href* attribute, each area has a *directActionName* attribute.

Very briefly, key-value pairs within curly braces ({}) represents a NSDictionary, whereas objects in a NSArray are represented by ("") separated by commas, and quoted items represent Strings.

This conforms to the ASCII property list standard. See *NSPropertyListSerialization* in the documentation for more info.

Now add a key to `Application.java` consisting of a variable `imageMap` and an accessor:

```
protected NSDictionary imageMap;

public NSDictionary imageMap() {
    if (imageMap == null) {
        InputStream inputStream = resourceManager().
inputStreamForResourceNamed("ImageMap.plist", null, null);

        // read in the data, log exceptions
        try {
        NSData mapData = new NSData(inputStream, inputStream.available());
        imageMap = (NSDictionary)
NSPropertyListSerialization.propertyListFromData(mapData);
        } catch (Exception exception) {
        NSLog.out.appendln("Application:  failed to read in image map");
        }
    } return imageMap;
}
```

First, the application resource manager locates the file named `ImageMap.plist` and goes a step further by returning a handle to an InputStream for that file. Next the image map is read into a NSDictionary using property list serialization.

> **NOTE**
>
> A NSDictionary represents a set of key-value pairs. A NSArray in contrast, represents an ordered list of objects.

Before building, remember to add `import java.io.*;` to the import statements at the beginning of `Application.java`.

Using WORepetition

Next, we are going to generate the HTML image map from the Plist image map. With the WOMappedRollover component open in WebObjects Builder, select one of the WOArea elements.

Now click WORepetition icon to repeat this element over a list. Bind the WORepetition list attribute to `application.imageMap.areas` and the *item* to a new variable key, `area`, as in Figure 3.4.

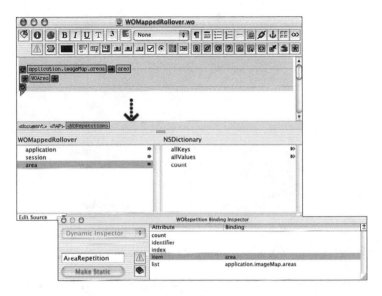

FIGURE 3.4   Bind the WORepetition list and item attributes.

We are taking advantage of the fact that both NSDictionary and NSArray conform to the key value coding APIs. That is, `imageMap.valueForKey("areas")` will return you the NSArray of *areas*. Similarly, `area.valueForKey("directActionName")` will return the *directActionName* String for that particular area. So, we can bind the WOArea attributes as follows:

```
Area: WOArea {
    shape = area.shape;
    coords = area.coords;
    directActionName = area.directActionName;
}
```

Remove the redundant WOArea elements, save and build and run.

Now convert WOMappedRollover to a nonsynchronized component. At the moment all that is involved is to have the method `synchronizesVariablesWithBindings()` return `false`. Open the component in WebObjects Builder and add three keys to its API: *imageName*, *imageFile,* and *imageMap,* as in Figure 3.5.

FIGURE 3.5   Define the WOMappedRollover API.

Rebind the WOImage attributes *name* and *filename* to ^`imageName` and ^`imageFile`, respectively. Rebind the WORepetition's list to ^`imageMap.areas`. The binding *usemap* should be set to a key of the same name:

```
public String usemap() {
    NSDictionary imageMap = (NSDictionary) valueForBinding("imageMap");
    String mapName = (String) imageMap.valueForKey("name");

    return "#" + mapName;
    }
```

Now when you open `Main.wo` in WebObjects Builder you will notice that the three new attributes of WOMappedRollover appear in the Inspector.

NOTE

When attributes are displayed in red it indicates that they are required bindings.

One or two things are left to complete before we can move on to the next section. One is to make the <map> dynamic. You might have to do this manually. To do so, switch to Source View, and then add the WOGenericContainer.

Set its element name to map, and then make sure the WORepetition copied, cut, and pasted inside it. Bind another attribute *name* to ^`imageMap.name`. Finally, we need to set the *usemap* attribute of the image to correspond to the `imageMap.name`. Add an accessor key usemap, which vends #mapname:

```
public String usemap() {
    NSDictionary imageMap = (NSDictionary) valueForBinding("imageMap");
    String mapName = (String) imageMap.valueForKey("name");

    return "#" + mapName;
    }
```

Next, we have to work around a feature of WOImage, which will attempt to locate a file of the same name, instead of allowing one to set its *usemap* attribute as a String. So, instead of the WOImage, use a WOGenericElement, setting its *elementName* to img. Remember to rebind the *name* and *usemap* attributes. For its *src* binding, create an accessor src to vend the image URL:

```
public String src() {
    WOResourceManager resourceManager = application().resourceManager();
    String imageFile = (String) valueForBinding("imageFile");

    return resourceManager.urlForResourceNamed
➥(imageFile, null, null, context().request());
    }
```

After that is completed build and run.

Adding Rollovers to Image Maps

So far we have abstracted out the component logic, template, and API for a WOMappedRollover component pretty well. But, the obvious is missing: the rollovers. Much of the work has already been done, however.

We still have to add a few more keys as accessors for onMouseOver, onMouseOut, and the JavaScript scriptString for image preloading:

```
public String onMouseOver() {
    String imageName = (String) valueForBinding("imageName");
    return imageName + ".src=" + imageName + index + ".src;";
    }

public String onMouseOut() {
    String imageName = (String) valueForBinding("imageName");
    return imageName + ".src='" + src() + "';";
    }
```

For the onMouseOver notice that we use an *index* counter. Add index as an integer variable key. Bind onMouseOver to the WOArea. Then bind onMouseOut to the

WOMap. Add a WOJavaScript element before the image map. Change to Source View and reuse the WORepetition used to repeat the WOArea, by copying the WebObejcts tags for, and placing it around, the WOJavaScript:

```
<webobject name=Repetition>
    <webobject name=JavaScript></webobject>
</webobject>
<webobject name=Map>
    <webobject name=Repetition>
        <webobject name=Area></webobject>
    </webobject>
</webobject>
<webobject name=Image></webobject>
```

CAUTION

Be careful when using WebObjects elements in this fashion. In particular, only do so if and when the WebObjects bindings are identical as in the previous example.

We are using the convenience of a repetition to help us construct the image preloading JavaScript(s). Bind the WOJavaScript *scriptString* to a key of the same name. The index is incremented by the WORepetition, so make sure that it is bound to the *index* attribute of the WORepetition.

```
public String scriptString() {
        WOResourceManager resourceManager = application().resourceManager();
    String filename = (String) area.valueForKey("imageOnMouseOver");
    String url = resourceManager.urlForResourceNamed(filename, null, null,
                                                    context().request());
    String imageName = (String) valueForBinding("imageName");

    // image pre-loading
    return imageName + index + " = new Image();\n" +
imageName + index + ".src = '" + url + "';\n";
    }
```

We are making a minor compromise here by not including the main image in the preloading. This is done to keep the component simple. Finally, don't forget to add the *onMouseOver* attribute to the WOArea component, then build and run.

Voilà! You should now have a mapped rollover element.

Making Stateful Components

A second method or technique for improving performance of applications is to make components *stateless* where appropriate.

The best way to discover statelessness is to look at a component that is *stateful*. In other words, look at a component that can't be made stateless.

Examining a Stateful Component

In this subsection we're going to a simple component, WOToggle, as an exercise. It is a component switch that can be toggled between an *on* and *off* state.

Create a new project, *WOToggleTest*, and add a new component, *WOToggle*, to the *Application Server*, as normal.

Copy in the images `PowerSwitch_Off.gif` and `PowerSwitch_On.gif` from */System/Library/WebObjects/JavaApplications/JavaMonitor.woa/WebSeverResources/* into the *Web Server Resources* group. (Remember to copy them into the *Web Server* target when doing so). Open `WOToggle.wo` in WebObjects Builder, then make it a partial document.

Add a WOConditional from the WebObjects menu and inside it place a WOActiveImage. Set the active image filename to `PowerSwitch_On.gif`. Bind the conditional's *condition* to a new boolean variable of the same name.

> **NOTE**
>
> A *WOConditional* is a WebObjects element that displays its contents if its *condition* is true. It can be made to display its contents if the *condition* is false, by setting the *negate* attribute.

Repeat for the second image `PowerSwitch_Off.gif`. Only this time the conditional must be set to *negate*. To display the *off* active image in the second conditional, click the conditional's plus icon. This should turn it into a minus, as shown in Figure 3.6.

Finally, add a `toggle` action in the event a user clicks the toggle to switch its state:

```
public void toggle() {
        condition = !condition;
}
```

Bind the two active images *action* attributes to `toggle`.

Add a WOToggle element to the Main component, then build and run.

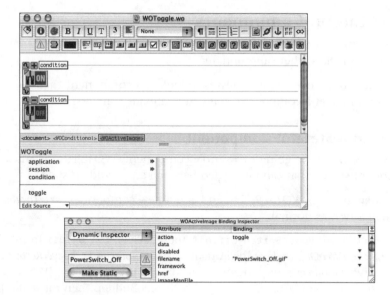

FIGURE 3.6 Bind WOToggle.

You might have noticed that we didn't make this component *nonsynchronizing* or *stateless*. It is indeed possible, however.

I leave it as an exercise for you to make WOToggle into a *nonsynchronizing* component. (Hint: the hard part involves *pushing* a value back into the parent. Use takeValueForBinding() to do that).

Observing Component Memory

In the last exercise we got a glimpse of what it is for a component to have state. In other words, what it is for a component to have memory.

Although it is possible to make WOToggle both a *nonsynchronizing* and *statelesss* component, the most natural place to maintain the on/off state is in the WOToggle component itself.

When we look at *direct actions* in the next chapter, we will see that it is not possible for direct action pages to use WOToggle as implemented, for the very reason mentioned previously.

Now we'll take a more detailed look at component state or memory by creating WOCollapsibleListContent. This is a component very similar in nature to WOToggle, except it is a *container* that displays its contents based on whether it is *on* or *off*, as shown in Figure 3.7.

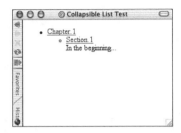

FIGURE 3.7   Outlining a WOCollapsibleListContent.

Start as usual by creating a project to develop the component in *WOCollapsibleListContentTest*. Create a component *WOCollapsibleListContent*, then add the boolean variable `condition` and a null action `toggle` as we did previously for WOToggle. In addition, add a variable String key `label`.

This time however, instead of an active image, we'll have a list and a hyperlink. Click the unordered list icon to add a list to the *WOCollapsibleListContent* in its WebObjects Builder window.

Add a WOHyperlink, and delete the contents of the hyperlink and bind its *string* attribute to `label`. Bind its *action* to `toggle`.

Position the cursor just after the hyperlink, but still inside the list item. (You might have to do this by changing to Source View). Add a WOConditional and bind its *condition* to the key of the same name.

So far, we have created noncontainer components. But *WOCollapsibleListContent* will be a *container*. Much like WORepetition or WOConditional or WOHyperlink.

To make *WOCollapsibleListContent* a *container*, we need to add a WOComponentContent element from the WebObjects menu. This indicates where in the component the content should go. Place the WOComponentContent inside the conditional. So the contents will only be displayed if the condition is met. You might want to place a break within the conditional. Compare it with Figure 3.8.

Before using it in the Main page, you will have to define its API.

Set the *condition* binding to *Will Set* and its *Value Set* to *boolean*. What *Will Set* means is that the *WOCollapsibleListContent* will change the state or value of that key. So, if it is bound it will set the condition value in its parent component. Make the *label* binding *Required*, then Save and Build.

Now drag in a *WOCollapsibeListContent* container into the Main page component. Nest a second one inside of the first, and label both components and go play.

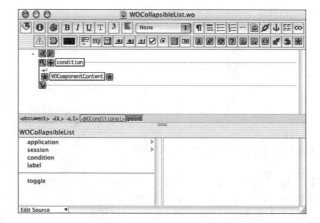

FIGURE 3.8   Compare the layout of WOCollapsibleListContent in WebObjects Builder.

When running the application you should get to open and close *nodes* like an outline view, as shown in Figure 3.7. Now, here we are clearly seeing each *WOCollapsibleListContent* component. Remember if it is open or closed?

It would be rather difficult to use such a component if it were made stateless. Where and how would the state of the conditions be kept? Perhaps you should play around with it and see.

Using Stateless Components

Now that we've had a look at *stateful* components, I think we have a better understanding of when a component is *not stateful*, more commonly known as *stateless*.

Making a Component Stateless

To set a component that isn't stateful as stateless is simple. Make sure the accessor isStateless() returns true. Let's return to WOMappedRolloverTest and set both reusable components WOMappedRollover and WOArea as stateless:

```
public boolean isStateless() {
    return true;
}
```

After this is completed build and run.

There should not to be any observable difference. So what's all the fuss about?

Observing Singleton Component Instantiation

When a component is set to stateless, only one such component is created in every application. It is reused by each and every component that uses it.

The alternative is a scenario where the component is instantiated each time it is used, for example, on each page called twice. Or on separate pages that use the same component. Let's have a look at this in action.

Add a debug line to the WOMappedRollover constructor:

```
// debug
WOComponent.debugString("WOMappedRollover: init");
```

Disable the stateless setting by making isStateless()return false. Build and run the application.

Click the refresh button a few times. Notice how the statement is printed in Project Builder's console. This indicates that a new instance of the component has been created. Now turn statelessness on and Build and Run again.

Notice this time however, that the message is only printed once. Only one instance of WOMappedRollover was created.

When to Use Nonsynchronization and Stateless Components

For reusable components, try to make them nonsynchronizing if appropriate and possible. We've already seen cases where it is not appropriate, for example WOCollapsibleListContent, and to some extent WOToggle. If the component can be made nonsynchronizing, the chances are that it can be made stateless as well.

Remember that appropriate use of these techniques can yield applications with significantly smaller memory footprints, which in turn can produce excellent results, performance wise.

However, you might find that in a typical application, it is a well-designed object model that affects both the performance and success of a site. We'll look at this more later in the book.

Using a DHTML Splash Page

Finally, it's time to incorporate our work on WOMappedRollover into *DynamicMovies*.

It might seem like a lot of work to produce a simple image map with rollovers, but you've actually done much more than that. The WOMappedRollover that you've created is fairly generic and can be reused again in another page or application. Next time, it's a matter of dragging in the component and hooking it up.

Copy the WOMappedRollover and WOArea components, and their associated files into the DynamicMovies application. Don't forget to copy over the images into the *Web Server* and the `ImageMap.plist` in the *Application Server*. Also remember to add the `imageMap` key to the `Application.java`.

Oh, you might want to hook up the direct action names in the `ImageMap.plist` to the ones in the *DynamicMovies* application. (Hint: they are the same ones we used for the ToolbarComponent) Finally, add a title image from the file download associated with this chapter from the companion Web site (`www.samspublishing.com`) and build and run the application.

Summary

In this chapter we looked at optimizing WebObjects applications and components by using nonsynchronization and statelessness while developing a component to render a DHTML splash page.

4

Building Bookmarkable Applications

"The only way of discovering the limits of the possible is to venture a little way past them into the impossible."

—*Arthur C. Clark*

Finally, we get a chance to look at direct actions and how to build a stateless application in this chapter.

Those developers familiar with direct actions might want to skip over this chapter or at least the first section. In particular, this chapter will look at creating a direct-action application, handling form values in direct actions, and "the browser backtracking problem."

Throughout this chapter, you might find ideas and concepts on which you would like a more thorough explanation. For more resources, please visit Apple's WebObjects Developer's site at `http://developer.apple.com/techpubs/webobjects/`.

Creating a Stateless Application

If you weren't already aware of it, you have been using and developing a direct-action application. The *DynamicMovies* example that you've been developing is a direct-action application.

So really we've been holding off on discussing direct actions long enough. It's time to take an in-depth look at them.

Introduction to Direct Actions

So far, when running a WebObjects application we have always been presented with the Main component as the starting page. For most applications this is the only way to enter an application.

The advent of direct actions changed this. Now, you are allowed to enter a WebObjects application from any one of these direct-action pages. Hence the name direct action.

This rather small idea turned out to have a greater significance. It opened avenues of new applications to WebObjects and it provided a solution to a nagging problem: The backtracking limitation of WebObjects.

We'll look at both in this chapter.

Setting Direct Actions as Default

Let's start by making a direct-action version of the *Hello* application. Duplicate the project and rename it *HelloDirect*. Later we are going to compare both applications.

In order to prevent the first page being vended as a session-based page, the application's direct request handler must be set as default.

Add the following two lines to the Application constructor:

```
public Application() {
    super();
    WORequestHandler directActionRequestHandler = requestHandlerForKey("wa");
    setDefaultRequestHandler(directActionRequestHandler);
}
```

Handling User Input with Direct Actions

Let's add a *greetingsAction*. First, edit *DirectAction.java* and add a direct-action method similar to the *defaultAction*. Open the Main component in WebObjects Builder.

Now that the Main page is to become a direct action, we must remove the reference to session. In particular, we are not going to use session.username to store the user's typed input.

Instead, we are going to make that key local, so add a username key as a variable to Main.

Rebind the *WOTextField value* to username.

Set its name to username. This is to identify the text input in the form submission. Later we'll retrieve this value from the direct-action request using this as its key.

Remove the action binding on the *WOForm* and instead bind its *directActionName* to *greetings* from the drop-down menu.

Remember to make your submit button static, as the direct action is being handled by the *WOForm*.

NOTE

Every direct action is implemented with the suffix "Action." In other words, the method "greetingAction" implemented in a DirectAction class, represents a direct action called "greeting."

Save it and return to the *greetingAction* in *DirectAction.java*.

The caveat of using direct actions is that unlike standard WebObjects actions, it does not possess the convenience of an automatically synchronizing component state from one page to the next; this must be done manually. Values must be pulled from the request and then placed in the component.

Change the *greetingAction* to get the username value from the request, and then pass it onto the *Greeting* page.

```
WOComponent nextPage = pageWithName("Greeting");
String username = request().stringFormValueForKey("username");

// set values
nextPage.takeValueForKey(username, "username");

return nextPage;
```

The key value coding like method `stringFormValueForKey("username")` will return the string `Ravi` from a direct action URL in the form:
`.../wa/greeting?username=Ravi`.

Then to set the value we turn to key value coding API `takeValueForKey()`.

Using Hyperlinks in Direct Action Components

Now we must alter the back link on the `Greeting` page.

To do so open the component in WebObjects Builder and rebind the *WOHyperlink* to use `directActionName` "default," instead of a WebObjects action. Add the username variable to the component and bind it to the *WOString*.

Finally, in order to pass the username value back to the Main page, when the back link is clicked, add an attribute ?username to the back link and bind it to username.

By setting a *WOHyperlink* binding prefixed with ?, we are able to append form values onto the URL. Then make sure the username value is parsed in by the defaultAction. Add the code required to take the form value from the URL and then place it in the Main component. Finally, save, build, and run.

TIP

Developing stateless applications, one must make sure that spurious Sessions aren't created. A simple way to keep track of Sessions is to add a debugString() to the Session() constructor, which will inform you whenever a session is accidentally created.

Using Direct Actions

In this section we shall look at the merits and demerits of statelessness and direct actions, as well as build a second, more sophisticated, example application.

Observing Transient State

This is an ideal time to compare both the original *Hello* application and the *HelloDirect* application. To do so, open a browser window to both applications; enter some text, submit, and repeat. Notice how the results are pretty much identical.

But how is this? *HelloDirect* is a *stateless* application. How does it appear to maintain state? Well, the state of the *HelloDirect* application can be considered to be *transient*. It lives neither on the browser nor the server but in limbo, passing between pages via the URL.

Another thing you might like to try is bookmark a page from both applications. Then stop and restart the applications. When the applications are running try accessing the bookmarked pages.

Avoiding the Backtracking Problem

There is one other thing you might have already noticed when using the *Hello* application: the browser backtracking problem.

To replicate the problem:

1. Type in name1, hit return, click the back link and repeat for a second string, name2.

2. Return to the first instance of the Main page by using the browser back button.

3. Retype something over name1 and submit.

You will find that you lose your input.

You have just observed the browser backtracking problem. This is largely a limitation of storing state on the server, and a limitation of typical WebObjects applications.

Fortunately, there are ways around it. One solution, which is applicable to the Hello example, is to set the Application default to `setRefreshesOnBacktrackEnabled(true)`. This vends each WebObjects page as preexpired, forcing your browser to refresh.

Again however there are limitations of this workaround, which is most notable in larger WebObjects applications. The best solution in many cases is to circumvent it altogether by employing direct actions and using statelessness wherever possible.

Advantages of Direct Actions and Stateless Applications

Let's take a brief look at some advantages of using direct actions in stateless applications.

- Circumvent or minimize effects of the browser backtracking problem.

- Performance and Efficiency: A typical WebObjects application must cache instances of pages in a session. This defaults to 30 pages per session. In nontrivial applications, that can amount to a mighty load. Direct action pages are not cached. They are created and disposed of with each request, making their use more memory efficient. This produces the effect of a more responsive application.

- Deployment is simpler.

- Pages are Bookmarkable.

- Appropriate for small or Mini-Applications where there isn't a need for full-fledged session management.

When to Use Direct Actions

We have pointed out the advantages of using direct actions and statelessness in applications. However we have not looked at their disadvantages.

The most obvious disadvantage is that there might be a steep learning curve associated with direct actions.

Although sometimes, the concept of direct actions can be more intuitive, or natural, to developers. Particularly, if they are up on other server-side technologies like PHP, JSP, and Perl, which use form values to pass state between pages.

Given that as a preference, I would want to use direct actions wherever possible. But when would I not use it? A simple rule to go by is to not use statelessness whenever there is a user login or a personalized experience of a Web site. In that case a typical WebObjects application is a better and more natural solution.

Remember, however, that you don't have to decide on one or the other. The solutions are not mutually exclusive. Most of the time, applications can employ both statelessness and statefullness at the same time.

Building Mini-Applications Using Direct Actions

In this next section we're going to build a simple *Feedback* form as a stateless mini-application. Mostly as an exercise in using direct actions, but we'll also learn about e-mail composition and delivery using WebObjects.

Using E-mail Delivery in WebObjects

Create a new WebObjects Application project *Feedback*.

Follow the instructions for setting up the basic application:

1. Make the application handle direct-action requests by default.

2. On the Main page, add a form and static fields for from, subject, and a *WOText* element for the contents. You might want to layout the form in a table. See Figure 4.1

   Make sure the form elements are named from, subject, and contents. These define the keys used for the values filled out by a user.

   Add the variable String keys from, subject, and contents, and then bind them.

   Bind the *WOForm* to a direct action named feedback.

3. Add a feedbackAction method to the DirectAction class. For now simply pull the form values into variables. Return a page named ThankYou.

4. Create a basic ThankYou page to return after the feedback has been submitted.

Build and run the application to make sure the basic application works. Finally, we are going to add a bit of code to the feedback method to generate and send e-mails:

```
WOMailDelivery sharedInstance = WOMailDelivery.sharedInstance();

// send email
sharedInstance.composePlainTextEmail(from, to, null, subject, message, true);

// log
logString("DirectAction: email sent from: " + from);
```

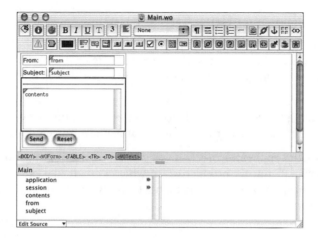

FIGURE 4.1   Laying out the feedback form component.

Add the key to representing the address the e-mail is being sent to:

```
protected static NSArray to = new NSArray("me@my.com");
```

The method composePlainTextEmail() composes and sends e-mail via the WOSMTP default mail server, but this default must be set for e-mails to get sent. The most convenient place to do this is as an application launch argument.

Select the Feedback target from the Targets tab. Then select the Executables tab to set a command-line argument. Click on Add to set WOSMTPHost, as in Figure 4.2, and build and run.

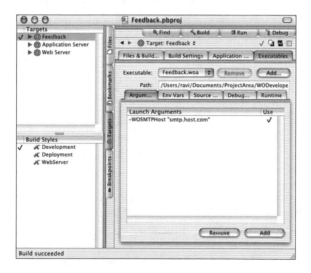

FIGURE 4.2   Adding a command-line argument to the application.

Localizing a Direct-Action Application

The principles behind localizing a direct-action application are about the same as a typical WebObjects application. In fact, there are more options available for a typical application. Here we'll look at techniques that are applicable to both styles of application.

The simplest strategy for localization is to create separate apps for each language. In practice this is what happens for larger sites that get administered locally.

However, for smaller applications, the hassle of administrating separate apps for each language can make it counter productive. In which case, it makes sense to employ some of the localization techniques available to WebObjects applications, which we'll look at next.

Localizing Components

In this subsection and the next, we are going to localize *HelloDirect* for both French and Japanese.

Start by duplicating the *HelloDirect* project. Call it *LocalHelloDirect*.

We are going to localize `Main.wo`:

1. Select the component in Project Builder's Groups & Files pane.

2. Bring up the Inspector by choosing Project, Show Info.

3. Select Make Localized from the Localization & Platforms drop-down menu, as shown in Figure 4.3. Now within the component directory you will notice a further directory named English. This represents the English version of the component.

4. To add a French version, select Add localized variant from the Localization & Platforms drop-down menu. Then, from the panel that appears enter **French** for the name of the locale (see Figure 4.4). This should add a `French` directory under the component folder as in Figure 4.5.

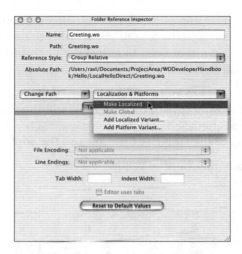

FIGURE 4.3   Examining file locales from the Project Builder Inspector.

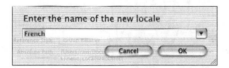

FIGURE 4.4   Choosing a language locale.

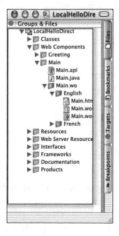

FIGURE 4.5   Editing a localized component in Project Builder.

Now open the French version of the Main component. Change the document title to `Bonjour tout le monde` and the submit button label to `Entrez votre nom`. For the sake of consistency, you might want to relabel the English version's submit button `Enter your name`. Then, save and build.

Now add French to your browser's list of language preferences. In Internet Explorer, that would mean choosing Explorer, Preferences, and then adding French to the languages list in the Language/Fonts panel. Make French your default language by moving it to the top of the language list. Now run the application.

Voilà! You should automatically be vended the French version of the Main page. See Figure 4.6.

FIGURE 4.6   Running a French Hello World.

Now that there are separate components for each language, you are free to create and add localized images like the `HelloWorld.gif`.

As an additional exercise, you might want to localize the Greeting page. The strings you need are `Bonjour` and `Retour à la page Main`.

Supporting Japanese

Localizing a component for Japanese is pretty much identical, but there are a few things to look out for. In particular the character encoding.

Create a new Main component locale for Japanese. Open and edit the component in WebObjects Builder Source View. Now copy in the appropriate strings from the Web site (see companion Web site at `www.samspublishing.com`) as in Figure 4.7.

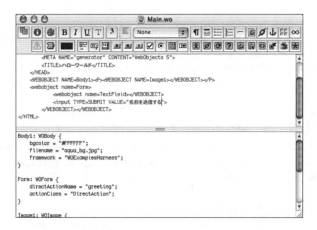

FIGURE 4.7   Adding Japanese strings in WebObjects Builder.

Repeat for the Greetings component. Edit the HTML source in Project Builder or WebObjects Builder source mode. Notice that the HTML templates for the components will have saved the Japanese characters in the HTML character equivalents:

```
<webobject name=Form>
    <webobject name=TextField></webobject>
    <input TYPE=SUBMIT
           VALUE="&#21517;&#21069;&#12434;&#36865;&#20449;&#12377;&#12427;">
</webobject></webobject>
```

This is the reason for performing the copy and paste via WebObjects Builder, so that it would perform the character conversions automatically. Save and run.

FIGURE 4.8   Running the Hello application in a Japanese browser.

NOTE

Testing the application in a Japanese browser can be a little more challenging. On MacOS X, this requires setting Japanese as the preferred language in both System Preferences and Internet Explorer. In addition, the default character set of Japanese-Shift must be set in IE.

Other Facilities for Localization

The way in which WebObjects determines the language locale to choose in order to vend a component, is from the request. Programmatically this can be obtained from: `request.browserLanguages()`.

Explicitly Setting Language Preference

When dealing with Sessions, there is another place you can set and get the language preference of the user. That is in the Session: `session.languages()`.

Note that this feature is unavailable to stateless applications for obvious reasons.

Also, unless it is an absolute requirement, which it might be, then using automatic language preference detection is probably a superior solution even for applications with sessions.

Using String Locales

There might be cases where you need to obtain a string locale in your code, to dynamically generate some JavaScript, for example. In which case you may maintain a strings file for each locale. The localized string can be fetched using `resourceManager().stringForKey()`.

However, I would only use this if absolutely necessary. Again, using localized components is a simpler and more elegant solution.

Setting the Database Encoding

When developing database driven applications, it is important to remember to set up databases with the correct locale in mind. You don't want to store Japanese text in a database that supports only ASCII.

Summary

In this chapter we introduced the concepts behind direct actions and stateless applications.

Hopefully, it has given you the impression that direct actions are really not very difficult, in fact they are easy. If used appropriately and for the right application, they can be used to develop full-featured and comprehensive applications like their stateful counterparts.

5

XHTML and WebObjects

Seymour Skinner: "I have caught word that a child is using his imagination and I've come to put a stop to it."

—The Simpsons

In this chapter we are going to dig deeper into the WebObjects Component architecture, while developing a WebObjects application that serves XHTML.

We'll look at creating an XHTML WebObjects application. Prototyping a XHTML component. Handling component actions. Implementing XHTML components as dynamic elements and the WebObjects request-response loop.

Introduction to XHTML

Before we begin let's take a moment for a brief introduction to XHTML and what it is.

XHTML is a redefinition of the HTML 4.0 specification in XML. Because it is based on HTML 4, it is backward compatible with HTML 4.0 browsers. Hence, it promises to be the bridge between the Web of the past (based on HTML) and the Web of the future (based on XML).

Looking at the Differences Between XHTML and HTML

On the whole you will notice that XHTML is stricter and less forgiving than HTML. Therefore, we must be a little more careful when developing XHTML applications.

So, before we begin to develop a WebObjects application in XHTML, let's take a quick overview of the new XML and XHTML conventions we are going to have to stick to.

Lowercase Tags

To conform to the XML specification, all tags must be lowercase.

To set the WebObjects Builder preference to use lowercase tags, choose Preferences from the WebObjects Builder application menu. In the HTML panel, select lowercase markers in the When prettyprinting option, as in Figure 5.1

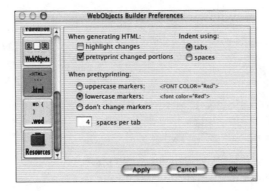

FIGURE 5.1   Setting WebObjects Builder to use lowercase tags as a preference.

Quoted Attribute Values

It is no longer sufficient to have attribute values as in the example `<td width=5>`, it is now necessary to place attribute values within quotation marks, `<td width="5">`.

So, when using WebObjects Builder make sure those number values are enclosed in quotes. Again, this is a convention of XML.

Document and XML Declaration

To indicate conformance to the XHTML spec, a document must contain the declaration

```
<!DOCTYPE html
➥PUBLIC "-//W3C//DTD XHTML 1.0 Transitional//EN" "DTD/xhtml1-transitional.dtd">
```

In addition, it ought to have the XML declaration specifying the document encoding:

```
<?xml version="1.0" encoding="UTF-8"?>
```

This will require manually replacing the `!DOCTYPE` declarations in each of the page components with the previous ones.

WebObjects Builder might complain about the XML declaration unless you have set a preference to ignore the semantic and syntax errors it finds. See Figure 5.2.

FIGURE 5.2   Setting WebObjects Builder preferences to ignore HTML validation exceptions.

Noncontainer Elements Must Be Terminated

It is no longer sufficient to declare a noncontainer element, such as <hr>, as such. Instead, it is necessary to declare it as <hr/>. Which is a simplification of the empty XHTML element <hr></hr>.

Well-Formed XML

Finally, it is important to properly nest XML elements and to close your elements such as <p></p>.

For further reference see http://www.w3.org/TR/xhtml1/.

Building a XHTML WebObjects Application

Before plunging into writing our *Hello* application in XHTML, let's take a look at what is required. In particular, let's highlight the HTML of the first page that has to change:

```
<!DOCTYPE HTML PUBLIC "-//W3C//DTD HTML 3.2//EN">
<HTML>
    <HEAD>
        <META NAME="generator" CONTENT="WebObjects 5">
        <TITLE>Hello World</TITLE>
    </HEAD>
    <body background="/cgi-bin/WebObjects/HelloDirect.woa/wr?wodata=%2FLibrary%2F
Frameworks%2FWOExamplesHarness.framework%2FWebServerResources%2Faqua_bg.jpg">
        <p><img src="/cgi
          bin/WebObjects/HelloDirect.woa/wr?wodata=%2FUsers%2Fravi%2F
```

```
            Documents%2FProjectArea%2FWODeveloperHandbook%2FHello%2FHelloDirect%2F
            hello_world_title.gif" width="225" height="150"></p>
    <form method="post" action="/cgi-bin/WebObjects/HelloDirect.woa/wa/greeting">
            <input type=text value="ravi" name="username">
            <input type=SUBMIT>
    </form>
        </body>
</HTML>
```

Preparing Page Components for XHTML

First and foremost, the document declaration should be changed.

Having made a duplicate of the *HelloDirect* project and renamed it *XHelloDirect* appropriately, we can proceed to make the required changes.

From within Project Builder, you might want to edit the Main.html template to use the XHTML document declaration. Also, add the XML declaration.

Now change all the uppercase tags to lowercase.

TIP

In WebObjects Builder, there is a neat feature that allows you to reformat and prettyprint HTML according to your preferences. Change to Source View and choose Format, Reformat HTML. This ought to do the trick.

Finally, in source view, edit the submit button element, placing its type attribute value, "submit", within quotation marks. Also remember to close the tag with /> according to XML/XHTML conventions.

Do the same for the <meta> tag.

Implementing a WebObjects XHTML Element

What remains to be converted are the <img> and the text <input> elements. Unfortunately, just to add a / before the closing > requires us to re-create XHTML components for them. We'll start with prototyping the XHTML <img> element.

Prototyping Basic XHTML Elements

As usual, we are going to develop the WXImage in isolation. So create a development project *WXImageTest*. Add a new component *WXImage* and make it a partial document.

NOTE

There is an example framework called WOComponentElements, which does use the WX prefix. Do not confuse these WX elements with those WebObjects example components.

To prototype *WXImage*, we are going to use *WOXMLNode* instead of *WOGenericElement* as we did before. *WOXMLNode* terminates tags according to XML convention so it is preferable when developing XML elements.

1. Add a WebObjects custom component *WOXMLNode* and set its *elementName* to "img". *WebObjects, WOXMLNode.*

2. Set WXImage as a nonsynchronizing component.

3. Make the API identical to WOImage. With the exception of the *otherTagString*, which is not applicable to XML elements and data, replicate the API of *WOImage*, as in Figure 5.3. Also make *filename* a required binding.

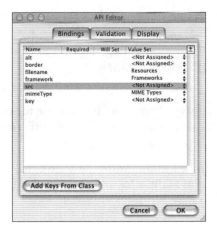

FIGURE 5.3   Setting the WXImage API.

4. Bind the WOXMLNode as in Figure 5.4.

5. Add an accessor for the key src. We'll use the filename and the framework bindings to serve the WebObjects URL for the image:

```
public String src() {
    String framework = (String) valueForBinding("framework");
    String filename = (String) valueForBinding("filename");
    WOResourceManager resourceManager = application().resourceManager();
    WORequest request = context().request();
```

```
   return resourceManager.urlForResourceNamed(filename, framework,
➡ null, request);
}
```

6. Make the component stateless.

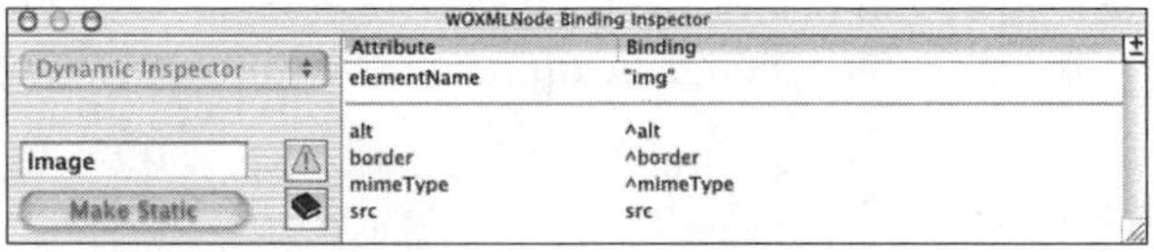

FIGURE 5.4   Binding WOXMLNode.

Finally, incorporate it into a Main page, which has been converted to XHTML. Add in an image for test purposes, and then build and test.

You will notice that your browser probably displays the Main page correctly, even though it doesn't really conform yet to the XHTML spec.

Setting Component API Validation

There are two keys, data and src, which haven't been bound or used.

These are mutually exclusive alternatives to filename for providing the source of the image. In other words, you might provide a static URL, or even the image as data, but you can only have one of these bindings set.

To specify that one of these bindings must be set we define a validation condition for WXImage. Open the API Editor for WXImage and click the Validation tab.

1. Highlight the first Error Condition.

2. Click the Add button to add a second entry and choose src from the attribute pop-up.

3. Double-click the validation message to edit it. Change it to "One of the bindings 'filename' and 'src' must be set." Compare it with Figure 5.5.

So far we've defined a validation rule to generate an error if the keys filename and src are left unbound. However, a second rule must be added to make sure that *only* one of them is set.

For this we are going to have to make sure that a validation error will be raised if both filename and src are bound.

Add a second validation message by clicking on the plus/minus icon. Add the validation conditions as before, only this time set them as bound.

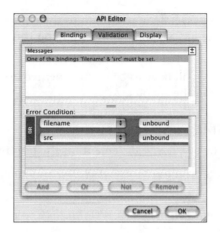

FIGURE 5.5   Creating a WXImage validation rule.

Using Mutually Exclusive Keys

Now we have to alter the src accessor to reflect the changes we have made to the API.

```
public String src() {
    WOResourceManager resourceManager = application().resourceManager();

    if (hasBinding("filename")) {
        String filename = (String) valueForBinding("filename");
        String framework = (String) valueForBinding("framework");

        return resourceManager.urlForResourceNamed(filename, framework, null,
                                                  context().request());
    } else return (String) valueForBinding("src");
}
```

We use hasBinding() to determine if and when a particular binding has been set. In this case, if it is filename, we execute the same code as before. Otherwise, the value for the src binding is vended.

Test the component using the src binding by pointing it to some graphic ("/PoweredByMacOSXLarge.gif", for example) located on your Web server. Make sure that the Web server is active.

For another experiment, try adding the nonAPI bindings *width* and *height* to a *WXImage*.

You will notice that they do not get passed on to the component. A limitation of implementing an element as a component is that you can't set any additional bindings as appropriate.

To do that, the *WXImage* will have to be reimplemented as a Dynamic Element. We'll attempt this later in the chapter.

Prototyping XHTML Form Elements

Next, let's prototype the *WXTextField* element for the user input.

Create a development test project *WXTextFieldTest* and add a component for the *WXTextField* element.

1. Make the document *Partial*. Add a *WOXMLNode* to represent the XHTML `<input>` element.

2. Make the component nonsynchronizing.

3. Add an accessor key `name`. Bind it to the WOXMLNode *name* attribute.

    ```
    public String name() {
            String name = (String) valueForBinding("name");
        return (hasBinding("name")) ? name:context().elementID();
        }
    ```

4. Add only the name and value keys to the API. The value is settable.

5. Make the component stateless.

6. Add the method `takeValueFromRequest()`:

    ```
    public void takeValuesFromRequest(WORequest request, WOContext context) {
        super.takeValuesFromRequest(request, context);

        // get the value from the request
        Object value = request.formValueForKey(name());

        // push the value to the parent
        setValueForBinding(value, "value");
    }
    ```

The `takeValuesFromRequest()` is the first method we've encountered that participates in the request-response loop. In particular, it is responsible for managing the state of the textfield.

The name plays a critical role in this. The method `context().elementID()` is a utility that will generate a unique number for the text field. This is, in the event that a name is not provided.

Given that the text field identifies itself in the document by the unique name, the text field can synchronize itself by pulling the form value for that key.

This is perhaps the first time we've witnessed state synchronization in the raw. It is amazingly simple.

I might add that the component is far from complete. You might have noted that we omitted the *dateFormat* and *numberFormat* bindings. This was deliberate.

It might be fairly trivial to push and pull values from requests. However, the advantage of this simplicity is that it allows us to achieve greater sophistication and functionality elsewhere. Implementing the date and number formatting is one such case.

Now you should test the component. So place it inside a *WOForm* in the Main page, and add the appropriate keys and bindings to test a component action and perhaps a direct action, too.

When you are satisfied with the functioning of the *WXTextField*, move onto prototyping the last component for the chapter: a *WXHyperlink*.

Prototyping an Actionable XHTML Element

In this subsection we're going to look at prototyping the third, and last, type of dynamic element as a component.

NOTE

The standard WOHyperlink will work correctly in an XHTML document. The WXHyperlink as prototyped here conforms to the XML/XLINK specification. As such it may render correctly depending on the browser.

WXHyperlink differs from *WXImage* and *WXTextField* in that it is an element that must also handle a user action. In this case return a new page when the user clicks on the link.

Start again by creating a development project *WXHyperlinkTest*, adding a component for the *WXTextField*, and making it a *Partial Document* and *nonsynchronizing*.

1. Place a *WOXMLNode* in the component template using "a" as its *elementName*.

2. Add a binding "xlink:href" to the *WOXMLNode*. (Include the quotation marks to avoid WebObjects from incorrectly parsing in the component.) Bind it to an accessor for href.

3. Set up the API for the component as in Figure 5.6.

FIGURE 5.6   Defining the WXHyperlink API.

4. Add a *WOString* and a *WOComponentContent* to the *WOXMLNode* to represent the content for the link. Bind the *WOString* value to `"^string"`. See Figure 5.7.

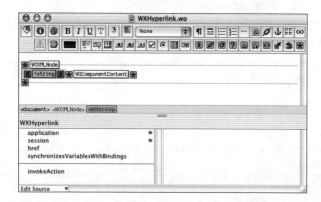

FIGURE 5.7   Laying out WXHyperlink.

5. Edit the `href` accessor to return the appropriate URL:

```
public String href() {
    if (hasBinding("href"))
        return (String) valueForBinding("href");
    else if (hasBinding("action") || hasBinding("pageName"))
        return (String) context().componentActionURL();
    else if (hasBinding("directActionName")) {
        String directActionName = (String) valueForBinding("directAction-
Name");
        NSDictionary queryDictionary = (NSDictionary)
                                        valueForBinding("queryDictionary");

        return context().directActionURLForActionNamed(directActionName,
                                                       queryDictionary);
    } else return null;
}
```

Returning a static URL bound to the *href* key is fairly easy to vend. Simply use `valueForBinding()` to fetch and return it.

However, things are not so obvious if the action is a WebObjects action.

In the case of a direct action, you can obtain its URL from the `context().directActionURLForActionNamed()` method. A *queryDictionary* can be used to append form values to the URL. Then when the user clicks on the direct action link, he is directed to that particular direct action.

When the hyperlink is bound to either *pageName* or *action*, the processing of the result is handled by the *WXHyperlink* component itself, therefore, it returns `context().componentActionURL()`. Clicking the link will call the `invokeAction()` method.

6. Add the `invokeAction()` method to handle a WebObjects action:

```
public WOComponent invokeAction()  {
        if (hasBinding("action")) {
            return (WOComponent) valueForBinding("action");
        } else if (hasBinding( "pageName") ) {
            String pageName = (String) valueForBinding("pageName");
            return pageWithName(pageName);
        } else return null;
    }
```

In the case of the hyperlink being bound to a WebObjects component *action*, all invokeAction() does is to forward the action to its parent using valueForBinding().

But if a *pageName* is bound, then the WXHyperlink component performs the page creation as any other component using pageWithName(), and then returns it.

7. Set a validation error condition if *pageName, action, directActionName,* or *href* is left *unbound.*

8. Add a second validation error condition if more than one of those mutually exclusive keys is set.

This is somewhat trickier.

It requires a compounded statement which says: Raise an error when (*pageName* and *action*) OR (*pageName* and *href*) OR (*pageName* and *directActionName*) OR (*action* and *directActionName*) OR (*action* and *href*) OR (*directActionName* and *href*) is *bound*. Whew!

Actually we can simplify this to: (*pageName* and (*action* OR *href* OR *directActionName*)) OR (*action* and (*directActionName* OR *href*)) OR (*directActionName* and *href*). A little simpler perhaps?

Compare your results with Figure 5.8.

FIGURE 5.8   Adding a second validation condition.

Now add the *WXHyperlink* to the Main page and test it with an *action* and a *pageName*.

You might have noticed that this has been the most comprehensively implemented component of the three XHTML components implemented so far. There is only one key remaining, the *actionClass* for direct actions, that should be implemented.

As a short exercise you might want to implement support for direct action classes other than that of the default *DirectAction.java*.

> **NOTE**
>
> Direct actions can be logically grouped together by implementing them in separate classes. So for example you might want to have all user-related direct actions implemented in a Users class. For instance, a direct action URL might look similar to:
>
> `.../wa/Users/login&name=...`

The place to find out how to do this would be the documentation for WOContext.

```
http://developer.apple.com/techpubs/webobjects/WebObjectsRef/Java/Classes/
WOContext.html
```

Implementing a WebObjects Dynamic Element

Finally, we get a chance to reimplement one of these XHTML components as a dynamic element. For this purpose we shall choose to reimplement *WXImage*.

First, a brief introduction to dynamic elements and how they differ from WebObjects components. They really are quite different, as we will soon discover.

Introduction to Dynamic Elements

A WebObjects Dynamic Element represents the smallest atom of the component architecture. They are lightweight objects that represent an HTML or XML element such as <img>, <body>, <a>, and <input>. As such, they lack many of the features available to WebObjects components.

You only need to implement anything as a dynamic element only on very rare occasions. One is when you need to develop an XHTML application, a clearly noncontrived situation that ideally requires us to create dynamic elements.

To be fair, it is not essential to create dynamic elements because we have quite satisfactorily prototyped the *WXImage* as a component. However, if we are to properly implement any of the other XHTML elements, then they should be constructed as dynamic elements.

Dynamic elements are supposed to be used for creating dynamic versions of HTML or XML elements. Whereas WOComponents are typically created for higher-level objects or document fragments.

Introduction to WebObjects Request-Response Loop

Perhaps now would be a good time to be introduced to the WebObjects request-response loop.

Every WebObjects component and element has been made to interact with, and respond to, the request-response loop.

We have already seen the mechanism by which WebObjects parses in user input and manages state from page to page with takeValuesFromRequest(). We have also witnessed how WebObjects performs actions using the invokeAction() method.

These are two of the three primary functions performed by the methods that take part in the request-response loop. The third function, which we will come to next, is the actual writing out of the HTML content to the response. This happens via appendToResponse().

So far we've not had the opportunity to use this at all. We've had the convenience of reusable components available for everything that was required.

However, when we rewrite *WXImage* as a dynamic element, we shall finally get a chance to witness how WebObjects generates its output at a lower level.

For further reading check out

```
http://developer.apple.com/techpubs/webobjects/DiscoveringWO/UserInput/
index.html
```

Using appendToResponse() to Generate the XHTML

Let's start by duplicating and renaming the *WXImageTest* project as appropriate.

1. Edit the WXImage class to extend WODynamicElement instead of WOComponent.

   ```
   public class WXImage extends WODynamicElement {
   ```

2. Remove the component constructor as well as the non-synchronization and stateless settings. They are not applicable to dynamic elements.

3. A dynamic element doesn't have the methods valueForBinding() and setValueForBinding() to synchronize variables with its parent. Instead it maintains the raw associations between the dynamic element and its parent. Add the following variables for the associations:

```
private NSMutableDictionary associations;
private WOAssociation srcAssociation;
private WOAssociation filenameAssociation;
private WOAssociation frameworkAssociation;
```

Note that there is a dictionary of associations. This is for additional bindings that we have not defined in the element's API.

4. We must add a constructor for the dynamic element:

```
public WXImage(String _name, NSDictionary _associations, WOElement _element)
{
        super(_name, _associations, _element);

        // set the associations
        associations = new NSMutableDictionary(_associations);

        // remove the public bindings/associations
        filenameAssociation = (WOAssociation)
                                associations.removeObjectForKey("filename");
        frameworkAssociation = (WOAssociation)
                                associations.removeObjectForKey("framework");
        srcAssociation = (WOAssociation)
                                associations.removeObjectForKey("src");
}
```

The constructor for a dynamic element is the ideal place to filter out bindings that are defined in the API and those which are not.

Those nonAPI bindings go into the associations dictionary. The method removeObjectForKey() will return you the removed object, which in the case of these associations, we keep a handle on.

5. Remove the accessor for src. Instead, the values for the src will be synchronized from within the appendToResponse() method.

6. Add the appendToResponse(), which writes out the XHTML content to the response:

```
public void appendToResponse(WOResponse response, WOContext context) {
    WOComponent component = context.component();
    String src = null;
    // open tag
    response.appendContentString("<img");
```

```
    // src
    if (srcAssociation != null)
        src = (String) srcAssociation.valueInComponent(component);

    // filename
    else if (filenameAssociation != null) {
    WOResourceManager resourceManager = WOApplication.application().resource-
Manager();
        String filename = (String) filenameAssociation.valueInComponent(com-
ponent);
        String framework = null;

        // set the url
        if (frameworkAssociation != null)
            framework = (String) frameworkAssociation.valueInComponent(compo-
nent);

        src = resourceManager.urlForResourceNamed(filename, framework, null,
                                            context.request());
    }

    // append image src
    response.appendContentString(" src=" + "\"" + src + "\"");

    // append other bindings
    if (associations.count() > 0) {
        Enumeration keyEnumerator = associations.keyEnumerator();

        while (keyEnumerator.hasMoreElements()) {
            String key = (String) keyEnumerator.nextElement();
            WOAssociation association = (WOAssociation) associations.object-
ForKey(key);
            Object value = association.valueInComponent(component);

            // append attribute
            if (value != null)
                response.appendContentString(" " + key + "=" + "\"" + value +
"\"");
        }
    }
```

```
// terminate tag
response.appendContentString("/>");
}
```

Notice first that the XHTML tag is written out to the response using appendContentString() on the response.

Next we construct the *src* string from the bindings *src, filename, framework.*

The way a dynamic element synchronizes its bindings is by taking the values from its associations using valueInComponent().

The URL for the image is vended in the usual way using *WOResourceManager* to locate the resource for a *filename* from a *framework.*

Then we append the key-value pairs for the remaining bindings from the associations dictionary.

Finally, the <img> tag is terminated by appending /> onto the end of the response.

7. Remember to change the *mimeType* API to lowercase *mimetype.*

8. Include the import statement in the class file:

```
import java.util.Enumeration
```

9. Last but not least, delete the contents of the WXImage.wo template and definition, without removing the component itself.

Because we are writing out the XHTML content explicitly, the *WOXMLNode* in the component template is redundant. Hence, we remove everything within the template and definitions file.

There is no reason to remove the WXImage.wo component itself though. Leave the component intact, even though it is empty. This is so that WebObjects Builder can see the component.

Now, the dynamic element is ready for testing, so build and run.

Test the *WXImage* again. This time test the use of additional nonAPI bindings *width* and *height* and see what happens.

Summary: Completing the XHTML Application

Finally, you can incorporate the fully implemented *WXImage,* and the prototype components *WXTextField* and *WXHyperlink,* into the *XHelloDirect* application.

It has been a lot of work to achieve something as subtle as XHTML content. But in the process, we have learned more about the WebObjects Component Architecture and dynamic elements and how they interact with the request-response loop.

We might have also caught a glimpse of the shape of things to come.

6

SVG and WebObjects

"The Best Things in Life are Free"

From the song of the same title
—Janet Jackson and Luther Vandross

In this chapter you'll explore using WebObjects to generate images dynamically. In particular we'll look at vending images in the XML graphics format known as SVG.

Introduction to SVG

In this chapter we are going use WebObjects to vend an altogether different content from that of Web interfaces. In particular, we are going to use WebObjects to generate images on the fly.

What Is SVG?

It is an open standard published by the W3 Consortium and has an impressive lineup of applications that support it, including Adobe Illustrator 10, Adobe Golive 6, CorelDraw 10, Quark XPress 5. Not to mention a host of Java classes and libraries to generate and process SVG content.

SVG as a format is most often compared with Flash, which is another popular vector format on the Web. However, the most important feature of SVG is that it is based on XML. In other words, the format is in a human-readable form, unlike Flash, which is neither an open standard nor is it in a human-readable form.

For further reference take a look at these resources:

```
http://www.adobe.com/svg/
```

```
http://www.w3.org/Graphics/SVG/
```

Generating Graphics with WebObjects

In this section we're going to revisit the *Hello* application. This time however, we're going to vend the greeting response as a SVG graphic.

Vending SVG Content

Start by duplicating the *HelloDirect* application to *SVGHelloDirect* or something similar. You'll find more on this in Chapter 4, "Building Bookmarkable Applications."

Edit the *Greeting* HTML template in WebObjects Builder source mode. Copy the following SVG into it from the file named `Stripes.svg` located in the file download of the Web site companion to the book (www.samspublishing.com).

```
<?xml version="1.0" encoding="iso-8859-1"?>
<!DOCTYPE svg PUBLIC "-//W3C//DTD SVG 20000303 Stylable//EN"
"http://www.w3.org/TR/2000/03/WD-SVG-20000303/DTD/svg-20000303-stylable.dtd">

<!-- Generator: Adobe Illustrator 9.0, SVG Export Plug-In  -->

<svg xml:space="preserve" viewBox="0 0 950 200" style="fill-rule:nonzero;clip-
rule:nonzero;stroke:#000000;stroke-miterlimit:4; font-size:195;">
    <text transform="matrix(0.9775 0 0 1 0 162.3291)"
style="stroke:none;">Hello World</text>
    <text transform="matrix(0.9775 0 0 1 0 162.3291)"
style="fill:none;stroke-width:10;">Hello World</text>
    <text transform="matrix(0.9775 0 0 1 0 162.3291)" style="fill:none;
stroke:#FB0F0C;stroke-width:6;stroke-dasharray:12;">Hello World</text>
</svg>
```

For now we're simply displaying the string `Hello World`. We'll change this later to display the text the user typed in dynamically.

To ensure that the browser interprets the response as a SVG image, we need to set the content encoding. This is done in the `appendToResponse()` of the Greeting component:

```
public void appendToResponse(WOResponse response, WOContext context) {
    super.appendToResponse(response, context);

    // set the header
    response.setHeader("image/svg-xml", "Content-Type");
}
```

Select build and run. You might like to resize the greeting window to see the scalable effect of SVG.

> **NOTE**
>
> To view your SVG graphics, you have to download and install the SVG plug-in for your browser from `http://www.adobe.com/svg/`.

You should get results similar to Figure 6.1.

FIGURE 6.1   Hello World in SVG.

Now, to make the graphic truly dynamic, replace the text string Hello World in the Greeting template, with a WOString. Note that you might find more than one occurrence of the string Hello World. Bind the *value* to username to display the text the user typed, and refresh.

Generating Typographic Effects on the Fly

In addition to changing the text that is displayed in the graphic, we can also change the typographic effect.

First, let's factor out the component responsible for the current textual effect.

1. Create a new component called *SVGStripesText*.

2. *Cut* and *Paste* the following SVG from the Greeting template into the *SVGStripesText* template. Use WebObjects Builder source mode to do this.

```
<svg xml:space="preserve" viewBox="0 0 950 200" style="fill-
rule:nonzero;clip-rule:nonzero;stroke:#000000;stroke-miterlimit:4; font-
size:195;">
    <text transform="matrix(0.9775 0 0 1 0 162.3291)"
style="stroke:none;"><webobject name=Text></webobject></text>
    <text transform="matrix(0.9775 0 0 1 0 162.3291)"
style="fill:none;stroke-width:10;"><webobject name=Text></webobject></text>
```

```
    <text transform="matrix(0.9775 0 0 1 0 162.3291)" style="fill:none;
stroke:#FB0F0C;stroke-width:6;stroke-dasharray:12;">
<webobject name=Text></webobject></text>
</svg>
```

3. In addition, you will need to copy the WebObjects definition for the WebObjects element named Text from the .wod file.

4. In the Greeting template, insert a *WOSwitchComponent* in place of the SVG. Select *WebObjects, WOSwitchComponent* from the WebObjects Builder menu. We'll take a look at what WOSwitchComponent does later.

5. Enter SVGStripesText as the *WOComponentName* from the WOSwitchComponent Inspector. Bind username to an additional binding called *text*.

6. Make the *SVGStripesText* component and *stateless*. This also makes the component nonsynchronizing.

7. Rebind the *WOString* value to ^text. Add *text* to *SVGStripesText* API, and then build and run the application.

The results should be the same as before. However, we needed to factor out the SVG responsible for the text effect to prepare the application for additional SVG effects components.

Now, create a second *nonsynchronizing* component *SVGGradientText* with the content. Copy in the SVG source from the file of the same name from the file download obtained from the companion Web site (www.samspublishing.com).

```
<svg xml:space="preserve" viewBox="0 0 950 200" style="fill-rule:nonzero;
➥clip-rule:nonzero;stroke:#000000;stroke-miterlimit:4; font-size:195;">
        <g>
            <linearGradient id="aigrd3" gradientUnits="userSpaceOnUse"
x1="81.9229" y1="-21.4438" x2="279.5647" y2="176.1994">
                <stop offset="0" style="stop-color:#E2E1E1"/>
                <stop offset="0.1999" style="stop-color:#DBDBD9"/>
                <stop offset="0.3779" style="stop-color:#C9C8C5"/>
                <stop offset="0.5476" style="stop-color:#ADABA7"/>
                <stop offset="0.7123" style="stop-color:#898682"/>
                <stop offset="0.8717" style="stop-color:#605E5C"/>
                <stop offset="1" style="stop-color:#404040"/>
            </linearGradient>
            <linearGradient id="aigrd4" gradientUnits="userSpaceOnUse"
x1="112.6865" y1="-52.2075" x2="310.3284" y2="145.4357">
```

```
            <stop offset="0" style="stop-color:#E2E1E1"/>
            <stop offset="0.1999" style="stop-color:#DBDBD9"/>
            <stop offset="0.3779" style="stop-color:#C9C8C5"/>
            <stop offset="0.5476" style="stop-color:#ADABA7"/>
            <stop offset="0.7123" style="stop-color:#898682"/>
            <stop offset="0.8717" style="stop-color:#605E5C"/>
            <stop offset="1" style="stop-color:#404040"/>
        </linearGradient>
    </g>
    <text transform="matrix(0.9775 0 0 1 0 162.3291)"
style="fill:url(#aigrd4);
➥stroke:none;"><webobject name=Text></webobject></text>
    <text transform="matrix(0.9775 0 0 1 0 162.3291)"
style="stroke:none;fill:url(#aigrd3)"><webobject
name=Text></webobject></text>
</svg>
```

Duplicate the WebObjects definition for the WOString to match that of the *SVGStripesText* component.

Adding a WOPopupButton
Now, a pop-up button must be added to the Main page so we can select the style of greeting that will be displayed.

1. Open the Main page in WebObjects Builder. Add a *WOPopupButton* to the form.

2. Bind its *list* attribute to a key of the same name list. This should be of type *NSArray*:

```
protected NSArray styles = new NSArray(new String[]{"Stripes", "Gradient"});
```

3. Similarly, bind the *item* and *value* of the *WOPopupButton* to a key, style. *Name* the *WOPopupButton* style. This is how it will be identified in the form. This is important because the form is bound to a direct action.

Swapping WebObjects Components
Next, we must swap in the appropriate component to generate the desired SVG effect.

1. Change the *greetingAction* to pass the value for the style from the request into the SVG Greeting page:

```
public WOActionResults greetingAction() {
    WOComponent nextPage = pageWithName("Greeting");
```

```
        String username = request().stringFormValueForKey("username");
        String style = request().stringFormValueForKey("style");

        // set values
        nextPage.takeValueForKey(username, "username");
        nextPage.takeValueForKey(style, "style");

        return nextPage;
    }
```

2. Add the style key, as a String variable, to the Greeting page. In addition add a key componentName as an accessor:

```
public String componentName() {
    return "SVG" + style + "Text";
}
```

The componentName returns the name of the SVG component to use with a user-selected style.

3. Rebind the WOSwitchComponent *WOComponentName* attribute to componentName. Then build and run.

Figure 6.2 is an example of the SVG greeting using the gradient effect.

FIGURE 6.2   View the SVG Gradient Effect.

Building WebObjects Applications Using SVG

In this we are going to build an *eCards* application with SVG and WebObjects. The aim is to demonstrate that WebObjects, together with SVG, can be used to generate a simple solution to certain applications. We can use the *Feedback* application created in Chapter 4.

Before we begin to add SVG components and content to the *eCards* application, let's prototype the application by generating HTML *eCards*. Start by copying the *Feedback* project and renaming it *eCards*.

Managing Form Values with Direct Actions

In this subsection we are going to consolidate our components and direct actions in preparation for expanding our Feedback form.

There is no extra overhead being created here.

When a WebObjects application receives a direct action request, a *DirectAction* is instantiated, and then released at the end of the request-response loop. Any variables created for it are garbage collected along with it.

1. Add the variables for `message`, `from`, and `subject` to `DirectAction.java`:

```
protected String from;
protected String subject;
protected String message;
```

2. Add a static array to represent the keys always accessed from the request:

```
protected static NSArray keys = new NSArray(new String[]{"from", "message",
"subject"});
```

3. Take the form values for the request in the *DirectAction* constructor:

```
public DirectAction(WORequest aRequest) {
    super(aRequest);
    takeFormValuesForKeyArray(keys);
}
```

This is another key value coding, similar to convenience, which has the effect of taking values from the request on the *DirectAction*, for each of the keys in the request. Refer to the documentation on *DirectAction* for more information on this method.

The documentation is particularly useful in this case because all of our direct actions in both the *Feedback* application and the *eCards* application have the same set of form values in their requests.

4. Amend the *feedbackAction* by removing the local instances of `from`, `subject`, and `message`:

```
public WOActionResults feedbackAction() {
    WOMailDelivery sharedInstance = WOMailDelivery.sharedInstance();

    // send email
    sharedInstance.composePlainTextEmail(from, to, null, subject, message,
false);
```

```
// debug
debugSring("DirectAction: " + this);

return pageWithName("ThankYou");
}
```

TIP

It might be a good idea to set *WOMailDelivery* to not send e-mails while you're developing and testing. You can do this by passing the last argument of `composePlainTextEmail()` to *false*.

---

5. Place a to key in the component to identify the e-mail address(es) the e-mail should be sent to:

```
protected static NSArray to = new NSArray(emailAddress);
    // emailAddress should be a string
```

6. Finally, build and run to test the results.

Adding Additional Form Values

Before we generate the page that previews an *eCard*, we must update the *Main* page component to accept more information.

1. Add a to field and a pop-up button to select the `image` for the *eCard,* as shown in Figure 6.3. Remember to *name* the input elements `to` and `image`.

TIP

You can insert a row into the table by selecting or highlighting a table, row, or cell; then clicking on the insert table row icon from the *Inspector*.

---

2. Add the keys' `images` (as an array) and `image` for the image selection. Copy in the images from the file download associated with this chapter from the companion Web site (www.samspublishing.com). Add the images into the Web Server Resources group in the project. Make sure that when copying the images, you add them to the Web Server target of the project. Select *Copy items...*, and use the *Default* reference style.

```
protected NSArray images = new NSArray(new String[]{"leila.jpg",
"snowboard.jpg"});
protected String image;
```

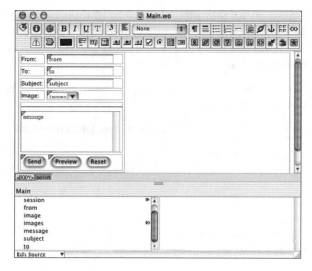

FIGURE 6.3   Layout the eCards Main page as shown in the Figure.

3. You will need to add image to the set of keys to be parsed in by the direct action class.

```
protected static NSArray keys = new NSArray(new String[]{"from", "to",
"message", "subject", "image"});
```

4. Add the key to as a variable. Unlike the feedback application, the *eCard* isn't sent to a particular e-mail address or addresses.

5. Rename the key contents to message, to bring it in line with the new actions we'll be adding to the Main page. Remember to rebind the *WOText name* attribute to message, as well.

Handling Multiple Submit with Direct Actions

In Figure 6.3 you might have noticed that we've added another submit button to the *Main* form.

This means that depending on whether the user clicks on the Preview button or the Send button, a different action must be invoked.

1. First add another submit button for *Preview* to the form, as shown in Figure 6.3. This time don't make it a static button, but leave it dynamic. Label it Preview by setting its *value*. Bind its *directActionName* to Preview.

2. Make the form static. Select the *WOForm,* and then from the *Form Inspector,* click *Make Static* to convert the dynamic element into a static element. Also, because this form has more than one submit button, we must set the *multipleSubmit* attribute of the form to true.

3. Change the *Send* button into a dynamic element and bind its directActionName to send.

Now the form is ready to handle the multiple direct actions *preview* and *send*:

```
public WOActionResults previewkAction() {
    WOComponent nextPage = pageWithName("Preview");

    // set values
    nextPage.takeValueForKey(subject, "subject");
    nextPage.takeValueForKey(message, "message");
    nextPage.takeValueForKey(image, "image");

    return nextPage;
}

public WOActionResults sendAction() {
    return pageWithName("ThankYou");
}
```

The old feedbackAction can be removed as it has been superceded by the sendAction method.

Creating an HTML Card

Now we need to add a component for the *Preview* page to display the *eCard* we've created.

Create a new page component for *Preview*. Add the keys subject, message, and image as variables, then layout the *eCard* as you please. Use Figure 6.4 as a guide.

Here I've used a nested table with a Grey background and small spacing to produce a border around the card.

Before building and running the application, add the variables to and image to the DirectAction class. Also, remember to add them to the key array. Add an appendToResponse to the Preview class to send the Content-Type header of the response to image/svg.

Now build and run the application.

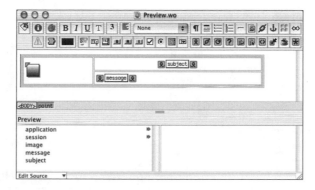

FIGURE 6.4   Layout of eCards Preview page.

Test the multiple submit direct actions and the *eCard Preview* page.

Using WebObjects to Compose HTML E-mail

When an *eCard* is composed and sent, we must deliver an e-mail informing the recipient that he has received an *eCard*. In that e-mail you can provide a link directly to that *eCard*—this is where it's important to use direct actions.

Similarly, you need to notify the sender that an *eCard* has been sent on his behalf. Given that we need to include a link in the e-mail, composing the e-mail as HTML would seem most appropriate.

WOMailDelivery has another convenient API that enables you to deliver e-mail composed from WebObjects components.

Creating a WebObjects E-mail Component

The e-mail messages themselves are composed as WebObjects components. So now we'll create the two pages to represent the HTML e-mails sent to the recipient and sender.

1. Create and add a page to the project called *RecipientEmail*.

2. Layout your card similar to Figure 6.5. The most important element is the hyperlink to the *eCard* itself.

3. Bind the hyperlink to the direct action named preview. Given that the preview action requires the message, subject, and image to compose a card, we bind these keys to the link prefixed with ?, as shown in Figure 6.6.

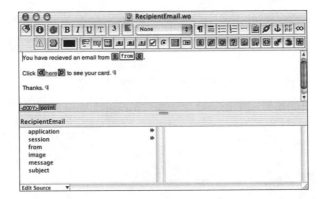

FIGURE 6.5   Use the figure as a guide to layout the Recipient E-mail.

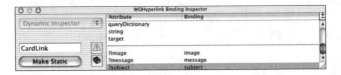

FIGURE 6.6   Binding additional form values onto a Hyperlink.

Similarly, add a page *SenderEmail*, which is used to notify the sender that the card has been sent. The main difference is that the card will say: You have sent a card to…

Using WOMailDelivery to Send Components

WebObjects has utility methods to use WebObjects components as defined previously as the contents of e-mail messages. Here we'll use WOMailDelivery to send the HTML e-mails.

1. In the *DirectAction* class, add the functionality to generate the recipient e-mail as an accessor:

```
public String recipientEmail() {
        WOComponent nextPage = pageWithName("RecipientEmail");
    WOMailDelivery sharedInstance = WOMailDelivery.sharedInstance();

    // set values
    nextPage.takeValueForKey(subject, "subject");
    nextPage.takeValueForKey(message, "message");
    nextPage.takeValueForKey(image, "image");
    nextPage.takeValueForKey(from, "from");
```

```
    // compose email
    return sharedInstance.composeComponentEmail(from, new NSArray(to), null,
subject, nextPage, false);
    }
```

Here we use composeComponentEmail() to generate an e-mail from the component. This is done after setting the required variables to compose the e-mail.

2. Next, amend the *sentAction* method to perform the sending. You can send the e-mail instantly, however for purposes of development and debugging, it might be helpful to split the two operations into *compose* then *send*:

```
public WOActionResults sendAction() {
    WOMailDelivery sharedInstance = WOMailDelivery.sharedInstance();

    // send emails
    sharedInstance.sendEmail(recipientEmail());
    sharedInstance.sendEmail(senderEmail());

    return pageWithName("ThankYou");
    }
```

3. Implement a similar accessor for *senderEmail*, to compose the e-mail to the sender:

```
public String senderEmail() {
        WOComponent nextPage = pageWithName("SenderEmail");
    WOMailDelivery sharedInstance = WOMailDelivery.sharedInstance();

    // set values
    nextPage.takeValueForKey(subject, "subject");
    nextPage.takeValueForKey(message, "message");
    nextPage.takeValueForKey(image, "image");
    nextPage.takeValueForKey(to, "to");

    // compose email
    return sharedInstance.composeComponentEmail("eCards", new NSArray(from),
null,
subject, nextPage, false);
    }
```

4. Select build and run. This time test the sending of an *eCard*.

Figure 6.7 shows an example *eCard*.

FIGURE 6.7   An eCard.

NOTE

The added advantage of using WOMailDelivery to compose e-mail messages from
WebObjects components is that it renders the URLs as absolute instead of relative URLs.

Adding SVG Effects to the Graphics

What benefit if any could SVG give to an already satisfactory HTML *eCard*? Adding a
SVG typography effect to the subject text wouldn't be all that great. The text is too
small for it to have much impact. However, we can add an SVG graphic effect to the
raster image. So what we'll try to do is replace the HTML image in the *eCard* with an
SVG graphic.

Prototyping a SVG Embed Component

SVG can be embedded in HTML pages by using the <embed> element. Because our
SVG is going to be WebObjects generated, we will need to develop a component to
do this.

1. Create a new *nonsynchronizing* component called *WOSVG*. Remember to make
   it a *Partial Document*.

2. Add a *WOGenericElement*from the WebObjects menu. In the Inspector, uncheck
   the Item is container box. Set the elementName to embed.

3. Add the other bindings, as in Figure 6.8. Most importantly, the *type* must be set to image/svg. This is to indicate that the content of the embedded object is SVG.

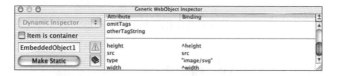

FIGURE 6.8   The Bindings for WOGenericElement in WOSVG should appear as in the figure.

4. Set the API of the component to include directActionName, queryDictionary.

5. Add an accessor key, src, to the component:

```
public String src() {
    String directActionName = (String) valueForBinding("directActionName");
    NSDictionary queryDictionary = (NSDictionary)
valueForBinding("queryDictionary");

        return context().directActionURLForActionNamed(directActionName,
queryDictionary);
    }
```

The SVG embed will be vended as a direct action in the *eCard* application.

For our purposes we don't need to implement other methods of vending SVG content, that is, we don't need to add support for *action*, *pageName*, or *src*.

A fully implemented *WOSVG* component can be found with the *SVGObjects* Framework at http://www.svgobjects.com.

Creating an SVG Dynamic Element
We are also going to need an SVG dynamic element to point to the images vended as WebObjects Resources. What we are looking to develop is a dynamic element for the SVG <image> element. This is practically identical to the dynamic element we created for *WXImage* in Chapter 5, "XHTML and WebObjects."

1. Create a new component called *SVGImage*. Empty its WebObjects template and definition as you did for *WXImage*.

2. Copy the contents of the *WXImage* class into *SVGImage*. Change any *WXImage* references to *SVGImage*.

3. Make sure the *SVGImage* element tag is image instead of img, according to the SVG specification.

4. Also change the *src* attribute to xlink:href conforming to the XLINK specification, which is part of SVG.

5. Add *filename, height,* and *width* to the API.

Vending SVG as a WebObjects Page
Now we need to add the WebObjects component to the SVG content.

1. Add a component for the SVG graphic called *Picture.*

2. Locate the file named picture.svg from the file download associated with this chapter. Copy in the SVG source from that file.

```
<svg>
    <defs>
        <filter id="emboss" filterUnits="objectBoundingBox" x="0%" y="0%"
width="100%" height="100%">
            <feColorMatrix type="luminanceToAlpha" result="dot"/>
            <feComponentTransfer result="dot">
                <feFuncA type="table" tableValues="1 0"/>
            </feComponentTransfer>


            <feDiffuseLighting resultScale="1" surfaceScale=".015"
diffuseConstant="1" lightColor="gray" result="diffuse">
                <feDistantLight azimuth="135" elevation="60"/>
            </feDiffuseLighting>
            <feSpecularLighting in="dot" surfaceScale=".015"
specularConstant="1" specularExponent="6" lightColor="white" result="specu-
lar">
                <feDistantLight azimuth="135" elevation="60"/>
            </feSpecularLighting>
            <feComposite in="diffuse" in2="specular" operator="arithmetic"
k1="0" k2="1" k3="1" k4="0" result="litPaint"/>
        </filter>

        <filter id="gray" filterUnits="objectBoundingBox" x="0%" y="0%"
width="100%" height="100%">
            <feColorMatrix type="luminanceToAlpha" result="dot"/>
            <feColorMatrix type="matrix"
values="0 0 0 1 0  0 0 0 1 0  0 0 0 1 0  0 0 0 0 1"/>
```

```
        </filter>
     </defs>

     <g transform="scale(400)">
        <image width="1" style="filter=url(#emboss)" height="0.7"
xlink:href="leila.jpg">
             <clipPath id="clip1">
            <rect x=".15" y=".2" width=".4" height=".3"/>
        </clipPath>
        <g style="clip-path:url(#clip1)">
           <g style="filter:url(#gray)">
              <image width="1" height="0.7" xlink:href="leila.jpg ">
                 </g>
        </g>

        <clipPath id="clip2">
           <rect x=".4" y=".08" width=".45" height=".25"/>
        </clipPath>
        <image width="1" style="clip-path=url(#clip2)" height="0.7"
xlink:href="leila.jpg">
     </g>
</svg>
```

3. Set the *filename* of the *SVGImage* elements to the key image, which should be added as a variable to the *Picture* component.

Embedding SVG in a HTML Component

Now we are ready to use the *Picture* component in place of the *WOImage* in the *eCard*.

1. Open the *Preview* component responsible for the display of the *eCard*.

2. Remove the *WOImage* and replace it with a *WOSVG* component. Use the *WOCustom element* icon to enter in a *WOSVG* element. Type WOSVG in the panel, as in Figure 6.9, and press Return.

3. Bind the directActionName to picture.

```
public WOActionResults pictureAction() {
       WOComponent nextPage = pageWithName("Picture");

       // set values
       nextPage.takeValueForKey(image, "image");
```

```
        return nextPage;
    }
```

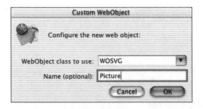

FIGURE 6.9   Adding a custom WebObjects Element to a component.

4. Set the *height* and *width* to 300 and 400, respectively.

5. Add a new key queryDictionary as an accessor and bind it to the attribute of the same name in WOSVG:

```
public NSDictionary queryDictionary() {
    return new NSDictionary(image, "image");
    }
```

This simply wraps the image as a dictionary, so that we can pass it onto the direct action. Finally, you are ready to Build and Run the *eCard* application.

On previewing a card you should get results similar to that of Figure 6.10. An *eCard* with raster graphics effects courtesy of SVG!

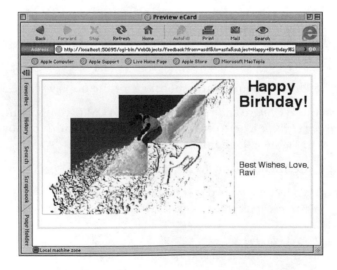

FIGURE 6.10   An SVG/HTML eCard.

Summary

In this chapter we looked at using WebObjects to generate SVG graphics and applied it to an example *eCards* application. A complete expose of SVG components and dynamic elements can be found at `www.svgobjects.com`. The *SVGObjects* Framework contains the two components *WOSVG* and *SOImage* prototyped in this chapter.

7

A Game of Crazy Eights: Beginning Enterprise Objects

"...Because the people who are crazy enough to think they can change the world, are the ones who do."

—Apple Computer

So far, this book has successfully avoided discussion of the crown jewel of WebObjects, Enterprise Objects. The focus of Part I of the book was strictly on the *view* or interface layer of WebObjects. Enterprise Objects is the *model* layer of WebObjects.

It is a robust and time-tested object-relational tool. It is also terribly sophisticated and sometimes daunting. However, it is my personal opinion that Enterprise Objects has unjustly received that reputation.

There are some very simple rules and some common sense guidelines, which when used can help the new Enterprise Objects developer deploy small to mid-sized applications with relative ease.

Often the successful implementation of an application rests on a thorough and well-designed object model. A bad model is sure to fail an application, whereas a well-designed and properly tested model will most certainly help to deliver the project successfully and on time.

In this chapter we shall look at doing something fun with Enterprise Objects. That is, use it to create a card game: Crazy Eights.

I'd like to give credit to an article from a *MacAddict* magazine (June 2001) titled "A Fistful of FileMaker," for inspiring the construction of a Crazy Eights game using WebObjects.

The article is aptly subtitled "Create a Relational Database (Yawn) to Make a Game of Crazy Eights (Cool!)." Quite right too! Databases don't conjure up the kind of excitement or enthusiasm that games often do.

So, instead of starting off with a more practical but serious application to model, I thought an introduction to Enterprise Objects with an excursion into game territory would be more appropriate, or fun at the very least.

We are going to develop a card game of Crazy Eights using Enterprise Objects.

Defining the Object Model

The objectives of this section are to learn the ins and outs of the Enterprise Object tools and how to put together a simple model.

What Is Crazy Eights?

For those unfamiliar with the game, here is an excerpt from the article "The Rules of the Game," that explains the rules of Crazy Eights, as it appeared in the June 2001 issue of *MacAddict*:

> The object of Crazy Eights is to be the first player to discard your entire hand of cards. Each player starts with seven cards (or five in games with more than two players, but here you just dual the computer, mano a Mac-o). The dealer turns over a card from the draw pile to start the discard pile. Players alternate turns and can discard any card in their hand that matches the topmost card of the discard pile in either rank or suit. The only exception is eights, which players can lay down at any time. When players lay down an eight, they can change the suit to one that will allow them to play out as many of their own cards as possible. If players have absolutely no playable cards, they must draw cards from the deck until they pick up a playable card or until the draw pile runs out. When that happens, players add the values of the cards in their hands (aces count as 1 and face cards as 11) and the player with the lowest score wins the game and can declare Crazy Eights superiority.

Outlining the Crazy Eights Object Model

Enterprise Objects does allow greater flexibility than FileMaker for relational database design. However, we are going to stick to the FileMaker database as described in the *MacAddict* article, as close as possible.

Essentially all we have to model is the deck of cards. This is quite straightforward, especially as the number of cards is static or remains constant. We'll maintain and manage the game at the application level to keep the model as simple as possible.

Creating the Database

Before we begin to create the model, we need to set up a database to store our information.

Open the *OpenBase Manager* application using the *OpenBase Manager app icon* from */Applications/OpenBase/*, as shown in Figure 7.1.

FIGURE 7.1   Start up OpenBase Manager.

From the *OpenBase Manager* window select *localhost* and choose *Database, New* from the menu. Type `CrazyEights` and check the box labeled Start Database at Boot, as shown in Figure 7.2.

FIGURE 7.2   Create a New Database with OpenBase Manager.

Select the *CrazyEights* database from the main window and click the start button icon. Now we are in a position to go and create the model for the game.

Creating a Model

Start up *EOModeler* from */Developer/Applications/*. This is the tool with which you will spend most of your time developing and designing an applications model. You will get to know it well.

Choose *Model, New* from the menu to create a new model. This will open the *New Model* wizard, as shown in Figure 7.3. Select *JDBC* and click *Next*.

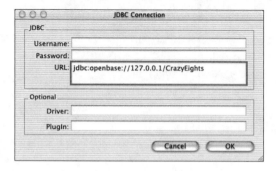

FIGURE 7.3   Create a New Enterprise Object Model.

In the *URL* field enter `jdbc:openbase://127.0.0.1/CrazyEights` and then click *OK* as in Figure 7.4. This is the JDBC connection information specifying the database server, the machine and the name of the database we are connecting to.

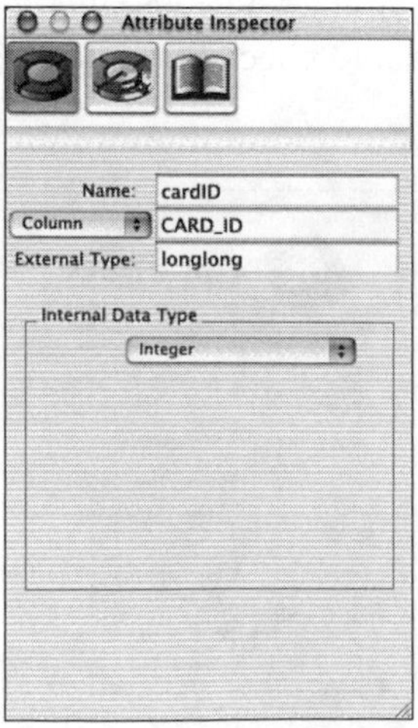

FIGURE 7.4   Connect to the Database from the JDBC Panel.

Click *Finish* to exit the wizard. We have created a model from an empty database so the remaining panels are of no relevance. Save the Game as CrazyEights in a suitable location by choosing *Model, Save.*

Adding an Entity

Now we need to add a class or an *entity,* as they are known in Enterprise Objects terminology, to represent a *Card.*

1. Click the *New Entity* button to add one.

2. Double-click the *Name* field and enter the name of the entity. In this case, Card.

3. Double-click the *Table* field and enter the name of the table: CARD.

NOTE

It is SQL database convention to use uppercase names for both tables and columns.

Before you can save changes, a primary key must be added.

What Is a Primary Key?

Every Enterprise Object must have a unique number to identify it: Card#1, Card#2, and Card#3 for example.

NOTE

The requirement for a unique identifier for each row or a primary key for each object is a *strict* adherence to the relational database paradigm.

This is because relational databases stem from classical set theory, which don't allow for duplicate objects in a set.

However, as in this example, this number is irrelevant to the model. It doesn't matter if the Ace of Spades is Card#1, or any other for that matter. As a result the primary key is an *abstract* attribute of the entity.

Adding a Primary Key

1. Select the entity you want to add the primary key to. In this case, the Card entity. Click the *New Attribute* button to add one.

2. Give the attribute a column name. In this case sticking with convention, give it CARD_ID.

3. From the *External* drop-down menu select *longlong*. This represents the value type in the database.

4. Enter the name of the primary key in the *Name* field: cardID.

5. Open the *Inspector* panel. Select *integer* from the *Internal Data Type* pop-up as in Figure 7.5. This is the value type as represented as an object.

6. Set the attribute as *abstract* by clicking on the *diamond* to deselect it as a class property.

7. Finally and most importantly, you must ensure that the attribute is set as the *primary key*. Do this by clicking on the *key icon* in the attribute row.

Now you're in a position to save changes made to your model.

NOTE

Sometimes, not all columns are displayed in EOModeler. To display another column, click the *Add Column* drop down and select the desired column, as shown in Figure 7.5.

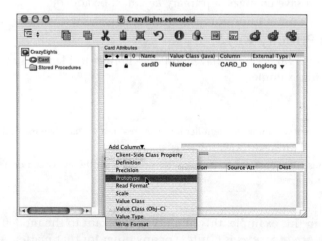

FIGURE 7.5   Add a Column to EOModeler.

Adding Other Attributes

A Card is going to have the attributes *rank, suit, name, filename* and *value*. (The *file-name* is to be the name of the image representing the card).

The *rank, suit, filename,* and *name* attributes will be Strings while the value is going to be a Number.

Adding a String Attribute

Add an attribute as you would add a primary key; paying attention to these particular differences:

1. Set the *External Type* to char.

2. From the Inspector set the *Internal Data Type* to String.

3. Then set a width to represent the limit of the size of the string. For simplicity set *rank*, *suit*, *filename*, and *name* to be of width 50. (We know that the name of the card is not going to exceed 50 characters.) See Figure 7.6.

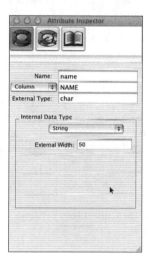

FIGURE 7.6   Set the External Width of the String from the Attribute Inspector.

Note that it is unnecessary to set the string attribute either as abstract or as a primary key.

Adding a Number Attribute

Now add an attribute for the value field.

1. Set its *External Type* to long.

2. Set the *Internal Data Type* to *Integer* from the Inspector.

TIP

Often a good way to add attributes to entities is to copy and paste them from an example EO model (for example, *Movies* from the *JavaBusinessLogic* Framework, which can be found in */Developer/Examples/JavaWebObjects/Frameworks*).

Creating the Tables from EOModeler

Now we can proceed to creating the database tables from EOModeler. Click the icon labeled SQL in the EOModeler toolbar to open the *SQL Generation* panel as in Figure 7.7.

FIGURE 7.7   Generate the Database Tables.

Then click *Execute SQL* to create the tables. Because you are creating the tables for the first time, you need to deselect the Drop Tables and Drop Primary Key Support check boxes from the panel.

The database is now ready to be populated with cards.

Populating and Testing the Model

One of the most important steps in modeling an application is testing it. It is very important to do this as early on in the development and design stage as possible. For our purposes, we are going to use a *DisplayGroup* application to test and populate the database.

Creating a DisplayGroup Application

Very briefly, a *DisplayGroup* is a class from the *control* layer of WebObjects that handles the fetching, sorting, and displaying of Enterprise Objects from the database.

A *DisplayGroup Application* is an Assistant generated WebObjects application that uses a display group controller to handle user interactions. We'll use one as a test application for our card object model.

1. Open *Project Builder* and select *File, New Project…* from the menu.

2. This time however, from the *Project Assistant*, choose *DisplayGroup Application* as in Figure 7.8.

FIGURE 7.8   Choose the DisplayGroup Application project template from the Project Assistant.

3. Give the project a suitable name; CrazyEightsTest would do in this case.

4. Ignore the *Enable J2EE Integration* panel. Click Next to proceed onto the Choose EOModels screen that prompts you to choose *EOModels*. Click *Add…* to navigate to the CrazyEights.eomodeld file that you created and select it. It should now appear in the *EOModel* list, as shown in Figure 7.9. Proceed to the next step.

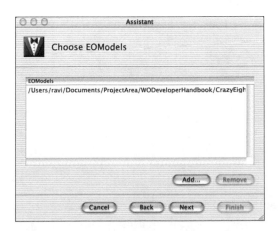

FIGURE 7.9   Add the EOModel to the project.

5. Choose *Card* from the *Choose Main EOEntity* panel. This decided what entity or class of objects we'll browse and edit.

6. From the *Choose a Layout* panel select which style or template you want to present the application in. For the purpose of populating the database with 52 cards, choose the *Selected Record/Display All Records* combination, as in Figure 7.10, then proceed.

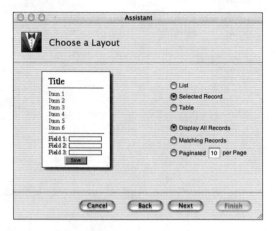

FIGURE 7.10   Choose a Layout for the Web Interface.

7. Now choose the attributes of your entity that you want to edit. Select all and click the >> button to include them (see Figure 7.11).

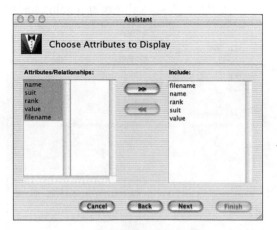

FIGURE 7.11   Select to display all the Card attributes.

8. Similarly, in the *Choose an Attribute for the Hyperlink* panel, pick one attribute that will display as the link to select. The *name* of the *Card* will do.

9. Finally, click *Finish* to enable the Assistant to create the project for you. Build and run the application.

Testing the Model and Populating the Database

Before populating the database, it is advisable to perform some rudimentary tasks like inserting a new object, editing it, and then deleting it.

Inserting an Object

Click the icon labeled *Insert/New* from the running application in the browser. Enter in the details for the *Ace of Spades*. Click *Save to Database* to commit the changes. Use Figure 7.13 as a guide.

Editing and Deleting an Object

You should also edit a field of the object just for testing purposes. Change the value of the card from *1* to *2* and save changes. You can revert back by changing the value back to *1* afterwards. To delete an object, click the Delete icon then save.

Populating the Database

To save you the hassle of entering the data for the 52 cards yourself, you can restore the *OpenBase* database from the Web site (see companion Web site at www. samspublishing.com).

> **NOTE**
>
> To *restore* the populated database, you will need to *stop* and *delete* the old database first.
>
> Then from *Openbase Manager*, with *localhost* selected, choose *Tools, Restore from ASCII* to navigate and select the database file.
>
> Name it the same as the database it is replacing and make sure it is set to startup at boot as before.

Copy the images for the cards from the Web site (see companion Web site at www.samspublishing.com) into the test project's Web Server Resources. Make sure again that the images are copied into the correct target Web server and with the correct reference style, *Project Relative*. Also check the *Copy Resources If Needed* box.

Open the Main component in WebObjects Builder and add a *WOImage* to display the card graphic. Bind the *WOImage filename* to cardDisplayGroup.selectedObject.filename, as in Figure 7.12.

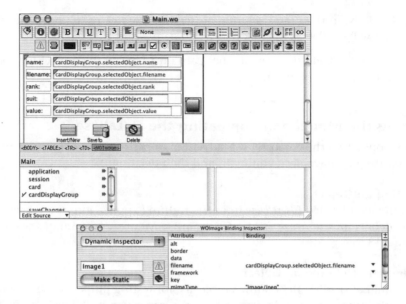

FIGURE 7.12   Examine the Main component layout of the DisplayGroup Application from WebObjects Builder.

Build and run the application. You should get something similar to Figure 7.13.

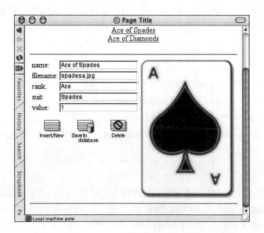

FIGURE 7.13   Run CrazyEights: The CrazyEights data entry screen.

Constructing the Game

We have created the database, defined the model, tested it, and populated it; now we are ready to build the game around it.

For the first step, we are going to create a one-person version of the Crazy Eights game. That is one without the computer player.

Start by creating a new *WebObjects Application* project entitled CrazyEights.

Now copy into the project the CrazyEights model that we created earlier. The model is normally placed in the Resources group or folder of the project and it should be associated with the Application Server target.

Fetching Objects from the Database

First, let's define the main variables we need in the Main component. Add the following variables to Main.java:

```
protected NSMutableArray deck;
protected NSMutableArray myHand = new NSMutableArray();
protected EOEnterpriseObject discard;
```

The three variables represent the draw pile, the user's hand of seven cards and the top card of the discard pile. Note that the enterprise objects are always typed as *EOEnterpriseObject*.

In the constructor, we setup and fetch the draw pile from the set of cards in the database:

```
public Main(WOContext context) {
      super(context);

   // fetch the Cards
   NSArray cards =
➡EOUtilities.objectsForEntityNamed(session().defaultEditingContext(), "Card");
   deck = new NSMutableArray(cards);

   // deal my hand
   while (myHand.count() < 7) myHand.addObject(card());

   // start the discard pile
   discard = card();
   }
```

To fetch the *Cards*, from the database, we use a WebObjects control layer class called *EOEditingContext*. The defaultEditingContext is used.

> **NOTE**
>
> An *EOEditingContext* is a controller that is responsible for executing database transactions such as fetching, editing, and deleting.

We use the convenience class *EOUtilities* and its method objectsForEntityNamed() to perform the fetch for us. We create a mutable copy of the card array for us to play with.

Next, we deal the seven cards of the user hand. This uses the accessor card, which randomly selects a card from the draw pile:

```
private EOEnterpriseObject card() {
    int i = (int) Math.floor(Math.random()*deck.count());

    // deal a random card from the deck
    EOEnterpriseObject card = (EOEnterpriseObject) deck.objectAtIndex(i);
    deck.removeObjectAtIndex(i);

    return card;
    }
```

The *NSArray* objectAtIndex() and removeObjectAtIndex() are used to draw a card from the deck of cards. Finally, the last thing required for a new game is to start the discard pile.

Using WOTable to Layout Components

Now we need to layout the Main component. What we want to produce is something along the lines of what's shown in Figure 7.14.

First, copy in the images of the cards into the *CrazyEights* project. Then, open the Main component in WebObjects Builder.

1. Place a 2x2 table for the draw and discard pile. Make the first row header cells and label them Discard Pile and Draw Pile, respectively.

2. Add to the Discard Pile column a *WOImage* in its second row. Bind the *WOImage value* to discard.filname. This is to display the top card of the discard pile.

3. In the Draw Pile column, similarly add a *WOImage*. But bind this to `cardimage.jpg`. This is so that we don't reveal the face of the cards in the draw pile.

4. Wrap the image in a *WOHyperlink*. Clicking on the draw pile should add a card to our hand. Bind its *action* attribute to a new action draw:

```
public void draw() {
    // draw a card
    myHand.addObject(card());
}
```

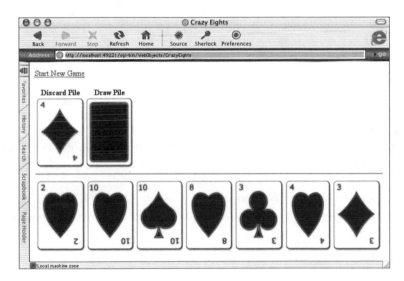

FIGURE 7.14   Fancy a game of Crazy Eights?

To make sure that we don't draw a card when the draw pile is empty, add a *WOConditional* to the hyperlink and image. That is, select both the hyperlink and the image then choose WOConditional from the WebObjects menu. Bind its *condition* to deck.count.

This has the effect of making the draw pile disappear when the deck is empty.

5. Add a horizontal rule to separate the draw and discard piles from your playing hand. Then add a *WOTable*.

NOTE

A *WOTable* is useful when you need to dynamically adjust a table to a situation.

In this case, when the player draws more than 7 cards, a *WOTable* will display the additional cards on a second (or third) row.

Bind its *list* attribute to myHand. Add a variable key aCard (of type *EOEnterpriseObject*) and bind it to the *WOTable* item. The *WOTable* acts like a repetition on the contents of the cell. Set its *maxColumns* to 7.

6. Place a *WOImage* wrapped in a *WOHyperlink* inside the *WOTable*. This is to display the hand of cards.

7. Bind the *WOImage* filename to aCard.filename and the *action* to a new action called play. The player clicks on a card to discard it:

```
public void play() {
    // discard the card you selected
    discard = aCard;
    myHand.removeObject(aCard);
}
```

8. Add a hyperlink to the top of the component to Start New Game. Bind its *pageName* to Main. When a user clicks on this a new instance of Main is vended along with a new game.

9. Finally, scale the images to half size. That is, set its *width* to 99 and *height* to 145. Also set the *border* to 0, if you want the image links not to be displayed with a border.

Now you should be ready to build and run the game of *CrazyEights*. You should get something similar to Figure 7.14. Play a game! (To test it of course.)

Note that the *WOTable* automatically renders a second row when there are more than seven cards.

Adding Logic to the Game Play

You might have noticed that we've not restricted what hand can be played. Although it is not entirely essential when you are playing yourself, it is not very difficult to do.

Alter the play action to add the condition:

```
public void play() {
    // check to see if the card is of the same suit or rank or an 8
    if (aCard.valueForKey("suit").equals(discard.valueForKey("suit"))
    || aCard.valueForKey("rank").equals(discard.valueForKey("rank"))
    || aCard.valueForKey("rank").equals("Eight")
```

```
    || discard.valueForKey("rank").equals("Eight")) {
        // discard the card you selected
        discard = aCard;
        myHand.removeObject(aCard);
    }
}
```

This ensures that the card played will be either of the same suit or rank unless it is an eight, which can be played at any time. Playing an eight has the additional effect of allowing the player to change the suit.

Refining the Model

In general, it is a good idea to develop a functional first iteration of an application. There are several tradeoffs that have been made in the Crazy Eights game so far.

In this next section, however, we'll look at refining both the model and the application a little. In the process we can achieve some performance improvements as well.

Design Pattern #2

We have developed WebObjects components and applications long enough to be able to make another observation about design. For most intents and purposes, the methods we defined in WebObjects components are of these types:

- Accessors

  Accessor methods to retrieve and set variables have been used only where necessary. Private accessors are rarely ever used.

- Request-Response methods

  The methods that fall into this category include appendToResponse(), takeValueFromRequest(), and invokeAction().

- Actions

  These include null or void actions, as well as those that return other components.

  This goes without mentioning the often mandatory component settings like isStateless(), synchronizesVariablesWithBindings(), or even constructors.

As the book develops you will notice that we rarely ever veer from using these methods exclusively in our component, session, or even application logic.

Modeling a Non-Enterprise Object Entity

Taking a look at the Main component you will notice that we have broken this trend by using the private accessor card. Also perhaps somewhere along in the development of the *CrazyEights* game you might have wondered whatever happened to modeling a *Deck* or perhaps even the draw piles.

First, I should add that it ended up being simpler to model the draw pile as a mutable array. The discard pile was not even necessary. All we really needed was the top card of the discard pile. The players' hand was also best managed as a mutable array. However, perhaps what was missing was an abstraction of the *Deck*.

So let's go ahead and create this object. It would be possible to model the *Deck* as an Enterprise Object. However, given that it is a singleton (there will be only one deck), it is probably best modeled as a Non-Enterprise Object.

Adding a Non-Enterprise Object to the Project

We'll now add the Deck class to the project:

1. Choose the *Classes* group in the *Groups & Files* panel in Project Builder.

2. Select *File, New File…* from the menu.

3. Choose *WebObjects/Java Class* from the *New File Assistant*. Name this file `Deck.java`.

Using Shared Enterprise Objects

First we need to talk about what it is to share Enterprise Objects. So it might be worth taking a look at what happens behind the scenes when a game starts.

Turning on SQL logging

Select the *CrazyEights* target from the *Targets* panel in Project Builder. Then add an application argument to the executable (from the *Executables* tab):
`-EOAdaptorDebugEnabled YES`.

Now run the application. Notice the `SQL SELECT` statement appears in the *Run* panel, as shown in Figure 7.15.

If you click *Start New Game*, you will see another fetch being performed.

Given that the set of cards remains constant, this might seem excessive. Surely, fetching this set once, and sharing it between all games is probably more efficient?

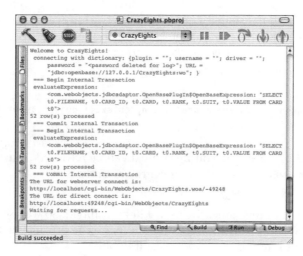

FIGURE 7.15   Examine the SQL Output from the Run Panel.

Using Shared Enterprise Objects

This is exactly what we are going to do next. Open the `CrazyEights.eomodeld` from the *Resources* group in the project. Select the *Card* entity. Click *info icon* to open the inspector. Then select the *Shared Object Inspector*.

Finally, choose the *Share All Objects* radio as in Figure 7.16.

FIGURE 7.16   Enable Object Sharing from the Shared Object Inspector.

Now the *Cards* are set as shared Enterprise Objects. However this is not all that needs to be done. The objects need to be fetched into and retrieved from a special editing context, an *EOSharedEditingContext*. Return to the *Deck*, where we will need to access the set of cards, add cards as a variable key to Deck.java:

```
protected NSMutableArray cards = ((NSArray)
EOSharedEditingContext.defaultSharedEditingContext().objectsByEntityName().
valueForKey("Card")).mutableClone();
```

Objects fetched into a shared editing context can be retrieved from the dictionary of objects, objectsByEntityName(). So the array of *Cards* is objectByEntityName().valueForKey("Card").

During the course of the game, the deck will be emptied. So we use mutableClone() to make a mutable copy of the array. Cut and paste the private card accessor from *Main* component into the *Deck*, and make it public.

```
public EOEnterpriseObject card() {
    int i = (int) Math.floor(Math.random()*cards.count());

    // deal a random card from the deck
    EOEnterpriseObject card = (EOEnterpriseObject) cards.objectAtIndex(i);
    cards.removeObjectAtIndex(i);

    return card;
    }
```

For convenience we add the *boolean* key hasCards():

```
public boolean hasCards() {
    return (cards.count() > 0);
    }
```

Now we need to force fetch the set of cards into the shared editing context. A suitable place to do this is in the *Application* constructor:

```
    // fetch the cards
    EOFetchSpecification fetchSpec =
➥EOFetchSpecification.fetchSpecificationNamed("FetchAll", "Card");
    EOSharedEditingContext.defaultSharedEditingContext().
bindObjectsWithFetchSpecification(fetchSpec, "FetchAll");
```

Using Fetch Specifications

You might have noticed that when making the set of Cards *shared objects*, a fetch specification called `FetchAll` was added to the *Card* entity.

NOTE

A fetch specification describes what entity to fetch from the database and what conditions to apply. It encapsulates a SQL fetch.

When fetching the card, we can refer to the fetch specification created in the *CrazyEights* model by entity and name using `fetchSpecificationNamed()`.

Now return to the Main component and replace the type of the `deck` from mutable array to *Deck*:

```
protected Deck deck = new Deck();
```

The Main constructor is simplified. Gone is the need to fetch the set of cards for each game:

```
public Main(WOContext context) {
      super(context);

   // deal my hand
   while (myHand.count() < 7) myHand.addObject(deck.card());

   // start the discard pile
   discard = deck.card();
   }
```

Change the draw action to use `deck.card()` as well:

```
public void draw() {
   if (deck.hasCards()) {
      // draw a card
      myHand.addObject(deck.card());
   }
   }
```

Because the deck's cards are protected, the `deck.hasCards` key is useful to indicate if the deck is empty or not.

Lastly, rebind the Main component's *WOConditional condition* to `deck.hasCards` instead of `deck.count`. Now you are ready to build and run the refined game of *CrazyEights*.

Summary

In this chapter we've created a game of Crazy Eights, using it as an introduction to Enterprise Objects and its tools.

8

Case Study I: Online Forum

"True Refinement seeks simplicity."

—*Bruce Lee*

Chapter 7 "A Game of Crazy Eights: Beginning Enterprise Objects," was a fun introduction to the tools and techniques of the WebObjects model layer.

Now it is time to look at a more serious application to model, not to say that it won't be fun. I hope you will find modeling applications such as these at least as satisfying as developing the game Crazy Eights. However, we need to turn our attention to some practical and important applications to model with Enterprise Objects starting with modeling an online forum.

In this chapter we will cover object-relational mapping, how to create a to-one relationship, how to use to-many relationships, and testing the Object Model using DirectToWeb.

Overview of Enterprise Objects

It is time to take a look at the theory behind the magic of Enterprise Objects. In particular, what exactly Enterprise Objects do.

Introduction to Object Persistence

We have seen what it is for an object to have *state* and we have often referred to it informally as its *memory*.

However, the state of say a session object, would last the duration of a session. The state of an application would last until it is quit, so that the next time the application is started the state of the application object returns to its initial settings.

NOTE

Typically the state of all objects in an application is lost when the application process has terminated.

What it means for an object to be *persistent* is for its state to transcend its scope or the duration of its process. Informally a persistent object is one that remembers its state forever.

Object persistence can be achieved in many ways. One is to save its data to file. We touched on using plists in Chapter 3, "Optimizing WebObjects Components."

However, another way to achieve object persistence is to save the state of an object to a database. This is perhaps the most robust method of providing object persistence services to an application.

This is in fact what Enterprise Objects do—provide WebObjects with a framework for object persistence.

Introduction to Object Relational Mapping

Saving the state of an object to a database is a sophisticated way of achieving persistence. Particularly so when the database is *relational*.

However, the mapping between objects and relational databases is really a natural one.

- *Entities* or *Classes* map to *Tables*.
- *Attributes* map to database *Columns*.
- Each *Object* is equivalent to a *Row* in a database table.

From the Crazy Eights example, the *Card entity* was mapped onto a *CARD* table. The 52 cards in a pack were represented by the 52 rows in the table.

The *name* of a *Card* was mapped to a column *NAME* in the *CARD* table; the suit of the Card was mapped to the SUIT column, and so on.

This is in fact the information contained in an EO model. A description of how object entities map onto the database. We have only scratched the surface of this mapping of structures between object model and database schema.

We'll review more of the object-relational mapping later. In the meantime though, it is necessary to know of or begin to understand this relationship between objects and their relational counterparts.

Designing the Database

When constructing an *entity-relationship* model for a new application, we effectively design two things: the *database schema* and the *object model*.

Often projects involve migrating legacy databases to the new ones designed specifically for the object model. These projects require a data migration phase in addition to designing, building, and testing an application.

Or sometimes, if you are unlucky, it involves modeling your objects on top of a legacy data source. This can often prove to be challenging for the experienced Enterprise Objects developer.

In this book however, when modeling applications, ideally we will create new databases specifically for the models we design.

Learning More About Relational Databases and SQL

It is important that you know something about relational databases and SQL. Heaps of books are written on the subject, therefore, I won't dwell on it at all, except within the context of Enterprise Objects and application modeling.

However, there are some good references and introductions that might be of interest to the budding database developer, starting with this one:

```
http://developer.apple.com/techpubs/webobjects/DiscoveringWO/
DatabaseBasics/Database_Structure.html
```

> **NOTE**
>
> A little history: Enterprise Objects was one of the first commercial object-relational mapping frameworks. In fact it predates WebObjects, when it was a separate product.

Modeling the Entities and Their Attributes

Hopefully our brief introduction to the concepts and the exercise of building a game with Enterprise Objects will be sufficient for us to begin modeling an online forum.

We are lucky that this is often a well-defined and very familiar application to model. As I am sure that you have come across an online message board system or discussion forum.

For this first stage we'll keep things simple by modeling an almost anonymous discussion forum where messages are posted with an alias. We can avoid introducing the concept of a User and logins to develop and test the object model for *Post*, *Topic*, and *Forum*. After we have done this we'll incorporate a User model into the Forum system.

Setting Up a Database and a Model

Before we begin on the model, refer back to Chapter 7 to create a database for the "Forum" application.

Then create a new model titled "Forum" and connect it to the newly created database. Now we are ready to add the entities for Post, Topic, and Forum.

Modeling an Entity for Post

A Post to the Forum will simply be posted by field instead of by a user. It will have a `timestamp`, a `message` field, and a `topic`.

NOTE

In practice, it can be very convenient to simply copy and paste similar attributes from an example model into yours.

In this exercise, we shall copy and paste attributes from the `Movies.eomodeld` located in the `JavaBusinessLogic` Framework: `/Developer/Examples/JavaWebObjects/Frameworks/JavaBusinessLogic/`.

So before you begin also open up the `Movies` model.

1. Create an entity `Post`. Set its table name to `POST`.

2. Add a primary key, as before, named `postID`.

3. Add a string attribute by of width 50. (This safely assumes that a user will not type an alias of more than 50 characters.)

4. To add the *timestamp* attribute, copy the *dateReleased* attribute from the *Movie* entity in the *Movies.eomodeld* and paste it into the *Post* entity. Rename the attribute `timestamp` and set its column to be `TIMESTAMP`.

5. Next we are going to add a field for the message. Copy the *summary* attribute of the PlotSummary entity (abbreviated to PlotSummary.summary) from the Movies model and paste it into *Post*. Rename the attribute `message` with column `MESSAGE`.

Given that a message can potentially be quite large or quite small, modeling it as a normal string column might be inefficient. So modeling it externally as an object turns out to be more appropriate in this situation.

Enterprise Objects is good in this way because it will automatically handle the conversion of the internal datatype, in this case a string, into the external datatype, which could be either a string or an object.

We are not quite finished with modeling Post just yet. We still have to model its topic, which will be modeled as a relationship.

> **NOTE**
>
> A *relationship* is a special *value* that is not a String, Number, or a Timestamp, but another Enterprise Object.
>
> Sometimes it is represented as an *array* of Enterprise Objects.

So first we need to model a Topic.

Modeling Topic

A Topic is a relatively simple entity. It has a name, belongs to a Forum, and has Posts.

1. Add an entity `Topic` and give it a table name `TOPIC`.

2. Add a primary key `topicID`.

3. Add a string attribute `name` of width 50.

4. Finally, make sure that all the attributes (bar the primary key) are set to *allows null*. That is, make sure that the attributes are checked in the allows null column.

Setting an attribute to allows null will bypass a feature of Enterprise Objects and relational databases, which will throw an exception if an empty value is inserted into a database.

> **NOTE**
>
> During the development and testing phase it can be very convenient to set as many attributes as possible to allows null.

Modeling Forum

Forum is very similar to Topic. It has a name and a list of topics.

Create a Forum entity mapping to a table named `FORUM`. Give it a primary key `forumID` and a String attribute name. The `forum.topics` is again a relationship that we shall define in the next section.

TIP

Naming your entities and attributes simply can help improve the transparency of your design.

For example, when naming attributes think about the *key path* the values form; for example, `forum.topics`, `post.message`, `post.by`, `post.topic.name`, *and so on.*

Defining and Using Relationships

So far we have modeled `Forum`, `Topic`, and `Post` without any of the links that tie them together. Each Post has a Topic, a Topic has several `Posts`, and a `Forum` has a list of `Topics`.

These "links" are commonly known as relationships.

Introduction to To-One Relationships

When we say that a Post has a Topic we mean more formally that each Post object has, or is related to, one Topic object. The way that this is modeled at the object level is as attributes of type Enterprise Object.

On the other hand, the way the database keeps track of relations is by using a *pointer*. Post#1 is related to Topic#1, Post#2 is related to Topic#2, Post#3 is related to Topic#1, and so on.

So the `POST` table will have a column `TOPIC_ID`, which keeps a copy of the primary key of the Topic that it references. More commonly, these pointers are known as *foreign keys*.

Like primary keys, these are *abstract* attributes, which by themselves have no real meaning. They are simply the mechanism behind a to-one object relationship.

For further reading go to

`http://developer.apple.com/techpubs/webobjects/DiscoveringWO/`
`DatabaseBasics/Relationship.html`

Adding a To-One Relationship

We need to add a relationship to the Post entity to represent its Topic.

1. Copy the primary key of Topic, in this case `topicID` and paste it into the Post entity.

2. Uncheck the class attribute to make it an abstract attribute.

3. Now click the New Relationship button to add one. Notice how relationships appear separate from attributes in EOModeler as in Figure 8.1.

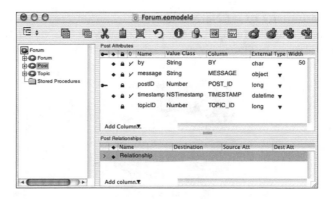

FIGURE 8.1   Adding a new relationship in EOModeler.

4. Open the Inspector. Highlight the topicID as the Source Attribute, then select Topic as the Destination Entity and choose its topicID as the Destination Attribute. Refer to Figure 8.2.

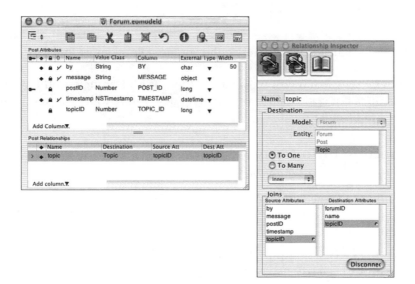

FIGURE 8.2   Setting properties using the Relationship Inspector.

5. Click Connect to establish the relationship.

Setting the Optionality of a Relationship

Click the Advanced Relationship Inspector. Then, choose the Mandatory radio from the Optionality box as in Figure 8.3.

FIGURE 8.3   Setting Optionality using the Advanced Relationship Inspector.

This is to indicate that a Post must have a Topic. It is meaningless otherwise. If a relationship is not made Mandatory, then it doesn't have to be set. In other words, it is allowed to be null valued.

Introduction to To-Many Relationship

Now we need to add the *Topic.posts* relationship.

This is different to the *Post.topic* relationship in that its cardinality is not *to-one* but *to-many*. Informally, a Post is usually made to only one Topic, whereas a Topic might have several Posts.

However, the two relationships do have something in common. That is, *Topic.posts* is the reverse or back relationship of *Post.topic*.

The way a to-many relationship is modeled in the database might not seem obvious at first. However, it might help to keep in mind that it is the reverse of a to-one relationship.

At the object level a to-many relationship is modeled quite simply. It is represented as a mutable array of Enterprise Objects.

Adding a To-Many Relationship

1. Add a new relationship to the entity, in this case to *Topic*.

2. In the Relationship Inspector, select the *To Many* radio.

3. Choose *topicID* as the Source Attribute. Select *Post* as the *Destination Entity*. Then, select *topicID* as the *Destination Attribute*.

4. Finally, click *Connect* to setup the relationship. Compare with Figure 8.4.

FIGURE 8.4 Setting up a To-Many Relationship.

Note that this time we didn't have to add any foreign keys to any entity. That is because the to-many relationship *Topic.posts* uses the foreign key *topicID* in the *Post* entity to determine its list of objects.

Next model the `Topic.forum` and `Forum.topics` relationship, similarly. Switching to Diagram View, your model should look like Figure 8.5. You can switch to Diagram View by choosing the drop down.

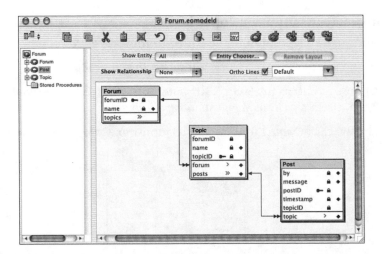

FIGURE 8.5   Looking at the Forum Model in EOModeler Diagram View.

Testing the Model with DirectToWeb

One of the most important parts of developing and designing an object model is the testing of it.

It is difficult to emphasize how important it is to test the model during the development phase. It might seem like an awful lot of time is spent on testing and fine-tuning your object model, but the dividends that pay are huge.

In many cases, the application just falls into place when you have a well-developed object model.

So most of your development time ought to be spent on developing your object model. This shouldn't mean spending time to add bells and whistles. As you might discover with experience, keeping the model as simple as possible is the key to being successful with Enterprise Objects. So instead, spend more time testing and refining your model.

By testing your object model, I mean performing rudimentary tasks like being able to fetch objects, insert objects, edit them, and delete them.

For this purpose, you would need to create a quick and dirty test application. In Chapter 7, we did this by using a WebObjects Assistant generated page to test the Card entity.

However, when you have a model such as the Forum model, you can use a remarkable tool known as *DirectToWeb* to create an instant application with a Web interface allowing you to perform all the previous tasks for each and every entity and relationship in the model.

Creating a DirectToWeb Application

Next, we are going to create a *DirectToWeb* application for the Forum model for purposes of testing and weeding our errors.

Before starting, make sure that you've generated your tables for the Forum model. Refer back to Chapter 7 on how to do this, if necessary. Launch Project Builder.

1. Choose File, New Project... to open the New Project Assistant. This time select Direct To Web Application. Give the project a suitable name ForumTest, and location.

2. Proceed to the Choose EOModels panel. Click Add... to navigate to and select the *Forum.eomodeld* file that you've been working on. See Figure 8.6.

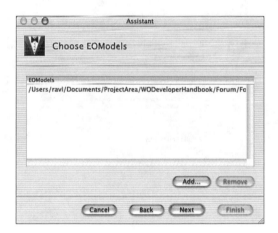

FIGURE 8.6   Adding a model to a DirectToWeb application.

3. Next, choose a look for the application. In this case select Neutral Look, as in Figure 8.7.

4. Finally, select Build and launch project now in the Project Builder by selecting the check box and clicking Finish. See Figure 8.8.

When the application launches just click Login to enter. You should now have a complete Web interface for manipulating objects in your model as in Figure 8.9.

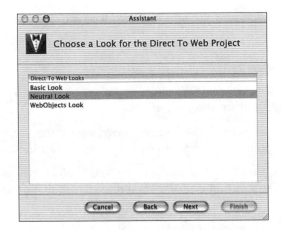

FIGURE 8.7   Choosing a Look for the DirectToWeb Application.

FIGURE 8.8   Launching the DirectToWeb Application.

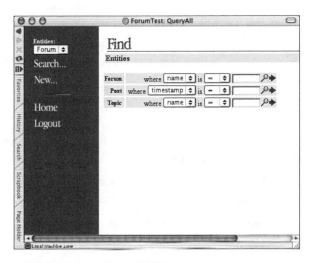

FIGURE 8.9   Using a DirectToWeb application.

Using a DirectToWeb Application

If the DirectToWeb interface is not obvious, here are some brief instructions to get you going.

Adding a New Object

1. Choose an entity from the Entities pop-up.

2. Click New... to open an Edit page.

3. Type the details and then always click Save to commit the changes back to the database.

Deleting an Object

1. First locate or search for an entity. You can do this from the Home page by clicking on the search button for the entity.

2. From the List page, click the trash can next to the object you want to delete.

Testing the Model

Make sure that you can add a new object, locate, edit it, and then delete it. As a guide, start by creating a Forum, then a Topic, and then a Post.

Also check to see that you can set relationships. In particular, when you create a new Post, make sure that you can set its Topic.

You will notice that you can't save a Post to the database unless you've set its Topic first. This is the *Mandatory optionality* of the relationship coming into play.

Set a `post.topic,` and then go and view the Topic. Notice that Enterprise Objects will automatically set the back-relationship `topic.posts` for you. It will include the post you just set to the Topic's list of Posts.

Here are some things to look out for:

- Make sure the tables and the object model is synchronized correctly. Renaming an attribute's column changes the database schema for example.

- Check to make sure the optional attributes are set to allows null. You don't want to be too strict at this stage when testing the model.

- Make sure the relationships are modeled correctly. Look out for foreign keys. They ought to be set as abstract otherwise the relationships won't get set.

Sometimes, an exception could be raised because of an application error. If this is the case, try performing the task in a different way.

Last but not least, I'd like you to try this out:

Create a new Forum; create a few Topics, and then add them to your Forum. Now delete the Forum.

If you've modeled it correctly so far, the DirectToWeb application won't allow you to delete the Forum, because the `Topic.forum` is a mandatory relationship.

To be able to do this, we need to set the delete rules.

Finessing the Model

It is imperative that even at this stage, the model is slick enough so that it allows us to do what we want.

It is useless being half way through a project and discovering that we have to adjust the model to perform a task such as object deletion.

Setting the Delete Rules

In the last testing exercise, we discovered that we are not allowed to delete a Forum, otherwise it would leave Topics orphaned. But in an Online Forum, a moderator would want to have the ability to delete Forums.

The way to do this is by setting a Delete Rule on the *Forum.topics* relationship. Select the relationship in EOModeler and open the Advanced Entity Inspector.

Then select Cascade as the Delete Rule, as in Figure 8.10.

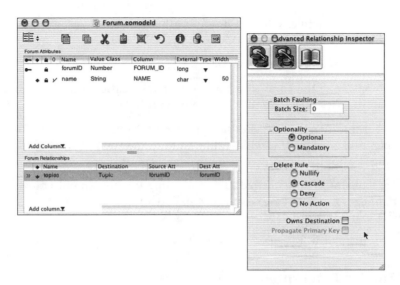

FIGURE 8.10   Setting the Delete Rule to Cascade from the Inspector.

This ensures that when you delete it, all its topics will be deleted along with it. Repeat this for `Topic.posts`.

Retesting Object Deletion

Now test object deletion again for both Forum and Topic.

You might also want to start looking at the SQL being generated by Enterprise Objects. A quick reminder: you do this by setting `-EOAdaptorDebugEnabled YES` as a command-line option.

> **NOTE**
>
> Unfortunately there are correct and incorrect ways of deleting an object when using DirectToWeb. For example a Post object may not be deleted directly. However, it may be deleted by removing it from a topic. This is because of the way it is modeled.

Introduction to Referential Integrity

Now you might want to perform another test. Say a moderator discovers someone has posted a naughty message and wants to remove it from the thread or Topic.

Mimic this by trying to remove a post from a `topic.posts` relationship. Notice again, the optionality of the `post.topic` relationship prevents you from doing this.

Now you might think, well, why bother setting these Mandatory options, if they are going to be so restrictive. Why not just allow the relationships `Post.topic` and `Topic.forum` to be optional instead?

In fact this makes an excellent exercise.

Make a duplicate of the ForumTest DirectToWeb application and remove all the referential-integrity rules, like the Optionality and Delete Rules.

Create a Forum, then a Topic; add the Topic to the Forum. Now delete the Forum. This time, unlike before, you will be allowed to delete the Forum object, thus orphaning the Topic.

What we have informally referred to as orphaning is when an object loses its *referential-integrity*. That is, we would now have a Topic that points to a Forum that no longer exists in the database. What results is a corrupt database.

Hopefully this makes it clear why setting these rules is absolutely important.

Fine Tuning Referential Integrity Rules

Having reverted back to the original ForumTest, let's set the last rule that will allow us to remove a post from a topic.

Select the `Topic.posts` relationship and open the Advanced Relationship Inspector. Check the Owns Destination box as in Figure 8.11.

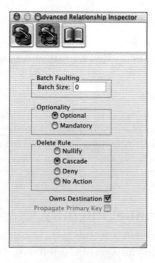

FIGURE 8.11   Setting the Owns Destination property of a relationship.

This deletes objects when they are removed from a relationship. So for example, a post will be deleted when it is removed from a topic, as required.

Summary

In this chapter we have studied and modeled a Forum system using Enterprise Objects and how to use DirectToWeb to aid in the testing and development of a model.

9

Prototyping with DirectToWeb

"There are two ways of constructing software design:

One way is to make it so simple that there are obviously no deficiencies and the other way is to make it so complicated that there are obviously no deficiencies.

The first method is far more difficult."

—*C. A. R. Hoare, Professor of Computing, Oxford University and inventor of the QuickSort algorithm, among other things.*

In this chapter we'll continue to define, test, and develop the object model for the first case study, an online forum we began in Chapter 8, "Case Study I: An Online Forum."

In addition, we'll look at using more of DirectToWeb to aid the prototyping of both the object model, as well as the user interface for the application.

Customizing DirectToWeb

What was not mentioned in the last chapter, was that DirectToWeb is a highly customizable *rules engine* for developing applications.

We used a Project Builder *Assistant* generated DirectToWeb application to test the Forum model. However, in addition, we could have customized it to streamline the user interface.

Using the DirectToWeb Assistant to Customize an Application

Start by launching the *ForumTest* DirectToWeb application. This time though, when logging in, check the *Assistant* box to enable the *DirectToWeb Assistant*. From the DirectToWeb home page, click the Customize link to open the *DirectToWeb Assistant*.

Open the *Edit Page for Forum* by selecting Forum in the entity popup, and then click *New...*. This will update the DirectToWeb Assistant, which should now appear, see Figure 9.1.

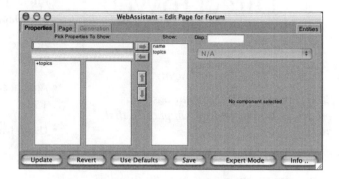

FIGURE 9.1   The DirectToWeb Assistant.

Changing the DirectToWeb Rule for a To-Many Relationship

We can simplify the user interface for selecting forum topics by using a browser.

1. Select topics from the *Properties to Show* view.

2. From the popup with *D2WeditToManyFault* selected, choose *D2WEditToManyRelationship* instead.

3. Select name from the *Target Key* view.

4. Now, from the *UI style* popup, select *browser*.

5. Click *Save* to save the rule, and then *Update* to refresh your browser. Refer to Figure 9.2.

Now, you should see a list of the forum.topics in a browser, which makes it much easier to select.

Repeat for *Topic.posts*.

Editing the DirectToWeb Rule for a To-One Relationship

We are going to change the rule for editing the *Topic.forum* relationship. Open the Edit page for Topic.

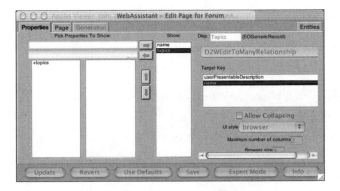

FIGURE 9.2   Setting a Rule for a To-Many Relationship.

1. Select the forum key in the *Properties to Show* view.

2. Change the *D2WeditToOneFault* to *D2WeditToOneRelationship*.

3. Select the name as the *Target Key*.

4. Change the *UI style* to *popup*.

5. *Save* and *Update*, and then compare with the Assistant screen in Figure 9.3.

The topic.forum should now appear in a popup button. This makes it much simpler to select.

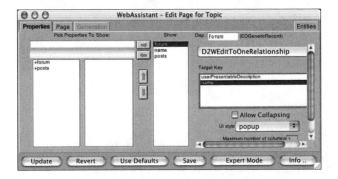

FIGURE 9.3   Setting a Rule for a To-One Relationship.

Setting Display Attributes and Formatters

Now open the Edit page for Post either by selecting a post for edit or by inserting a new one.

Changing a Text Editing Component

Notice that the Post's message is displayed in a text field, although ideally we want to be able to edit it in a text component.

1. Select the message key.

2. Choose the *D2WEditLargeString* component from the popup instead of *D2WEditString*.

3. Set the text view to be 5 *rows*, as in Figure 9.4

4. *Save* and *Update*.

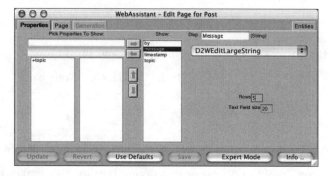

FIGURE 9.4   Using D2WEditLargeString.

Setting a Formatter

Next, we're going to change the date format.

1. Select the key timestamp.

2. Highlight the *Formatter* string and change it to %m/%d/%Y.

3. *Save* and *Update*.

You might have noticed that the *Post.by* field is rather generous at 50 characters. We designed it that way, however, we should be able to shorten it by changing the model.

This is an example of where testing an Enterprise Object model, as well as prototyping it with DirectToWeb can help to refine and root out bugs in the model.

Let's shorten the *Post.by* field to 10 characters max.

Altering the Object Model and Database

Open the Forum.eomodeld file from the *ForumTest* project.

Select the *Post.by* attribute in EOModeler and reset the width to 10 from 50. Save your changes.

Synchronizing the Model and the Database

For minor changes like the one we've just made, EOModeler has a very convenient tool that allows us to update the database to reflect the changes made to the model.

This enables us to circumvent recreating the tables and the database every time a small change is made. Hence, you don't lose your data.

This tool has its limits, but it's excellent for minor alterations to a model.

Choose *Model, Synchronize Schema …* from the menu.

This will open a panel such as the one in Figure 9.5.

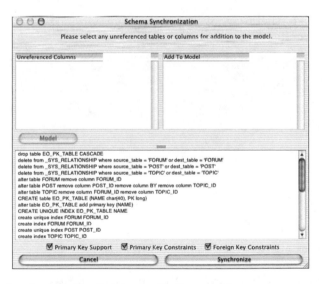

FIGURE 9.5   Synchronize the Database with the model.

Click the *Synchronize* button to execute the SQL.

Adding Logic to Enterprise Objects

Now, let's take a closer look at the way we have modeled the *Post* entity.

The timestamp attribute is exactly that, a timestamp. It is not meant to be a random date or one that you can set. It is to mark the time and date when a post is made. As such we can automate this. But to do that we have to write our first bit of Enterprise Objects logic. (You might have noticed that so far, we have developed basically a codeless application.)

Creating a Custom Class for Enterprise Objects

Until now, entities have been informally referred to as classes, so that it would be easier to conceptualize.

In reality, however, they don't have to be *separate* classes. Each of our Enterprise Objects uses a generic class to draw their functionality from. It is known as *EOGenericRecord*.

However, when we need to add custom functionality such as setting default values, we need to create custom subclasses.

1. Select the *Post* entity in the root model view, as shown in Figure 9.6.

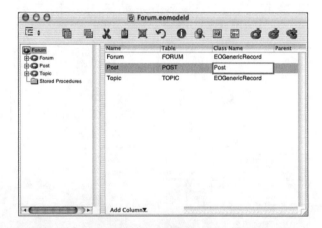

FIGURE 9.6   Set a Custom Class Name in EOModeler.

2. Change the Class Name from EOGenericRecord to Post.

3. Choose Generate Java Files from the Properties menu to generate the source code for the entity, in this case Post.java.

4. Save the file to the project folder as prompted, and save the changes to the model.

5. From the Project Builder add the new class file to the project, remembering to select only the Application Server target.

Removing Noncustom Accessors

Take a look at the file EOModeler generated:

```java
// Post.java
// Created by Apple EOModeler Version 5.0

import com.webobjects.foundation.*;
import com.webobjects.eocontrol.*;

public class Post extends EOGenericRecord {

    public Post() {
        super();
    }

    public NSTimestamp timestamp() {
        return (NSTimestamp)storedValueForKey("timestamp");
    }

    public void setTimestamp(NSTimestamp value) {
        takeStoredValueForKey(value, "timestamp");
    }

    public String message() {
        return (String)storedValueForKey("message");
    }

    public void setMessage(String value) {
        takeStoredValueForKey(value, "message");
    }

    public String by() {
        return (String)storedValueForKey("by");
    }

    public void setBy(String value) {
        takeStoredValueForKey(value, "by");
    }

    public EOEnterpriseObject topic() {
        return (EOEnterpriseObject)storedValueForKey("topic");
    }
```

```
    public void setTopic(EOEnterpriseObject value) {
        takeStoredValueForKey(value, "topic");
    }
}
```

Notice that it has generated a class with a constructor and accessors for each attribute.

Now these accessors are pretty much redundant if you adhere to the design philosophy of using key-value coding to access variables.

In fact, on closer inspection, these accessors are simply wrappers around a variant of the key-value coding interfaces. They use the methods storedValueForKey() and takeStoredValueForKey() to get and set variables.

> **NOTE**
>
> An *EOGenericRecord* stores its values as a dictionary. The methods storedValueForKey() and takeStoredValueForKey() simply get and set values from this dictionary of values.

Given that these methods are made redundant when using key value coding, we are going to remove them altogether. In fact, we are going to remove the standard constructor as well.

Your class should now look like this:

```
// Post.java
// Created by Apple EOModeler Version 5.0

import com.webobjects.foundation.*;
import com.webobjects.eocontrol.*;

public class Post extends EOGenericRecord {
}
```

> **NOTE**
>
> There are occasions when it might be *a* technical requirement or preference that your Enterprise Objects possess accessors. In which case, you must generate classes for every entity, and maintain the accessors as well.

Setting Default Values to an Enterprise Object

Next, let's add logic to the Post class so we can set the timestamp.

Add the following method to the class:

```
public void awakeFromInsertion(EOEditingContext editingContext) {
    super.awakeFromInsertion(editingContext);
    takeValueForKey(new NSTimestamp(), "timestamp");
}
```

The awakeFromInsertion() gets called whenever an Enterprise Object gets inserted in memory.

Setting the timestamp in a constructor would have the effect of resetting the timestamp every time a post is fetched from the database.

This happens because every time a post is fetched from the database, a *Post object* is instantiated and is used to store the data for that *row*.

For further reading on this topic see the Advanced Programming Topic on Assigning Default Values to Enterprise Objects on the WebObjects Documentation Web site.

Observing Automated Object Timestamping

Now, go ahead and add a new *Post* to the database. This time notice that the date is automatically set.

You also might realize that the field shouldn't be editable. So, add a DirectToWeb rule to make it a *D2WDisplayDate* instead of a *D2WEditDate* component, as shown in Figure 9.7.

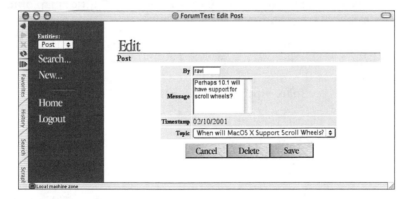

FIGURE 9.7   Edit a Post Page in DirectToWeb.

When Not to Use Custom Classes for Enterprise Objects

In general, if you don't need to add custom logic, then leave your classes as *EOGenericRecords*. There is that temptation to generate classes for each of your objects.

However, this only increases complexity without adding any functionality. It means that you will have to maintain and synchronize your classes with your model and database when you make changes; that is, if you use the generated accessors. In addition, it also adds in another possible point of contention if a problem does arise.

You want to do your best to keep it simple and minimize your code size, particularly in larger models.

Advanced Object Modeling

Having refined and tested the Forum model quite extensively, we are in a position to incorporate the concept of *Users* into the model.

A Forum will have two kinds of users: *Normal Users* and *Moderators*. *Moderators* will be given special privileges to delete posts and move topics, in addition to being allowed to delete entire topics.

Let's think about *Users* for a moment.

What are their properties (or attributes)? How are they different? The only difference between a Normal User and a Moderator should be the designation or class to which he belongs. Otherwise, they both share a (login) *name, password, e-mail, first name,* and *last name.*

Introduction to Enterprise Objects Inheritance

Thus far we have seen how objects map onto a database. Entities map onto Tables, Objects to rows.

What we have neglected to mention is that object orientation includes the concept of inheritance. For example, we can choose to model *Moderator* and *Normal User* as subclasses of *User*. In this case, it would make sense to model them using inheritance, given that they share attributes and features.

However, will we still be able to map these objects to a database?

The answer is yes. There are three methods for achieving inheritance with Enterprise Objects. In fact we are going to look at the first.

Using Single Table Inheritance

In this section, we are going to use inheritance to model the *Users* for our online forum. In particular, we are going to use the method known as *single-table inheritance.*

From a *relational* point of view, *single-table inheritance* might seem the most intuitive. It is when all the subclasses are mapped onto the same table.

For example, *Normal User* and *Moderator* would both map onto a USER table. The way Enterprise Objects distinguishes between a *Normal User* and a *Moderator*, is by having a special column to indicate the entity name. So, in this case, a *Moderator* would have an attribute className = *"Moderator"*, whereas a *Normal User* would have a className = *"NormalUser"*.

First, we are going to develop the *User* model in isolation from the *Forum* model. Hence, we are going to use a separate Enterprise Object model although we are going to use the same database.

Defining the Abstract Super Class

Create a new model linked to the *Users* database and save it as Users.

1. Add a new entity User, mapping onto a table USER.

2. Give it a primary key and attributes as in Figure 9.8. Note the attribute named className is *abstract* and should not *allow null*. By abstract we mean that in the subclasses of User, the className has no real world meaning or relevance. It is there as a mechanism to identify which class a User belongs to.

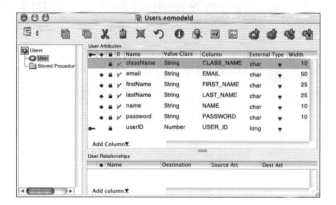

FIGURE 9.8   The User attributes.

3. In the Advanced Entity Inspector check the Abstract box to mark User as an abstract entity. See Figure 9.8.

4. Finally set the *className* to User.

FIGURE 9.9   Set the entity as Abstract.

Modeling a (Single Table) Inherited Enterprise Object

Next we'll model *Moderator*.

1. Duplicate the *User* entity: with the entity selected, press *copy* then *paste*. You should see a second entity labeled User1 appear, as shown in Figure 9.10.

FIGURE 9.10   Duplicating an entity.

2. Rename the duplicate Moderator.

3. Open the *Advanced Entity Inspector*. Uncheck the *Abstract* box because Moderator is a *concrete* subclass. Then, in the Parent view, select *User* and press *Set Parent*. Refer to Figure 9.11.

4. Finally, and most importantly, you must set a *qualifier* to filter only those *Moderator* rows in the USER table. In the *Qualifier* field type: (className = 'Moderator'), as in Figure 9.11.

FIGURE 9.11   Set the Parent Entity and Qualifier.

5. Save your changes and repeat the process for an entity called NormalUser. The only difference is that the qualifier will be (className = 'NormalUser').

Assigning the className as a Default

One final thing, when a new *Moderator* or *NormalUser* is created, the *className* must be set as a default. In other words, NormalUsers and Moderators must be mapped onto the User class. We have already seen how to set defaults earlier in the chapter, so this is not any different.

1. Generate the class for *User* and save it.

2. Replace the generated accessors and constructor with the one method awakeFromInsertion():

```
public void awakeFromInsertion(EOEditingContext editingContext) {
        super.awakeFromInsertion(editingContext);
        takeValueForKey(entityName(), "className");
    }
```

3. Make sure that the subclasses *Moderator* and *NormalUser* also use the *User* class as their className.

Using DirectToWeb to Test an Inheritance Hierarchy

Finally, we are in a position to take the *User* model for a spin. Generate the table for the *User* model as you've done before. Create a DirectToWeb application `UserTest` including the User model. Remember to add the `User.java` class file into the project.

There are a few things that need to be customized before you can use DirectToWeb with the inheritance hierarchy.

Hiding Entities in DirectToWeb

Build and run your application.

1. Login with the *Assistant* enabled. Click *Customize* to open the *DirectToWeb Assistant*.

2. Select the *Entities* tab.

3. Choose User from the *Read-Write Entities* view and click the left arrow button to move into the next column. Repeat to move it into the *Hidden Entities* column. Refer to Figure 9.12.

FIGURE 9.12   Hide the Abstract User entity in DirectToWeb.

4. Click Save, and then update.

Notice that in the home page of the application, only *NormalUser* and *Moderator* will appear.

Hiding Attributes in DirectToWeb

Open the Edit page for *Moderator*.

Select *className* in the *Show:* list, and then click the left arrow button to remove it. See Figure 9.13.

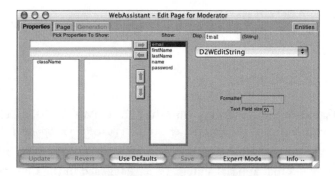

FIGURE 9.13   Hide the className attribute in DirectToWeb.

Save the rule and update. Repeat those steps for *NormalUser*.

You might also want to hide the password from the List pages for both *NormalUser* and *Moderator*.

Testing Inherited Object Insertion and Deletion
Add a new object to both entities, *NormalUser* and *Moderator*. Be sure that you can fetch them as well.

Creating a Custom Property-Level DirectToWeb Component

You might notice that when you edit a user, you get to see the password. Unfortunately, DirectToWeb doesn't come with a component for password fields. On the other hand, there is the facility to go and create one ourselves.

1. Add a new component to the DirectToWeb project called D2WEditPassword.

2. Open it in WebObjects Builder and make it a partial document.

3. Add a *WOTextField* to the component. From the static Inspector, make it a password field.

4. Add the keys object and key as variables:

```
protected EOEnterpriseObject object;
    protected String key;
```

5. Add two accessors for the key value and bind it to the WebObjects password element:

```
public String value() {
        return (String) object.valueForKey(key);
    }
```

```
public void setValue(String value) {
        object.takeValueForKey(value, key);
    }
```

6. Build your application.

Now when you run the application with the DirectToWeb assistant, choose the password key and change the component to *D2WCustomComponent*. You will have to navigate to an Edit page for a User if you are not already on one in order to do this.

Then, in the panel that appears, enter D2WEditPassword in the *Component* field. Compare it with Figure 9.14.

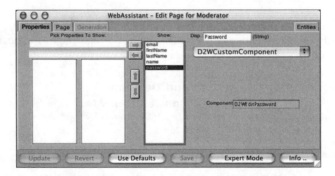

FIGURE 9.14   Using D2WCustomComponent for a password field.

The Edit page for *Moderator* should look like Figure 9.15. You might want to change the password component for *NormalUser* as well.

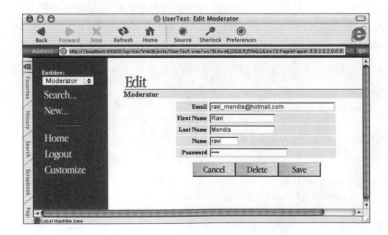

FIGURE 9.15   Viewing the customized Edit page for Moderator in DirectToWeb.

Using Multiple Models

When you are thoroughly satisfied that both the *User* model and the *Forum* model are functionally robust and stable, then you may proceed to linking them together.

Start by creating a new DirectToWeb application `UserForumTest`, with both the User model and the Forum model you've defined before. Make sure that the models are copied into the application for simplicity. Also copy in the custom-class files for the entitiess that you have defined.

Defining a Cross Model Relationship

Open the Forum model in EOModeler.

1. Copy the *User* primary key from the *User* model and paste it into the *Post* entity. Make sure that it is *abstract* and *doesn't allow null*.

2. Define a new to-one relationship to User as normal, except in the *Relationship Inspector* select *Users* from the *Models* popup as in Figure 9.16.

FIGURE 9.16   Define a Cross Model Relationship.

3. Set the relationship as mandatory.

Remove the redundant *Post.by* attribute, and then recreate the tables for the *Forum* model.

Testing the Cross Model Relationship

In the *UserForumTest* application, you might find that you have to repeat many of the customizations you made before to both the *UserTest* DirectToWeb application and the *ForumTest* application.

Guidelines Using Enterprise Objects Inheritance

Finally, before we end this chapter, there are some limitations and guidelines that you should be aware of when using Inheritance with Enterprise Objects.

- The different methods cannot be *mixed* and *matched* when modeling an inheritance tree. However, you can model different inheritance hierarchies within the same model if you want.

- Although Enterprise Objects can allow multiple levels of inheritance, it is best to avoid this. Most applications can be modeled using a *single* level of inheritance at very the most.

- Adhere very close to the standard inheritance methodologies and avoid straying from it. For example, always use *abtract* super-classes.

- Finally, do not make excessive use of inheritance; use it when absolutely necessary. Like other advanced features of Enterprise Objects, you are taking on a *risk* by adding significant *complexity* to your model and project by using it.

Summary

This chapter introduced customizing DirectToWeb applications, how to use DirectToWeb to test and prototype an object model, and how to use it to develop the *User* inheritance model.

10

Rapid Prototyping with WebObjects

(Using the Force, Yoda effortlessly frees the X-Wing from the bog)

Luke Skywalker: "I don't believe it."
Yoda: "That is why you fail."

—Star Wars: The Empire Strikes Back

Having designed, developed and tested the object model for the online forum, we are now in a position to start developing a Web interface for it.

This chapter will look at using detail display groups. Modeling a many-to-many relationship. Prefetching objects as an optimization. Using derived attributes to improve performance. And finally, batching enterprise objects

Building a First Application Prototype

Before we plunge in, let's briefly discuss the *requirements* of the application.

We want the online forum to be accessible by all. In other words, it should be readable by those who are not registered users, as well as those who are. However, we shall restrict the posting of topics and replies to those who are registered users only.

This doesn't necessarily suggest that we need to build the first few pages as direct actions, however, if we want to make the forum bookmarkable, then we'll indeed have to.

However, before we build the application with direct actions, as an intermediate step, let's build a quick and dirty *first prototype*. As such, this doesn't need to be direct actionable.

The objective of doing a first prototype is to refine our *requirements* and *object model* further, by giving us a glimpse of what we will eventually produce.

Creating the Home Page

Start by creating a new *WebObjects Application*. You can call it ForumPrototype1, or some other suitable name.

Copy in the *Forum* and *User* model files into the *Resources* group. That is, select the Resources group in the Groups & Files panel, then choose Add files from the Project menu. Check the Copy items box and add the models to the Application Server target. Also copy in the class files for *Post* and *User*.

Open the *Main* page in WebObjects Builder.

Open the *Forum* model file in EOModeler and drag in a *Forum* entity into the Main component. This will have the effect of adding a *DisplayGroup* controller, as you've seen before in Chapter 7, "A Game of Crazy Eights: Beginning Enterprise Objects."

Configure the display group to *fetch on load*.

From the WebObjects palette, select the *Premade Elements Palette*, and then drag a repeated table element, as in Figure 10.1, into the *Main* component.

FIGURE 10.1   Dragging a premade repeated table element into a component.

Bind the forumDisplayGroup.displayedObjects to the table repetition *list*. Add a variable key forum of type *Forum*, and bind it to the repetition *item*. Layout and bind the Main component, as shown in Figure 10.2.

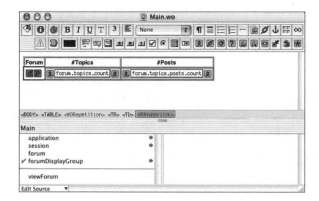

FIGURE 10.2   Layout the Main page to display the forums in a table.

Bind forum.name to the hyperlink *string* attribute. This is the text displayed in the link. Finally, bind a new action viewForum to the hyperlink's *action*.

Build and run the application to observe the Forum List in action.

NOTE

To obtain the number of topics and posts we use the count method accessor of *NSArray*.

Setting Up a Master-Detail Configuration

The next page we are going to create will list the Topics of a Forum. Unlike the forum list that we set up in the Main component, this page is somewhat different.

The *Forum* listing in the Main page is a complete listing of all forums, although the listing of a forum's topics is a listing of a selection of all Topics. Not just any selection either, but the *subset* of topics that belong to the forum selected.

A Display Group controller provides a convenient mechanism of handling this kind of relationship for us. It is known as a *master-detail* configuration. We are going to use this to create a forum's List Topics page.

To do this create a new page component ForumTopics to the application.

From EOModeler, select the *Forum.topics* relationship, and then drag it into the component. See Figure 10.3.

Add and configure the display group to fetch on load.

Notice however, that this time, the display group has been set up as a detail display group, as shown in Figure 10.4.

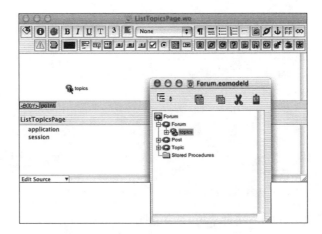

FIGURE 10.3   Setting up a master-detail display group configuration.

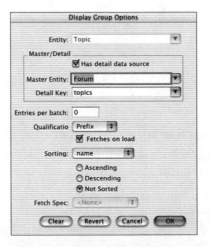

FIGURE 10.4   Configuring a Detail Display Group.

What remains to be done is to set the display group `masterObject` every time the page is used. In this case the `masterObject` is a forum.

NOTE

A detail display group fetches its objects by traversing the key path `masterObject.key`.

In the case of the Forum Topics List, it is `forum.topics`.

A good place to set the masterObject is in the action method that returns the page. Amend the viewForum action in the *Main* class to set the masterObject:

```
public WOComponent viewForum() {
    WOComponent nextPage = pageWithName("ForumTopics");

    // set the master object
    nextPage.takeValueForKeyPath(forum, "topicDisplayGroup.masterObject");

        return nextPage;
}
```

Now in the *ForumTopics* page, we want to display the topic name, the user who started the topic, the number of replies, and some details about the last post.

Layout the page as shown in Figure 10.5. Bind the table repetition to the display group as before, and add a variable key topic for the repetition *item*.

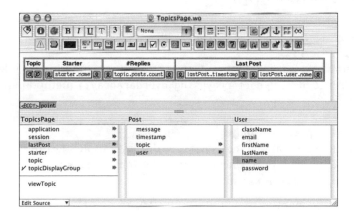

FIGURE 10.5 Layout the ForumTopics page similar to the Main page, except list details of topics instead of forums.

Bind the hyperlink to an action called viewTopic. The component as displayed in Figure 10.5 doesn't reveal the fact that the topic hyperlink *string* attribute is set. Bind it to topic.name. Add the following two keys as accessors to the component:

```
/** @TypeInfo User */
public EOEnterpriseObject starter() {
    NSArray posts = (NSArray) topic.valueForKey("posts");
    EOEnterpriseObject post = (EOEnterpriseObject) posts.objectAtIndex(0);

    return  post.valueForKey("user");
    }
/** @TypeInfo Post */
    public EOEnterpriseObject lastPost() {
        NSMutableArray posts = (NSMutableArray) topic.valueForKey("posts");

    // sort the posts by timestamp
    EOSortOrdering ordering = EOSortOrdering.sortOrderingWithKey("timestamp",
EOSortOrdering.CompareAscending);
    EOSortOrdering.sortArrayUsingKeyOrderArray(posts, ordering);

    return  posts.lastObject();
    }
```

Using Sort Orderings

In the custom accessor for the lastPost, we used a sort ordering to order the posts by date. EOSortOrdering sortArrayUsingKeyOrderArray() method performs this sort in memory.

Creating the TopicPosts page

Create another component, TopicPosts, to display a topic's List of Posts using a master-detail configuration. Drag and drop the Topic.posts relationship from EOModeler into the component window.

Layout the component as shown in Figure 10.6, and set the masterObject in the viewTopic action as you did before. (Hint: this time the masterObject is a topic.)

> **NOTE**
> To indicate repeated or conditional table rows and cells, that is elements wrapped in a
> WORepetition or a WOConditional, WebObjects Builder highlights the elements in blue.

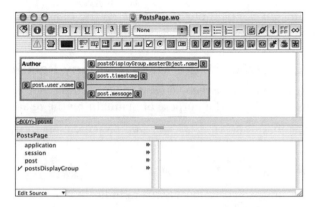

FIGURE 10.6   Layout the TopicPosts page as in the figure.

Refining the Object Model

Prototyping the user interface has some deficiencies in the requirements for the Forum.

Just as in reality, where it is not untypical for requirements to change or be altered during the course of a project, we have discovered some things that we want to add to the *Forum*.

- We need to assign moderators to forums

- Track the posts a user makes

- Monitor useful statistics (such as the number of posts in a topic or forum, when a last post was made to a topic, who made that post, and who started a topic)

In this section we'll amend and refine our object model to add these capabilities.

Given that there are changes being made to the model, we should test them as we did in Chapter 9, "Prototyping with DirectToWeb," by making these changes to the models in the *UserForumTest* project.

Introduction to Many-To-Many Relationships

First, we are going to add the capability to assign moderators to forums.

Typically, a forum can be assigned more than one moderator; a moderator can be assigned more than one forum. So, here we have an example of a *many-to-many* relationship.

A *to-many* relationship can be thought of as the reverse of a *to-one* relationship. So how do we model a many-to-many relationship?

Creating a JOIN table for the Many-To-Many Relationship

A *JOIN* table is used to model a *many-to-many* relationship. That is, an abstract, intermediate table used solely for the purpose of maintaining the relationship.

Open both model files in EOModeler, and add the JOIN table to the Forum model file.

1. Add a new entity titled ForumModerator.

2. Set its table name to FORUM_MODERATOR to indicate that it is a join of the FORUM table and the USER (Moderator) table.

3. Copy and paste the primary key for *Forum, forumID* into the table. Repeat by copying the primary key *userID* for *Moderator*.

4. Make sure that *both* keys are set as a primary key. This is a *compound* primary key.

NOTE

Primary keys can consist of more than one attribute. These are known as *compound* primary keys.

They are essential in special circumstances such as this, where they form the primary keys of JOIN tables in many-to-many relationships.

5. Add a to-one relationship to Forum, joining on the forumID. Make the relationship Mandatory from the Advanced Relationship Inspector. Make the relationship abstract.

6. Repeat with a similar to-one relationship to *Moderator*.

Now you should have an entity that looks similar to Figure 10.7. It is a purely abstract entity in that it has no real meaning or significance. It is there simply to represent the *many-to-many* relationship. Therefore, the relationships are marked as *abstract*.

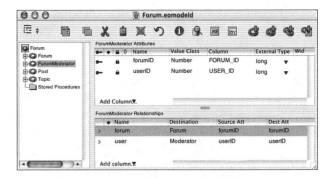

FIGURE 10.7   ForumModerator.

Using Flattened Relationships in a Many-To-Many Relationship

We haven't finished modeling the many-to-many relationship just yet.

We need to add the relationships to represent the many-to-many structure between *Forum* and *Moderator*.

1. Add an *abstract* to-many relationship from *Forum* to the JOIN table *ForumModerator,* on the `forumID` key. This relationship is abstract because it has no real meaning. It is part of the many-to-many structure.

2. Set it to *Propagate Primary Key* in the Advanced Relationship Inspector. This indicates that the primary key of *Forum* (together with the primary key of *Moderator*) will be made the primary key of *ForumModerator*.

3. Also set a Cascade Delete Rule and check the Owns Destination box.

4. Now double-click the `forumModerators` relationship to navigate to the destination entity.

5. Select the *user* relationship, and then choose Flatten Property from the Property menu to create a *flattened relationship*. Notice how it appears as bold.

NOTE

Flattened relationships are only necessary in special circumstances, such as when modeling a *many-to-many* relationship.

Otherwise, they are not normally required because you can traverse *key paths* to obtain values of related objects, for example, `post.topic.name` and `post.user.name`.

6. Rename the relationship something sensible. In this case `moderators` will do.

Now repeat for the forums relationship in *Moderator*, making sure that you flatten the *forumModerators.forum* relationship. Compare your results with Figure 10.8 and Figure 10.9.

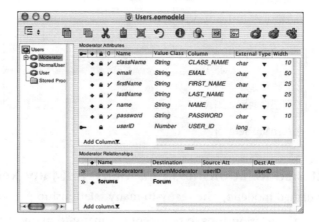

FIGURE 10.8   Using a flattened relationship in a many-to-many relationship.

Now the many-to-many relationship is complete. Test it by assigning forums to a moderator and vice versa. Check object deletion.

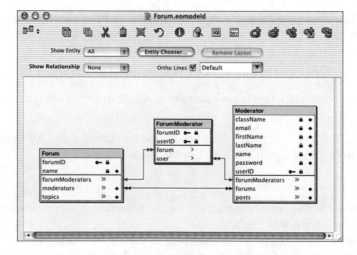

FIGURE 10.9   The forum-moderator many-to-many relationship.

Using EOModeler to Automatically Create a Many-to-Many Join

An alternative way to set up a many-to-many relationship is to use EOModeler to automate the previous steps for you. Select the two entities you want to join in a many-to-many relationship from the Entities view. Then choose Join in Many-to-Many from the Property menu. EOModeler should automatically set up a join table and entity along with the relationships needed to form a many-to-many relationship.

When To Use Back-Relationships

Lastly, we should consider adding the *User.posts back-relationship* to the model.

Notice that I've explicitly referred to this to-many relationship as a *back-relationship* because it is the *weaker* or *less relevant* direction in the *User-Posts* link: *Post.user* is a mandatory relationship, whereas *User.posts* is optional.

Don't be tempted to add them in just to avoid possible oversights in design. Use them only when it makes sense to do so, or when they are necessary.

Sometimes, you might find that an object graph might contain quite large to-many relationships, many of which often are *back-relationships*.

For example, you can be sure to expect that with significant use, if there are users with more than a hundred posts, then this back-relationship could be a performance bottleneck.

In this scenario back-relationships should be used with caution. However, here the requirements justify its use.

So, add the *User.posts* back-relationship to the model. Remember to copy the relationship to the subclasses of *User* before saving.

Building a Stateless Application Prototype

Now we are going to make a stateless version of the first prototype application.

Duplicate the project and rename it `ForumPrototype2`.

Preparing the Application for Statelessness

Set the application to use the direct action request handler by default, as you did in Chapter 4, "Building a Bookmarkable Application."

We are also going to use object sharing for performance.

In particular, the set of *Forums* in an online discussion board is unlikely to change, in the sense that new forums would be added or deleted very rarely. So these are the most likely candidates for object sharing.

Also, this version of the prototype is read only, so we shouldn't run into problems by sharing the object graph.

So, set *Forum* to *Share All Objects* as in Chapter 7.

Add the line to the Application constructor to fetch the *Forums*:

```
    // force fetching of shared EOs/rawRows
   EOSharedEditingContext sharedEditingContext =
EOSharedEditingContext.defaultSharedEditingContext();
    EOFetchSpecification fetchSpec =
EOFetchSpecification.fetchSpecificationNamed("FetchAll", "Forum");
    sharedEditingContext.objectsWithFetchSpecification(fetchSpec);
```

Now we are ready to make the necessary changes to the other components.

Converting Pages into Direct Actions

Let's start with the Main page.

Converting the Main page

Remove the display group by control clicking it in the WebObjects Builder, and then selecting *Delete forumDispalyGroup*. Select *Unbind* when prompted to do so.

Rebind the *WORepetition list* to the shared Forum objects `application.sharedEditingContext.objectsByEntityName.Forum`.

Add another column to the Main page to display the list of moderators next to a forum.

Place another repetition in the second row and bind `forum.moderators` to its *list*. Bind its item to a new variable key *moderator* of type *Moderator*. Place within it a *WOString* bound to `moderator.name`.

Now we've got to change the bindings for the hyperlink. It's got to use a direct action instead of the component action we used before. Hook it up to a new direct action named `topics`.

Because we are no longer using a component action, we won't be able to pass the object onto the next page as we did before. When using direct actions, we will still have to indicate which forum's topics we want to browse. The most concise solution is to pass the primary key via the request onto the next direct action.

We do this by adding a form binding `?forumID` to the hyperlink bound to a new accessor key of the same name:

```
public Integer forumID() {
    NSDictionary primaryKey = EOUtilities.primaryKeyForObject
    (forum.editingContext(), forum);
    return (Integer) primaryKey.valueForKey("forumID");
    }
```

Remember to add an import statement for *com.webobjects.eoaccess.** to your
Main.java class file.

NOTE

To accommodate *compound* primary keys or several primary keys together, a primary key of
an Enterprise Object is managed as a *NSDictionary*.

We obtain the *primary key value* using key-value coding for the particular key.

Add the direct action *topics* to DirectAction.java:

```
public WOActionResults topicsAction() {
    WOComponent nextPage = pageWithName("ForumTopics");
    Number forumID = request().numericFormValueForKey("forumID", new NSNumberFor-
matter());
    EOSharedEditingContext sharedEditingContext =
     EOSharedEditingContext.defaultSharedEditingContext();
    EOEnterpriseObject forum = EOUtilities.objectWithPrimaryKeyValue
    (sharedEditingContext, "Forum", forumID);

    // set variables
    nextPage.takeValueForKeyPath(forum, "topicsDisplayGroup.masterObject");

    return nextPage;
    }
```

Here as before, we use request().forumValueForKey() to access the *forumID* from
the URL. Then we use *EOUtilities* objectForPrimaryKeyValue() to convert that
primary key ID back into an object. We then set the *forum* as the masterObject in
the *ForumTopics* page, as we did in the component action.

Finally, we can remove the redundant component action.

Converting the ForumTopics page

Luckily, not much changes here. We simply need to change the action of the component. Rebind the hyperlink to a direct action named posts. Similar to what we did
with the Main component, add a form binding ?topicID and bind it to an accessor
key topicID, which presents the primary key value for the selected topic.

Add the *postsAction* that is analogous to the *topicsAction*. The only difference is to replace *forumID* with *topicID* and *Forum* with *Topic*.

Now remove the `viewTopic` action.

Converting the TopicPosts page

There is only one change that needs to be made to this component: an addition.

We are now in a position to display the number of posts made by a forum user.

In the author column, add another *WOString* below the first string and bind it to `post.user.posts.count`. This will traverse the *User.posts* back-relationship we added earlier to obtain the number of posts she has made.

Observing the Performance of the Application

Build and test your stateless prototype. Now turn on SQL Logging to observe the number of fetches being performed per page. Pay particular attention to the fetches the application performs on the first and subsequent request of a page.

Notice that in particular, the Main page fetches not only all the Forums, but also all its Topics!

Keep a note of all other inefficiencies you observe, and we'll take a look at them in the next section.

For a small Online Forum this might not be too much of a problem. However, we can do better than that.

Making Performance Optimizations to the Object Model

We're going to look at two methods of optimizing, the model and the fetches it performs.

Introduction to Prefetching

The first method we'll look at is a fairly simple method to use.

You might have noticed that displaying the list of *Forum.moderators*, on the Main page, resulted in the fetching of the moderators for each of the forums listed. This would have consisted of two fetches per forum. One for the JOIN table and the second from the USER table.

When an Enterprise Object is fetched, its related objects are *not* fetched along with it. This is for performance and efficiency.

Imagine if this were the case. Then an entire object graph would be pulled into memory when an Enterprise Object is first fetched. In large databases, that would quite possibly take forever.

Instead, related Enterprise Objects are fetched *on-demand*.

Prefetching enables select relationships to be fetched along with an object.

Again, as with any technique or optimization, be selective about what relationships you prefetch.

Actually, there is only a very minimal justification for prefetching *Forum.moderators*, given that the forum objects are already shared. This is to ensure that the fetching of moderators for each forum doesn't impact the performance of the first request of the Main page.

Using Prefetching to Optimize Performance

Open the *Forum* model and select the *FetchAll* fetch specification, under the *Forum* entity. This is the fetch specification created to fetch the objects into shared memory.

1. Click the *Prefetching* tab.

2. Choose the relationship you want to prefetch. In this case select *moderators*.

3. Click Add to select the relationship for prefetching. You will see it move to the bottom panel, as shown in Figure 10.10.

4. Save the changes.

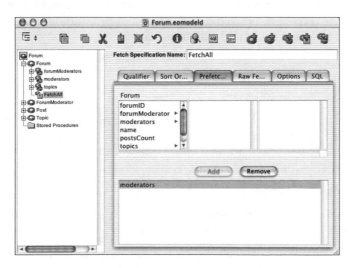

FIGURE 10.10   Prefetching objects.

The next time you build and run your application, the prefetching should be operational. In this case when the application starts up and *Forums* are loaded into shared memory, the *Forum.moderators* should be fetched as well.

For further reference check the WebObjects Documentation site for the Advanced Topic on Prefetching.

Introduction to Derived Attributes

In spite of the little performance boost we got by turning on object prefetching for *Forum.moderators*, you might be thinking that there are more pressing issues to deal with.

In particular, you should be alarmed at the inefficiency of fetching all Topics for a forum, and then all its Posts just to calculate the number of posts and topics per forum.

In effect, you are fetching most of the object graph for the database.

The next set of optimizations are more than just a refinement. In the case mentioned previously, performance would be essential to ensure that such an application is deployable, let alone robust and scalable.

We are going to use derived attributes to obtain the number of topics and posts in a forum. In addition, we'll use it to find the details of the last and first post of the topic.

Derived attributes are special attributes that are not mapped onto a table COLUMN of their own. They are usually derived from a combination or function of other COLUMNS. As such, they *are read-only* attributes. We can not write values to them because they are often calculated from other ones.

It is not new to Enterprise Objects, however as we will see next, *derived attributes* can prove to be an incredibly powerful feature.

Using Derived Attributes to Count Objects in a Relationship

The most glaring performance deficiency is the fetching of topics and posts for each and every forum, just to obtain their count. So instead, we'll try to obtain the count directly for #forum.topics and #forum.topics.posts.

Add a new attribute to *Forum* titled topicsCount.

1. Uncheck the *Lock* on the attribute by clicking the padlock icon in the Locking column, but make sure the attribute *Allows Null Value*.

2. In the *Attribute Inspector*, set the *Internal Data Type* to *Integer*. Set the *External Type* to *long* (in Openbase).

3. Enter (`SELECT COUNT(*) FROM TOPIC WHERE TOPIC.FORUM_ID = FORUM.FORUM_ID`) for the *Column*. Then change the *Column* pop up to *Derived*, as shown in Figure 10.11.

4. In the Advanced Entity Inspector, select Read Only as an Option.

5. Paste the same string you entered into as the *Column* into the *Custom Formatting Read* field. This is the vital setting, so make sure that it is correct. This is vital because these derived attributes are really defined by the custom read format and not by the column name.

6. Save your changes.

You can test that the derived field works correctly by doing a data browse from EOModeler. With the entity selected, choose Browse Data from the Tools menu. You should find a list of objects being fetched with the number of topics.

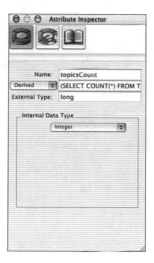

FIGURE 10.11   Derived Attribute Inspector.

Repeat for a derived attribute named `postsCount` on *Forum* with the SQL: (`SELECT COUNT(*) FROM POST, TOPIC WHERE POST.TOPIC_ID = TOPIC.TOPIC_ID AND TOPIC.FORUM_ID = FORUM.FORUM_ID`).

Using Derived Attributes and Other Aggregate Functions

Using *derived attributes* to count related objects is a useful solution to a common problem.

FIGURE 10.12   Derived Advanced Attribute Inspector.

However, we can use it to compute other *aggregate* relationships as well. For instance, we can use it to find the time of the last post made to a topic, or who started a topic.

In fact, we define these derived attributes in exactly the same way as we did for *Forum*.

- Add a postsCount attribute to *Topic* using the SQL: (SELECT COUNT(*) FROM POST WHERE POST.TOPIC_ID = TOPIC.TOPIC_ID).

- To *Topic*, add a *Date* attribute called timeOfLastPost with SQL: (SELECT MAX(TIMESTAMP) FROM POST WHERE POST.TOPIC_ID = TOPIC.TOPIC_ID).

- Add a *String* attribute called lastPostMadeBy to *Topic*, for the SQL: (SELECT NAME FROM USER WHERE USER_ID = (SELECT USER_ID FROM POST WHERE TIME-STAMP >= (SELECT MAX(TIMESTAMP) FROM POST WHERE POST.TOPIC_ID = TOPIC.TOPIC_ID))).

- Add a second *String* attribute called starter to *Topic*, with the SQL: (SELECT NAME FROM USER WHERE USER_ID = (SELECT USER_ID FROM POST WHERE TIME-STAMP <= (SELECT MIN(TIMESTAMP) FROM POST WHERE POST.TOPIC_ID = TOPIC.TOPIC_ID))).

- To *User*, add a postsCount *Integer* attribute using the SQL: You might have to replicate the properties of the attribute in the subclasses *Moderator* and *NormalUser*.

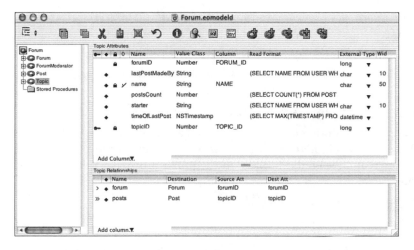

FIGURE 10.13 Topic Attributes in EOModeler.

Retesting the Object Model in DirectToWeb

It is a good idea to test your object model in DirectToWeb after you have made changes. Because there have been significant changes to the model, it is recommended that it is tested again at this point in time.

In particular, test that the derived attributes do display values correctly. You can use the DirectToWeb test application that you developed previously, by copying in the new object model files and classes and unsetting object sharing.

A limitation of DirectToWeb is that it doesn't support shared objects used in this fashion. Hence, object sharing must be explicitly turned off. Add the following line to the DirectToWeb Application constructor:

```
// turn off object sharing in D2W
EOSharedEditingContext.setDefaultSharedEditingContext(null);
```

This saves you from having to explicitly unset object sharing in the model files when you copy them over to the DirectToWeb project.

Binding WebObjects Components to Derived Attributes

Now you must return to the stateless prototype of the Online Forum and rebind the components to these attributes of the entities.

Most obviously, bindings made to posts.count and topics.count now bind to postsCount and topicsCount.

In the *ForumTopics* page, you can remove the redundant accessors `starter` and `lastPost`. Rebind the components to `topic.starter` and `topic.lastPostMadeBy` and `topic.timeOfLastPost`.

This time when you build and run the application, note the performance difference.

When to Use Derived Attributes

It might seem tempting to use these derived attributes at every corner. However, as we'll soon discover, there are other methods of optimization that might be simpler and more seamless; methods that don't require using SQL explicitly in the model or in code.

So use derived attributes sparingly.

Developing the Stateless Application Components

We have a stateless component that needs to be developed before the application can be fully stateless. That is, the stateless equivalent of the WebObjects component *WOBatchNavigationBar*.

Unlike the list of forums on the main page, which might be limited to one page, the lists of topics per forum and posts on a topic could overflow into several pages.

To organize and navigate these pages, we will need a direct action equivalent of *WOBatchNavigationBar*.

Converting a WOExtensions Component

We are fortunate enough to have the source to the *WOBatchNavigationBar* component. This will make customizing it easy.

Start by creating a development project *WABatchNavigationBarTest* to build the component in isolation.

1. Open the *WOBatchNavigationBar* component in the WebObjects Builder and save it as `WABatchNavigationBar` in your project directory. Create a class file for it when prompted to do so. You will find the WOBatchNavigationBar component in */Developer/Examples/JavaWebObjects/Source/JavaWOExtensions/*.

2. Place the newly added component files in a group folder by selecting *Project, New Group* from the menu.

3. Copy in the settings and accessors from the `WOBatchNavigation.java` into the class file.

4. Locate and delete the table cell containing the SortComponent because it is no longer required. Also delete the *WOForm* containing it. Remove the redundant hasSortKeyList accessor.

5. Convert the ItemsPerBatch element from a *WOTextField* into a *WOString*. That is, switch to Source View in WebObjects Builder and change the WebObjects declaration for the text field into a WOString. You can remove the *WOForm* wrapping it, by control clicking it in the midsection of the window and selecting *Unwrap Contents* from the contextual menu.

6. Bind the actions of the hyperlinks and the BatchNumberForm to use the ^directActionName of the ^actionClass and bind their *queryDictionary* to ^queryDictionary.

7. In addition add a form value key ?displayBatchIndex binding each of the action components i.e. the next and previous buttons to previousBatchIndex, currentBatchIndex, and nextBatchIndex defined as accessors.

```
public int nextBatchIndex() {
    int index = currentBatchIndex();
        return ++index;
}

public int previousBatchIndex() {
    int index = currentBatchIndex();
        return --index;
}

public int currentBatchIndex() {
        WODisplayGroup displayGroup = (WODisplayGroup) valueForBinding("dis-
playGroup");

        return displayGroup.currentBatchIndex();
}
```

8. Set the BatchNumber *WOTextField name* to currentBatchIndex, so that the value will be submitted as a form value to the direct action.

9. Finally, make the relevant changes to the API. In the API Editor, remove *sortKeyList* and replace it with *directActionName* (Direct Action Names), *actionClass* (Direct Action Classes), and *queryDictionary*. Save the changes.

Testing the WABatchNavigationComponent

Delete the Main page from the project. Add the Movies model file from the WebObjects Examples folder. Now re-create the Main component as an Assistant generated *Display Group Component*.

Choose the paginated option.

In the Main component that is generated, remove the elements above the horizonal rule. Then in place of the components and logic used to batch the display group objects, use a *WABatchNavigationBar* component.

Make the application handle direct actions by default. Bind the navigation bar to a new direct action:

```
public WOActionResults mainAction() {
      WOComponent nextPage = pageWithName("Main");
   String index = request().stringFormValueForKey("displayBatchIndex");

   // set values
   nextPage.takeValueForKeyPath(new Integer(index),
➡    "movieDisplayGroup.currentBatchIndex");

      return nextPage;
   }
```

Build and test the component.

Here you will notice that the batch index is explicitly pulled from the request and pushed back into that page.

Batching Objects as Pages

Now copy the component and its files into the *ForumPrototype2* project.

Add the component to the *ForumTopics* page and the *TopicsPost* page.

Bind the directActionNames to topics and posts, respectively. Additionally, binding the *queryDictionary* to an accessor primaryKey. This is to pass on the id of the forum and topic onto the batch navigation component.

Here is the method for ForumTopics:

```
public NSDictionary primaryKey() {
      EOEnterpriseObject forum = (EOEnterpriseObject)
➡    topicsDisplayGroup.masterObject();
   return EOUtilities.primaryKeyForObject(forum.editingContext(), forum);
   }
```

Amend the direct actions to handle the setting of the batch index. Here is the code for the topicsAction:

```
// set the batch index
Number index = request().numericFormValueForKey("displayBatchIndex ", new NSNumber-
Formatter());

    if (index != null) nextPage.takeValueForKeyPath(index,
""topicsDisplayGroup.currentBatchIndex"");
```

Now you are ready to build and test object batching. To set the size of batches, double click the display group to open the *Display Group Options* panel. Here you can set the *Entries per batch* to whatever you desire.

Summary

In this chapter, we've developed an advanced application prototype by iteration. Successively improving the model to match the requirements, and optimizing it to realize goals of satisfactory performance.

11

Managing Users, Sessions, and Personalization

"If you treat an individual...as if he were what he ought to be and what he could be he will become what he ought to be and could be."

—Johann Wolfgang von Goeth
German writer, scientist, master of poetry, drama, and novel.

In this chapter we'll look at adding session support to the direct action application. In particular, the ability for a user to login and submit a new post or reply.

At the same time, we'll see what kind of personalization options we can grant the individual, such as adding his own signature, for example.

Crafting the Interface for Posting Topics and Replies

If you are familiar enough with Enterprise Object control logic, and how to insert and save objects to a database, then you can skip this entire section.

Otherwise, it might prove to be a necessary exercise at extending a read-only interface that we have crafted for the online forum.

The purpose of this iteration is to create and define the interface for logging in, posting a new topic, and submitting a reply.

We are going to *branch* off the first application prototype we developed in Chapter 10, "Rapid Prototyping with

WebObjects," because this would be easier than implementing this functionality as a stateless, direct-actionable component. So start off by making a copy of the first forum prototype. Copy in the latest object model, but remember to turn off object sharing. That is, in the Shared Object Inspector of the Forum entity, choose to Share No Objects.

However, given that the reader should be rather familiar with these tasks by now, the outlined instructions will be more concise and brief.

Adding a Login Page

Add a new component, Login to the forum prototype application project.

Open the User model and drag in the *User* entity to add a display group to the *Login* page. Make sure it is configured to fetch *Users*.

Layout the component as in Figure 11.1

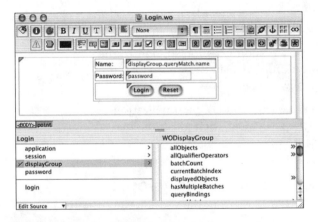

FIGURE 11.1   Laying out the Login Window.

Note that the username field is bound to displayGroup.queryMatch.name. This is a facility in a *WODisplayGroup* that allows you to perform a search on that key based on what is typed by the user.

The Login button is hooked up to the login action that initiates this fetch:

```
public WOComponent login() {
    displayGroup.qualifyDataSource();

    if (displayGroup.selectedObject() != null) {
        EOEnterpriseObject user = (EOEnterpriseObject)
```

```
displayGroup.selectedObject();
        String _password = (String) user.valueForKey("password");
                    if (_password.equals(password)) {

            // set the session user
            takeValueForKeyPath(user, "session.user");
            return pageWithName("Main");
        }
    } return null;}
```

We use the `qualifyDataSource()` on the display group to perform the fetch. Then, if a user is found to have the same name and password we register that user as the `session.user`.

For this add a key, user, to the *Session*. At the same time add a convenience accessor indicating whether a *Session* has a user or not:

```
protected EOEnterpriseObject user;

public boolean hasUser() {
    return (user != null);
}
```

Now you might want to add a `login` link to the three pages of the application. You can also wrap the link in a conditional, bound to the *negation* of `session.hasUser`, so to only display it if the user is not logged in.

Implementing a Reply Function

Add a new component `Reply`, and set up a master-detail display group on the relationship: *Topic.posts*. Darg in the Topic.posts relationship from EOModeler into the Reply component window.

Layout a simple form with a *WOText* to edit the reply and a *WOSubmitButton* to perform a save action. Bind the WOText *value* to `post.message`. Add a *WOString* to display the topic, and bind it to `post.topic.name`:

```
/** @TypeInfo Post */
public EOEnterpriseObject post() {
    EOEnterpriseObject post = (EOEnterpriseObject) postsDisplayGroup.selectedOb-
ject();

    // create a new post on demand
    if (post == null) {
        EOEnterpriseObject user = (EOEnterpriseObject)
```

```
valueForKeyPath("session.user");

        // insert a new post
        postsDisplayGroup.insert();

        // assign the user
        post = (EOEnterpriseObject) postsDisplayGroup.selectedObject();
post.addObjectToBothSidesOfRelationshipWithKey(user, "user");
    } return post;
}
```

The *@TypeInfo* is used by WebObjects Builder to identify the real type or entity of enterprise objects. Based on this information, it will display the object's keys in the lower half of a component window.

Note that here we are doing two things:

First, we insert a new post into the `topic.posts` array, by using `insert()` on the detail display group.

Second, we assign the mandatory relationship `post.user`, by setting the relationship using `addObjectToBothSidesOfRelationshipWithKey()`.

NOTE

The method `addObjectToBothSidesOfRelationshipWithKey()` is the default way to set *relationships* in Enterprise Objects.

Actually, it does double duty: it sets both the `post.user` relationship as well as the *back-relationship* `user.posts`.

Therefore, using `addObjectToBothSidesOfRelationshipWithKey()` takes precedence over setting the values of relationships using either key value coding API or accessor methods.

In the *TopicPosts* page add a `reply` link to each post, bound to an action of the same name.

```
public WOComponent reply() {
    WOComponent nextPage = pageWithName("Reply");
    EOEnterpriseObject topic = (EOEnterpriseObject)
postsDisplayGroup.masterObject();

    // set the master object
    nextPage.takeValueForKeyPath(topic, "postsDisplayGroup.masterObject");

    return nextPage;
}
```

Finally, bind the *Reply* page submit button to a save action:

```
public WOComponent save() {
    WOComponent nextPage = pageWithName("TopicPosts");

    // save changes    session().defaultEditingContext().saveChanges();

    // set the topic
    nextPage.takeValueForKeyPath(postsDisplayGroup.masterObject(),
"postsDisplayGroup.masterObject");

    return nextPage;
}
```

Here, changes to the *Session's* defaultEditingContext() are saved and you are returned to the *TopicPosts* page.

Adding a Page to Start a New Topic

This NewTopic component is very similar to the *Reply* page.

The main difference is that you add two detail display groups, one for *Forum.topics*, the other for *Topic.posts*.

When a startTopic action is called from the *ForumTopics* page, you set the forum as the topicsDisplayGroup.masterObject.

Bind the form elements to topic and post:

```
/** @TypeInfo Topic */
public EOEnterpriseObject topic() {
    EOEnterpriseObject topic = (EOEnterpriseObject)
topicsDisplayGroup.selectedObject();

    // create a new topic
    if (topic == null) {
        // insert
        topicsDisplayGroup.insert();

        // set it as master object of the postsDisplayGroup
        topic = (EOEnterpriseObject) topicsDisplayGroup.selectedObject();
        postsDisplayGroup.setMasterObject(topic);
    } return topic;
}
```

```
/** @TypeInfo Post */
public EOEnterpriseObject post() {
    EOEnterpriseObject post = (EOEnterpriseObject)
postsDisplayGroup.selectedObject();

    // create a new post on demand
    if (post == null) {
        EOEnterpriseObject user = (EOEnterpriseObject)
valueForKeyPath("session.user");

        // insert a new post
        postsDisplayGroup.insert();

        // assign the user
        post = (EOEnterpriseObject) postsDisplayGroup.selectedObject();
        post.addObjectToBothSidesOfRelationshipWithKey(user, "user");
    } return post;
}
```

This component performs two operations. It inserts and creates a new topic, as well as one for a new post.

The `post` accessor is identical to the *Reply* page accessor.

The big difference here is that the `topic` accessor will set the `postsDisplayGroup.masterObject` when it has created a new topic.

Also note that the layout of the component, although similar to the *Reply* page, will have a *WOTextField* in place of a *WOString* to display and edit `topic.name`.

The save action is pretty much identical, although it returns the *ForumTopics* page.

Build and test your application to see that you can add a new topic, and reply to one, without error.

Supporting Sessions in a Direct Action Application

In this next section we'll add a login page to the online forum to enable members to login and post replies and topics of discussion.

Using Direct Action Classes

The login page can be implemented as a stateless page.

It is not until the user has correctly typed in a username and password that we really have to create a session.

Revert back to developing the stateless application prototype again. Add a *UserLogin* page and lay it out pretty much as you did before.

The differences this time are that we us a direct action on the *WOForm*, and so must *name* the form elements as well. That is, you must specify the name attribute of the WOForm elements for them to work as a stateless direct action.

Bind the static submit button to a direct action named user and this time bind the direct action class to one called Login.

We are going to implement the actions relating to user login in a separate Direct Action class. This is useful to partition, or group, direct actions logically.

Add a new class to the project, Login. Make sure it *extends WODirectAction* and has a *constructor* and defaultAction similar to that of the default direct action class *DirectAction*. Have the defaultAction return to the *UserLogin* page.

Now add the userAction method:

```
public WOActionResults userAction() {
    String username = request().stringFormValueForKey("name");
    EOEditingContext editingContext = new EOEditingContext();
    NSArray results = EOUtilities.rawRowsMatchingKeyAndValue(
editingContext, "User", "name", username);

    // if there are user(s) matching the username
    if (results.count() > 0) {
        NSDictionary result = (NSDictionary) results.objectAtIndex(0);
        String _password = (String) result.valueForKey("password");
        String password = request().stringFormValueForKey("password");

        // check that the passwords match
        if (password.equals(_password)) {
            EOEnterpriseObject user =
➥EOUtilities.objectMatchingKeyAndValue(session().defaultEditingContext(),
 "User", "name", username);

            // set the session.user
            session().takeValueForKey(user, "user");

            return pageWithName("Main");
        } else return wrongPasswordAction();
    } return noSuchUserAction();
}
```

Note that the direct action uses the fact that the login form elements were labeled name and password, respectively.

However, of real importance here is the fact that we have been careful not to fetch the user as an object.

We have to work extra hard to prevent the login page from being included in the *Session*. The user object should be fetched into the *Session* defaultEditingContext, but we can't create a *Session* until we know that the username and password match the user info in the database.

So, first we fetch the user data as *raw rows*.

NOTE

A *raw row* is the data or set of values of a row fetched from the database. It is represented as a *NSDictionary*.

In addition, we use a transient-editing context. This is so the data we fetch is discarded at the end of the action. On successful login, we refetch the user from the *Session* defaultEditingContext.

Handling a Wrong Password or Incorrect User

We also implement the sub actions wrongPasswordAction and noSuchUserAction privately:

```
private WOActionResults noSuchUserAction() {
    WOComponent nextPage = pageWithName("UserLogin");

    // set variables
    nextPage.takeValueForKey("No such username. Try again.", "msg");

    return nextPage;
}

private WOActionResults wrongPasswordAction() {
    WOComponent nextPage = pageWithName("UserLogin");
    String username = request().stringFormValueForKey("name");

    // set variables
    nextPage.takeValueForKey(username, "username");
    nextPage.takeValueForKey("Incorrect password. Try again.", "msg");

    return nextPage;
}
```

This requires that we add a variable key msg to the *UserLogin* page. You can display the error msg in a different color font to assist the user.

Displaying a Conditional Login Link

Finally, you need to add a conditional hyperlink to the *Main* page to allow for user *Login* (only if one hasn't logged in yet).

Add the key hasSession to the *Main* page to bind to the login conditional:

```
public boolean hasSession() {
      String sessionID = context().request().stringFormValueForKey("wosid");
      return (super.hasSession() || sessionID != null);
   }
```

The conditional is necessary to prevent a user from repeatedly logging in.

Implementing Navigation as Direct Actions

It will be useful to provide the user with the ability to navigate the forums and topics of discussion.

Take a look at Figure 11.2 for some inspiration:

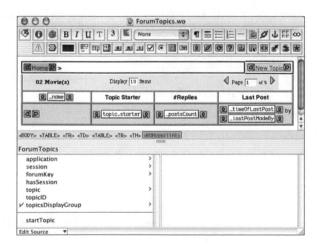

FIGURE 11.2   Navigation on the ForumTopics page.

You can add navigation to the *TopicPosts* page but also remember to add a form value binding forumID to the *topics* link to display the forum topics:

```
public Integer forumID() {
```

```
    NSDictionary primaryKey = EOUtilities.primaryKeyForObject(
forum.editingContext(), forum);
    return (Integer) primaryKey.valueForKey("forumID");
}
```

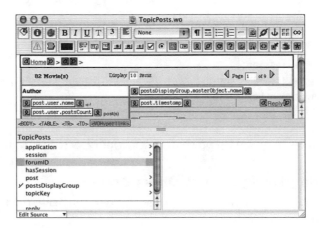

FIGURE 11.3   Navigation on the TopicPosts page.

Now we are in a position to add functionality to post a reply and submit a new topic.

First, an introduction to nested editing contexts.

Introduction to Default and Shared Editing Contexts

Every WebObjects session will create and use a `defaultEditingContext()` in which it performs fetches, edits, inserts, and deletes.

Because the application is using shared objects, it will use an *EOSharedEditingContext* as well.

> **NOTE**
>
> A *shared editing context* is a *read-only* editing context used exclusively to store commonly accessed objects.

The principal difference is that you will not be able to make changes to a shared object. However, when we need to submit a *Post*, we are invariably making changes to a *Topic*; similarly, when we post a new *Topic*, we are making changes to a *Forum*.

To make changes to a shared object, we must edit it in an editing context that is not in the shared editing context. The simplest way to achieve this is to break the relationship between the `application.sharedEditingContext` and the `session.defaultEditingContext`.

Adding the Post Reply Page

You can copy in the Reply page you created earlier on in the chapter and use it practically unchanged.

However, to use those components as is, we need to disable the nested editing context configuration of the *Session* `defaultEditingContext`.

Changing the Default Session Behavior

In the *Application* class we are given the opportunity to alter the *Session* creation behavior, so here is an ideal place to do this:

```
public WOSession createSessionForRequest(WORequest request) {
    WOSession session = super.createSessionForRequest(request);

    // disable object sharing for the session ec
    session.defaultEditingContext().setSharedEditingContext(null);

    return session;
}
```

Note that an alternative to the above would be to perform the Session customization in the Session constructor.

Here all we have to do to break the nested editing context configuration is to set the shared editing context of the `defaultEditingContext` to `null`.

Localizing Objects in Editing Contexts

There is one final alteration or change we must make to our existing code.

Because the two editing contexts are disjointed, objects fetched in one editing context are not necessarily known in the other. Hence, we need to *localize* them in the other editing context.

In the `reply` component action of *TopicPosts* we need to add one line:

```
public WOComponent reply() {
    WOComponent nextPage = pageWithName("Reply");
    EOEnterpriseObject _topic = (EOEnterpriseObject)
postsDisplayGroup.masterObject();
    EOEnterpriseObject topic = EOUtilities.localInstanceOfObject(
```

```
session().defaultEditingContext(), _topic);

    // set topic
    nextPage.takeValueForKeyPath(topic, "postsDisplayGroup.masterObject");

    return nextPage;
}
```

Here the topic instance was fetched into the `sharedEditingContext`. So, when we pass it onto the Reply page that uses the `defaultEditingContext`, we need to localize it. *EOUtilities* provides us with a convenience to create a local instance of an object in an editing context.

Adding the Start Topic Functionality

Again the *StartTopic* component can be copied in and used as is. Remember to local-ize the `forum` object before setting it as the `masterObject` in the *StartTopic* page.

When you build and run your application you might notice that when creating a new topic, the topic starter and the details of the last post are not displayed.

This is because these are precisely the derived values that are obtained only when the object is fetched from the database. Because the Enterprise Object has been created in the application, there is no need to refetch its values.

One way to circumvent this is to compute those values with accessor methods of the derived attributes if needed.

Computing Aggregates In-Memory

Use a custom class for the *Topic* entity, generate its class file, and include it in the project.

Remove all but the derived attributes, and add in the logic to compute those derived attributes from the object graph:

```
/*
* derived attribute accessors
*/
public Number postsCount() {
    Number postsCount = (Number) storedValueForKey("postsCount");
    return (postsCount != null) ? postsCount: (Number)
valueForKeyPath("posts.count");
}
```

```
public NSTimestamp timeOfLastPost() {
    NSTimestamp timeOfLastPost = (NSTimestamp)
storedValueForKey("timeOfLastPost");
    return (timeOfLastPost != null)
➥ ? timeOfLastPost: (NSTimestamp) valueForKeyPath("posts.@max.timestamp");
}

public String lastPostMadeBy() {
    String lastPostMadeBy = (String) storedValueForKey("lastPostMadeBy");
    if (lastPostMadeBy == null) {
        NSArray posts = (NSArray) valueForKey("posts");
        EOEnterpriseObject lastPost = (EOEnterpriseObject)
posts.lastObject();

        lastPostMadeBy = (String) lastPost.valueForKeyPath("user.name");
    } return lastPostMadeBy;
}

public String starter() {
    String starter = (String) storedValueForKey("starter");
    if (starter == null) {
        NSArray posts = (NSArray) valueForKey("posts");
        EOEnterpriseObject firstPost = (EOEnterpriseObject)
posts.objectAtIndex(0);

        starter = (String) firstPost.valueForKeyPath("user.name");
    } return starter;
}
```

Notice in particular, to work out the time of the last post, we use a key path
posts.@max.timestamp.

By traversing the first key posts, a *NSArray* is returned. The *NSArray* will evaluate the
@max aggregate in memory, working out the largest (or latest) such value.

Managing Client-Side State with Cookies

In this next section we will add functionality to remember login details the next
time a user visits from the same client (browser).

Introduction to Storing Session State on the Browser

WebObjects applications already have an excellent mechanism for managing *Session*
state on the server.

However, *Session* state is transient. When the Session ends, its state or memory is discarded with it. So for example, login details are lost when the user finishes with an application.

This means that the next time the user wants to use that application, she will have to log in again to retrieve settings.

Thankfully, WebObjects applications can take advantage of client-side technologies as well. In particular, browser cookies provide an excellent mechanism for *Session* state to persist, or be managed on the client.

We can use cookies to store user login details so that the next time a user wants to log into the online forum, her details will be "remembered."

Setting Cookie Values

First, we need to make a change to the *UserLogin* page.

Add two static radio buttons representing the yes and no values of whether to remember login details. In otherwords the yes radio should have value 1 and the no radio should have value 0. Name both elements isPersistent.

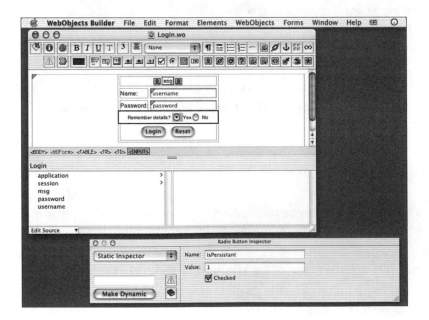

FIGURE 11.4   Adding radio buttons to the UserLogin page.

Now, change the *Login* userAction to retrieve this value from the direct action, and then pass it onto the next page.

```
if (password.equals(_password)) {
    EOEnterpriseObject user = EOUtilities.objectMatchingKeyAndValue(
session().defaultEditingContext(), "User", "name", username);
    WOComponent nextPage = pageWithName("Main");
    Number isPersistant = request().numericFormValueForKey(
"isPersistant", new NSNumberFormatter());

    // set the session.user
    session().takeValueForKey(user, "user");
    nextPage.takeValueForKey(isPersistant, "hasPersistantLogin");

    return nextPage;
}
```

In the *Main* class add a key.

```
protected boolean hasPersistantLogin;
```

This indicates whether to set the cookies or not. The setting of the cookies is actually performed in the appendToResponse() of the *Main* component.

```
public void appendToResponse(WOResponse response, WOContext context) {
    // set cookies to remember details
    if (hasPersistantLogin) {
        String username = (String) valueForKeyPath("session.user.name");
        String password = (String) valueForKeyPath("session.user.password");
        WOCookie nameCookie = new WOCookie("username", username);
        WOCookie passwordCookie = new WOCookie("password", password);
        NSTimestamp expires = new NSTimestamp()
    .timestampByAddingGregorianUnits(1, 0, 0, 0, 0, 0);

        // set timeOuts
        nameCookie.setExpires(expires);
        passwordCookie.setExpires(expires);

        response.addCookie(nameCookie);
        response.addCookie(passwordCookie);
    }

    super.appendToResponse(response, context);
}
```

A cookie is represented in WebObjects as a *WOCookie*. Here we create two, one for the *username* and the other for the *password*.

Next, we set the cookies to expire after one year. Then add the cookies to the response using addCookie(). Finally, the content along with the cookies is appended to the response.

Retrieving Cookie Values from a Browser

To obtain the cookie values back from the browser, all we need to do is change the *Login* defaultAction to pass the values onto the Login page.

```
public WOActionResults defaultAction() {
WOComponent nextPage = pageWithName("Login");

    // retrieve cookie values
    if (request().cookieValues().count() > 0) {
        String username = request().cookieValueForKey("username");
        String password = request().cookieValueForKey("password");

        // set the values
        nextPage.takeValueForKey(username, "username");
        nextPage.takeValueForKey(username, "password");
    }

    return nextPage;
}
```

Here the cookie values are obtained from the request using key-value coding such as methods cookieValueForKey().

Note that we could implement this functionality in the defaultAction of the *DirectAction* class, which would automatically logon the user from the first instance she accesses the application. However, we are making the decision to simply remember the login values for the Login page. This provides an opportunity for a different user to be logged in if required.

Now when you run your application, login with the option to have your details remembered. Open your browser preferences and look at the list of cookies. You will notice two cookies for the domain/IP address of the application.

You might need to fix the port number on which the application runs so the browser remembers the login details the next time you login to the forum. To do this add the command-line argument -WOPort 10000 (or some other unused port number) to the executable.

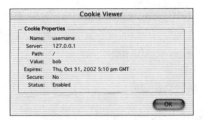

FIGURE 11.5 A cookie from the Online Forum.

Providing User Personalization and Preferences

Now we'll look at providing functionality for the user to change her password or signature when required.

Given that these functions are accessible only to those users who are logged on, we can implement them as standard WebObjects actions and components.

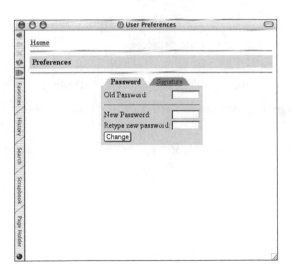

FIGURE 11.6 User Preferences.

Using WOTabPanel to Create a Tabbed Interface

First, add a new page component to the project: Preferences.

1. Place a *WOTabPanel* on the page. You might want to position it on the page using a table if appropriate.

2. Bind the *tabs* attribute to a new key of the same name. Bind *selectedTab*, similarly.

```
protected NSArray tabs = new NSArray(new String[]{"Password",
"Signature"});
protected String selectedTab;

public String selectedTab() {
    return (selectedTab != null) ? selectedTab: (String)
tabs.objectAtIndex(0);
}
```

3. Place a *WOSwitchComponent* inside the *WOTabPanel*. Bind its *WOComponentName* to a method accessor componentName:

```
public String componentName() {
    return selectedTab() + "Preference";
}
```

4. Create and add two partial components PasswordPreference and SignaturePreference to the project.

You might also add a home link back to the *Main* page. Remember to use the direct actions wherever possible. So bind this to the defaultAction.

What happens here is that the content for the *WOTabPanel* is provided by the *WOSwitchComponent*.

Add a link to *Preferences* from the *Main* page, on the condition that there is a user logged in.

Setting the User Password
Open the *PasswordPreference* component.

Place a *WOForm* with three password fields, one for the current or old password, and two for the new one. Use a static submit button.

Add three String variables to represent these oldPassword, password1, and password2.

You might add a msg to the component, to assist the user in making the change. Bind a change action to the *WOForm*:

```
public void change() {
    String _oldPassword = (String) valueForKeyPath("session.user.password");

    // check the passwords match
    if (_oldPassword.equals(oldPassword)) {
```

```
   if (password1.equals(password2)) {
       takeValueForKeyPath(password1, "session.user.password");
       session().defaultEditingContext().saveChanges();
       msg = "Your password has been changed";
   } else msg = "New passwords do not match";
} else msg = "The Current password is incorrect";}
```

The logic for the change password action is pretty straightforward. You compare the old password with session.user.password. In addition, if the two new passwords match, you set the session.user.password key path to the new password, and then save changes in the session().defaultEditingContext().

When you build and run your application you should have something similar to Figure 11.6.

Adding User Signatures to Posts

More useful than being able to reset your password, is the ability to post replies and topics with a signature.

To do this we need to make an addition to the *User* model.

Add a string attribute *signature* to the three *User* entities in the Enterprise Object model. Give it some reasonable width or size, and it should also *allow null*.

Now you will have to synchronize the model and the database.

Given that we have added just one column, you might synchronize the database manually. In Openbase Manager, view the *Database, Schema....*

Select the USER table and click the add column button. Name it SIGNATURE and give it type char and an appropriate length. Click the Save button to commit the alteration. Use Figure 11.7 as a guide.

As we have seen before an alternative is to synchronize the database from EOModeler.

You might check that the model and the database is synchronized by using the data browser on the *User* entities. Choose the Data browser from the Tools menu in EOModeler.

Open the *SignaturePreference* component and layout a *WOForm* with a *WOText* element to edit the session.user.signature. You can use a static submit button again. However this time, we can bind the *WOForm action* to session.defaultEditingContext.saveChanges directly, so we don't have to specially create a component action here.

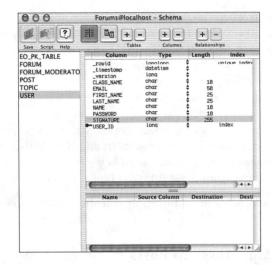

FIGURE 11.7 The database schema in OpenBase Manager.

Using WOCheckbox

Next, we need to add support for signatures in the *Reply* page.

Open the *Reply* page in WebObjects Builder and add a table row beneath the *WOText* element. Add a *WOCheckbox* as in Figure 11.8 labeled Use Signature and bind its *checked* attribute to a boolean key useSignature.

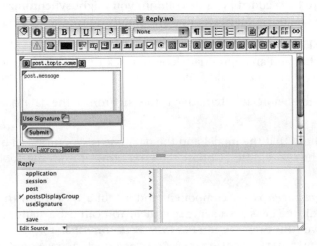

FIGURE 11.8 WOCheckbox.

You only want to display this option on the *Reply* page only if a user has a signature, so wrap the entire row in a conditional and bind its *condition* to `session.user.hasSignature`.

For this you will need to add an accessor to the User class:`public boolean hasSignature() {`
```
    return (storedValueForKey("signature") != null);
}
```

The *Reply* page save action also changes to append the signature before it saves changes to the `session().defaultEditingContext()`:

```
// append signature
if (useSignature) {
    String message = (String) post().valueForKey("message");
    String signature = (String) valueForKeyPath("session.user.signature");
    post().takeValueForKey(message + "<p>" + signature, "message");
}
```

Here we simply append the signature onto the `post.message` separated by an HTML paragraph.

Because we're saving the `post.message` as HTML, we must make sure that it is not escaped in the *TopicPosts* page. So make sure that the *WOString* representing `post.message` has *escapeHTML* set to `false`.

Build and run to ensure that you can save a signature as a forum user, and that you can post messages with a signature attached.

Perfecting Presentation of Pages Using Tables, Color, Fonts, and Rules

Now would be a good time to tidy up the presentation aspects of the page components.

I've used tables with appropriate spacing and alignments to position elements: font size, strong and italicized text to alter the emphasis of information; date formatters to display dates appropriately; color to display the *WABatchNavigationBar* and page headings on the *Main* page and the *Preferences* page; and horizontal rules to separate rows and table headings.

See Figures 11.9, 11.10, and 11.11.

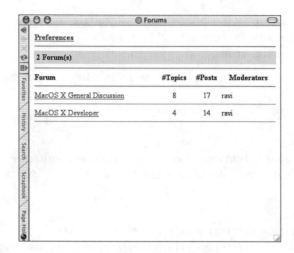

FIGURE 11.9   Forum home page.

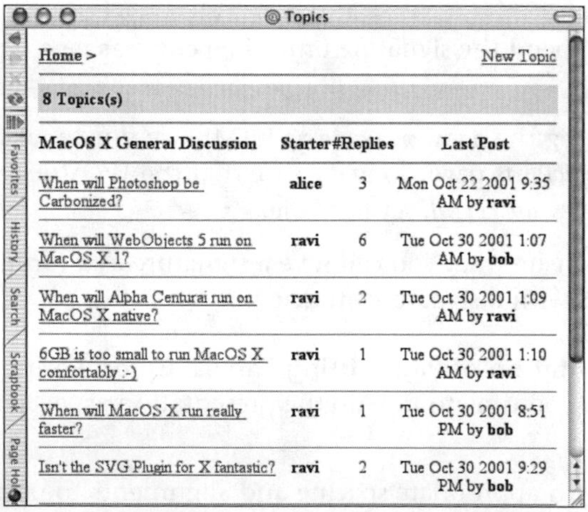

FIGURE 11.10   Forum topics page.

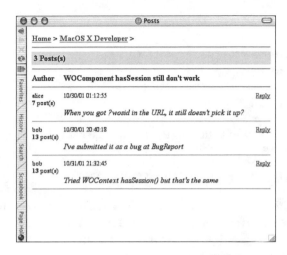

FIGURE 11.11   Topic posts page.

Implementing User Registration

As a last subsection in this chapter we'll look at enabling a user to register and use the forum immediately.

Similar to the user login, this will be implemented as *stateless* functionality.

Add a new component Registration to the project.

Lay out a *WOForm* and text fields for the *User* firstName, lastName, email, name as dynamic elements. Leave the two password fields as static. Use a static submit button.

Create a new direct action class *Register* to handle the user registration actions. Given that there are several form values to pass around, make them variables of the direct action class and parse them in using takeFormValuesForKeyArray():

```
protected static NSArray keys = new NSArray(new String[]{"username",
"firstName", "lastName", "email", "password1", "password2"});
protected String username;
protected String firstName;
protected String lastName;
    protected String email;
    protected String password1;
    protected String password2;

    /*
```

```
 * constructor
 */
public Register(WORequest aRequest) {
    super(aRequest);
    takeFormValuesForKeyArray(keys);
}
```

Bind the *Registration* form action to the *Register* userAction:

```
public WOActionResults userAction() {
    // check that the user has typed something in
    if (username != null) {
        EOEditingContext editingContext = new EOEditingContext();
        editingContext.setSharedEditingContext(null);
        NSArray results = EOUtilities.rawRowsMatchingKeyAndValue(editingContext,
    "User", "name", username);

        // check that the username isn't already taken
        if (results.count() == 0) {
            // check that passwords match
        if (password1 != null && password2!= null &&
    password1.equals(password2)) {
                // lock ec
                editingContext.lock();

                // create user
                EOEnterpriseObject user =
    EOUtilities.createAndInsertInstance(editingContext, "NormalUser");

                // set values
                user.takeValueForKey(username, "name");
                user.takeValueForKey(password1, "password");
                user.takeValueForKey(firstName, "firstName");
                user.takeValueForKey(lastName, "lastName");
                    user.takeValueForKey(email, "email");

                // save changes
                editingContext.saveChanges();

                // unlock ec
                editingContext.unlock();

                return pageWithName("Login");
```

```
        } else return passwordsDontMatchAction();
      } else return userExistsAction();
    } else return defaultAction();
}
```

The logic for the user registration is similar to that of user login, with one exception.

Here we are inserting the new user object before a session is created. Hence, we must use an editing context other than the defaultEditingContext. We can't use the Application sharedEditingContext either, because it is not allowed to insert objects into a read-only editing context. So, a new editing context must be created with the setting sharedEditingContext(null).

To be thread-safe, editing contexts are required to be *locked* before fetching and modifying objects. In this case, we must lock() the editing context before creating a new instance of *NormalUser*, and then unlock() it afterwards.

The private actions are fairly simple. As a convenience they pass on values to the new *Registration* page on a failed attempt:

```
private WOActionResults userExistsAction() {
    WOComponent nextPage = pageWithName("Registration");

    // pass values    nextPage.takeValueForKey("A user already exists with that
username",
 "msg");
        nextPage.takeValueForKey(firstName, "firstName");
        nextPage.takeValueForKey(lastName, "lastName");
        nextPage.takeValueForKey(email, "email");

        return nextPage;
    }

    private WOActionResults passwordsDontMatchAction() {
        WOComponent nextPage = pageWithName("Registration");

        // pass values
        nextPage.takeValueForKey("The passwords don't match", "msg");
        nextPage.takeValueForKey(username, "username");
        nextPage.takeValueForKey(firstName, "firstName");
        nextPage.takeValueForKey(lastName, "lastName");
        nextPage.takeValueForKey(email, "email");
```

```
    return nextPage;
}
```

Finally, add a `Register` link from the *Main* page to the default *Register* action.

Summary

This chapter has looked at managing *Sessions*, user preferences, and personalization from within a mostly stateless direct actionable application.

At the same time, hopefully, this chapter has started to reveal that building application functionality on top of a well-engineered object model is easy.

In the next chapter we'll continue the process of completing the online forum application.

12

File Uploads and Downloads

"Nothing is particularly hard if you divide it into small jobs."

—*Henry Ford*

The aim of this chapter is to finish developing the primary functions of the online forum.

Most importantly we want to have the ability to add attachments to posts. For example, a developer forum might want to attach small projects to posts. In addition, we want to add a search function to the online forum. This is often a standard requirement for many sites.

Uploading and Downloading Attachments

In this revision of the online forum we'll extend the object model to accommodate post attachments and add a facility to upload and download attachments.

Modeling Attachment

To avoid complexity and for performance, we are not going to model *Attachment* as a separate entity. Instead, we are going to model attachments as two attributes on *Post*.

We do this is in spite of the fact that modeling *Attachments* separately may be kosher or traditional.

> **NOTE**
>
> Adding a *data blob* attribute such as an attachment to an entity would have typically affected the performance of an application. Attachments can take up a fair amount of space on a database. Therefore, fetching posts with attachments can be slow. The way around this is to not fetch attachments with posts, by using raw rows in performance critical situations.

1. Add an *allows null* string attribute `filePath` to the Post entity, and give it a suitable length.

2. Add an attribute `attachment` of *Internal Data Type Data* and *External Type object*. It is similar in nature to the *Post.message* attribute. It should also *allow null*. There is no need to set an external width as data blobs can vary in size.

3. Alter the database schema for the POST table by adding the columns ATTACHMENT and FILEPATH from OpenBase Manager.

Using WOFileUpload

Now we need to edit the *Reply* post page to add support for attachments. Add a table row for the attachment field and place in it a *WOFileUpload* component. See Figure 12.1.

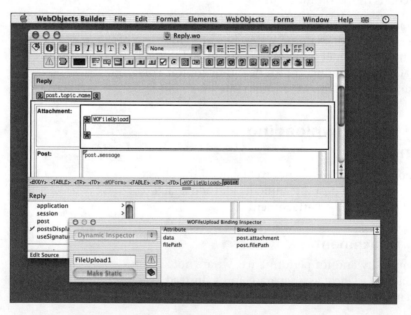

FIGURE 12.1   Adding a WOFileUpload component.

Bind the *WOFileUpload data* attribute to `post.attachment` and its *filePath* to `post.filePath`. More importantly, the *WOForm enctype* must be set to `multipart/form-data`.

Downloading an Attachment

The *TopicPosts* page is going to need a hyperlink on every post that has an attachment. The link will be bound to a direct action vending the post's attachment.

So, in a suitable location, perhaps after the post timestamp, add a conditional and bind it to post.hasAttachment. Add the hasAttachment accessor to the Post class:

```
public boolean hasAttachment() {
    return (valueForKey("attachment") != null ||
           !valueForKey("attachment").equals(""));}
```

Place a *WOHyperlink* inside the conditional. Bind its *string* value to post.filePath. Hook up its *directActionName* to file in a new direct action class Download. Add a new binding for a form value ?postID and connect it to an accessor that returns the primary key value for the post, which you must add to the component class.

Create and add a new direct action class, Download, to the project. Add the fileAction to the class:

```
public WOActionResults fileAction() {
    Number postID = request().numericFormValueForKey("postID",
 new NSNumberFormatter());

    if (postID != null) {
        EOEditingContext editingContext = new EOEditingContext();

        // lock
        editingContext.lock();

        // fetch attachment + create response
        EOEnterpriseObject post = EOUtilities.objectWithPrimaryKeyValue(
editingContext, "Post", postID);
        NSData data = (NSData) post.valueForKey("attachment");
        WOResponse response = new WOResponse();
        String filePath = (String) post.valueForKey("filePath");
        WOResourceManager resourceManager =
WOApplication.application().resourceManager();
        String contentType = resourceManager.contentTypeForResourceNamed(
filePath);

            // unlock
            editingContext.unlock();
```

```
        // set the content
        response.appendContentData(data);

        // set content type
        response.setHeader(contentType, "Content-Type");

        return response;
    } return null;
}
```

In this action we are not vending a WebObjects page. We are vending the post attachment as a file.

To do that we must create and return a *WOResponse*. We set its content data to be that of the post.attachment, then set the response header to describe the content type—be it a Word document, a Zip file, or a PDF document.

You are now ready to build and test your application.

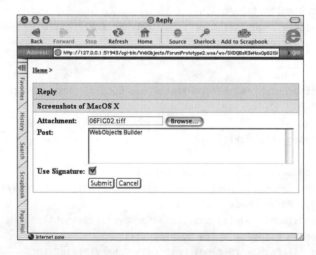

FIGURE 12.2   Post a reply.

In particular, upload and save a Zip file for example, then try and download it. Notice that if you are prompted to save the file, it will save as file.zip, as opposed to the filename of the attachment.

Sending the Attachment Filename to the Client

Normally to send the filename information to the client the content-disposition header would be used. However, because of a bug in certain browsers, this feature doesn't work well.

A simple workaround we can use is to make the action name the name of the file. Rebind the attachment download link in the *TopicPosts* page from `file` to `post.filePath`. Then we can override the default action handling behavior of the *Download* action class to always use the `fileAction`.

```
/*
 * action handling
 */
public WOActionResults performActionNamed(String anActionName) {
    // all actions dowload files
    return fileAction();
}
```

When we have an action of the form `.../wa/Download/SourceCode.zip?postID=...` it will automatically be directed to the `fileAction`.

Build and run again with SQL logging on, and then try to reply to a post without adding an attachment.

Look at the SQL log carefully and you will notice that a POST has been added with what looks like some attachment data. In reality, what has happened is that an empty data object has been stored in the database. This is not the same as leaving the attachment as `null`.

Using Enterprise Object Validation

Enterprise Objects has a very versatile, yet simple, mechanism for validating values and objects.

We can circumvent the previous scenario by adding some validation logic to the *Post* class. In particular, before an Enterprise Object gets saved, a `validateForSave()` gets called on it.

This would be an ideal time to make sure that we don't add a post with a basically empty (but not null) attachment:

```
public boolean hasFilePath() {
    String filePath = (String) valueForKey("filePath");
    return (filePath != null && !filePath.equals(""));
}
```

```
/*
 * validation
 */
public void validateForSave() {
    super.validateForSave();

    // leave data null if there is no filePath
    if (!hasFilePath()) takeStoredValueForKey(null, "attachment");
}
```

Here we are taking advantage of the fact that there won't be an attachment if the post.filePath hasn't been set. Now when submitting a post without an attachment, you will find that the attachment is left as null.

Adding a Cancel Button

Lastly, remember to add the attachment functionality to the *StartTopic* page.

One feature that we've neglected to add is a cancel button to both the *Reply* page and the *StartTopic* page.

To do so, set the *WOForm multipleSumit* to true. Then add another dynamic submit button, name it Cancel, and bind it to an action of the same name cancel. The only difference between the cancel and save actions is that the cancel action will discard changes made by using session().defaultEditingContext().revert().

Providing a Search Page

Any online forum deserves a good search function. We'll start developing the Search page and its results page as standard WebObjects component pages. We will, however, aim to make them stateless functions eventually.

Revisiting Fetch Specifications

We've come across fetch specifications before, in Chapter 7, "A Game of Crazy Eights: Beginning Enterprise Objects," where the standard *FetchAll* fetch specification was used to fetch forums as shared objects.

However, perhaps it is time to look at fetch specifications in more detail. In particular, how we can set up fetch specifications in Enterprise Object models without having to do so programmatically.

A fetch specification is quite a powerful and sophisticated mechanism for describing a fetch. Most notably, a fetch can be *qualified*. That is we can set conditions that determine the WHERE clause in an SQL statement.

In particular, in this section we'll add a fetch specification Search to the model. In addition, we'll qualify it to search for posts by message, topic.name, and user.name.

Adding a Fetch Specification to a Model

Open the *Forum* model in EOModeler and select the *Post* entity.

1. Click the add fetch specification icon or choose Add Fetch Specification from the Property menu to add one. Enter *Search* into the *Fetch Specification Name*.

2. In the *Qualifier* tab panel, select the field just below the logical operator buttons. Then select message from Post attributes list, press the *like* operator, and finally type $message and hit return. You should see something similar to Figure 12.3.

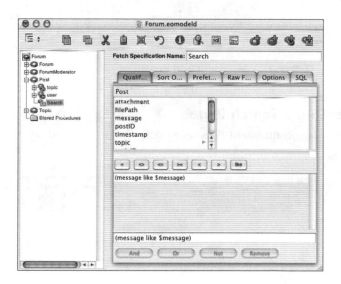

FIGURE 12.3   Qualifying a Fetch Specification in EOModeler.

3. Now, click the And button at the bottom of the panel. You should see a second qualifier field appear as shown in Figure 12.4.

4. Build a qualifier to match (topic.name like $topic). Click Add again.

5. Add the third and final qualifier (user.name like $username) similarly, and save the changes.

A *variable qualifier* is represented by the $ symbol. That is, it enables us to substitute the value of topic when a fetch is performed.

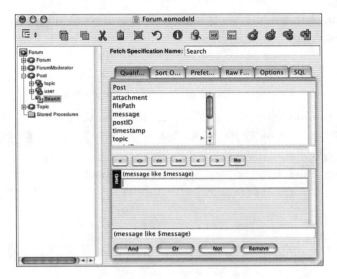

FIGURE 12.4   Defining a compound and qualifier.

Implementing a Search Page

Create a new page component `ForumSearch` to the project and lay it out as shown in Figure 12.5.

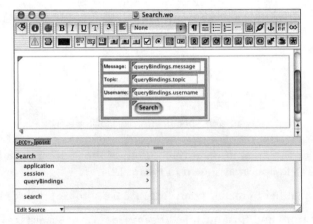

FIGURE 12.5   Layout the ForumSearch page as in the Figure.

Add a variable key, `queryBindings`, as a *NSMutableDictionary*. By taking advantage of key value coding APIs, the component will automatically set the dictionary values for message, topic, and username that the user types into the text fields.

```
protected NSMutableDictionary queryBindings = new NSMutableDictionary();
```

To simplify the Web interface and to keep it consistent with the rest of the application, the search results will be displayed on another page SearchResults. So create and add a component to represent the search results.

Open the *SearchResults* page in WebObjects Builder and drag in the *Search* fetch specification that was created earlier. Set up the display group to have 10 *Entries per batch* and *Sort* the search results in *Ascending* order by *timestamp*. See Figure 12.6.

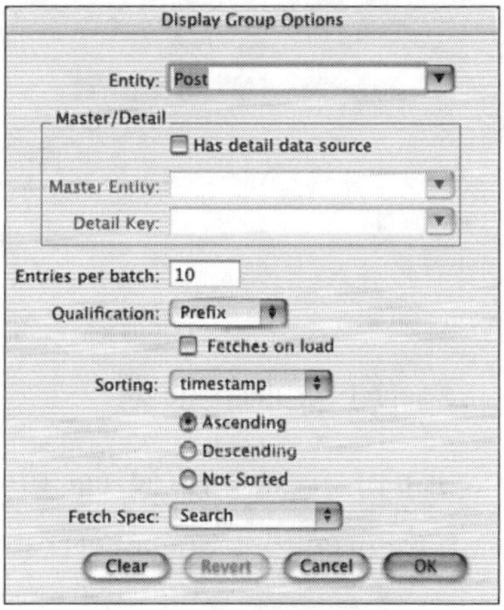

FIGURE 12.6 Configuring the Search Results display group.

Layout the *SearchResults* page as in Figure 12.7, using the *WOBatchNavigationBar* component to batch the results.

Display the post.topic.name as a hyperlink, which is bound to the posts direct action. Add a topicID key to vend the topicID as a form value in the direct action. Do not forget to add the post key as a variable.

Now, we need to define the search component action in the *ForumSearch* page. Add a search action to the *ForumSearch* page and bind it to the submit button:

```
public WOComponent search() {
    WOComponent nextPage = pageWithName("SearchResults");

    // Initialize your component here
    nextPage.takeValueForKeyPath(queryBindings, "queryBindings");

    return nextPage;
}
```

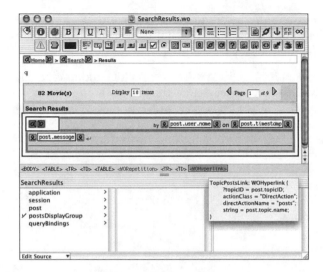

FIGURE 12.7   Layout of the SearchResults page.

The only thing we do here is pass the queryBindings onto the *SearchResults* page.

So, in the *SearchResults* page we need to define an accessor that sets the display group queryBindings:

```
public void _setQueryBindings(NSDictionary queryBindings) {
    // set the query bindings + fetch
    postsDisplayGroup.queryBindings().addEntriesFromDictionary(queryBindings);
    postsDisplayGroup.qualifyDataSource();
}
```

Here we set the bindings using *NSMutableDicitonary* addEntriesFromDictionary() then perform the fetch.

> **NOTE**
>
> WebObjects Builder won't display keys prefixed with an underscore. So you can define *private* key variables and accessors in this way.

Finally, add a link to the *ForumSearch* page from the *Main* component, Build your application.

Testing the Forum Search

When testing the search function, note that you might have to use the wildcard * to help perform searches. For example, to search for a message that has the string WebObjects type *WebObjects* into the *Message:* field.

This is something that we will automate after we have created a stateless search function.

Optimizing Fetches Using Raw Rows

If you had SQL logging on when you performed searches on the forum, you might have noticed that performing a search on posts yielded multiple fetches. Namely, for each posts' user and topic.

However, we can streamline this into one fetch if we want, by using raw rows.

Again, we have already been introduced to raw rows very briefly in the last chapter, Chapter 11, "Managing Users, Sessions, and Personalization." In particular, we fetched raw rows using *EOUtilities* rawRowsMatchinKeyAndValue().

When using a fetch specification however, we can be more explicit in terms of the attributes we want to fetch. In fact, we may even fetch values that traverse relationships; for example *post.user.name*, and *post.topic.name*.

Open and edit the *Search* fetch specification in EOModeler.

1. Click the *Raw Fetch* tab and select the *Fetch Specified Attributes as Row Rows* radio button. Notice that all the post attributes appear in the bottom half of the panel.

2. *Remove* the *attachment* and *filePath* attributes, given that they aren't used in the *SearchResults* page.

3. Highlight *topic.name* from the upper panel and click *Add*.

4. Repeat for *user.name,* and save changes.

5. Finally, you need to make some small changes to the *SearchResults* class. Change the type of the post variable to *NSDictionary*. Bind the topic hyperlink form value ?topicID to post.topicID, and then remove the redundant topicID accessor.

As the raw rows are not enterprise objects, their primary key and foreign key values are exposed. Because they are not hidden, as they would be in enterprise objects, they are convenient to use along with direct actions that normally do require key values.

Making a Stateless Search Function

Now we're going to convert the *ForumSearch* and *SearchResults* pages to be stateless direct actions.

Add a direct action class Search to the project with a default action vending the *ForumSearch* page.

Open the *ForumSearch* page in WebObjects builder. Make the three text fields static and name them *message, topic* and *username,* respectively. Remove the now redundant queryBindings variable.

Also remove the search component action. Make the submit button static and rebind the *WOForm* to a direct action named results, in the *Search* action class:

```
public WOActionResults resultsAction() {
    SearchResults nextPage = (SearchResults) pageWithName("SearchResults");
     Number index = request().numericFormValueForKey("displayBatchIndex",
new NSNumberFormatter());

    // set query bindings
     nextPage.takeValueForKeyPath(message,
"postsDisplayGroup.queryBindings.message");
    nextPage.takeValueForKeyPath(topic,
"postsDisplayGroup.queryBindings.topic");
    nextPage.takeValueForKeyPath(username,
"postsDisplayGroup.queryBindings.username");

    // fetch
    nextPage.fetch();

    // set the batch index
    if (index != null) nextPage.takeValueForKeyPath(index,
"postsDisplayGroup.currentBatchIndex");
    return nextPage;
}
```

Now that the search criteria message, topic, and username are being passed as form values to the direct action, we can append the wildcards to the search strings if need be:

```
static NSArray keys = new NSArray(new String[]{"message", "topic",
"username"});
String message;
String topic;
String username;

    public SearchAction(WORequest aRequest) {
        super(aRequest);
```

```
    // take values from the request
    takeFormValuesForKeyArray(keys);

    // append wildcards
    if (message != null) {
        if (!message.startsWith("*")) message = "*" + message;
        if (!message.endsWith("*")) message = message + "*";
    } if (topic != null) {
        if (!topic.startsWith("*")) topic = "*" + topic;
        if (!topic.endsWith("*")) topic = topic + "*";
    } if (username != null) {
        if (!username.startsWith("*")) username = "*" + username;
        if (!username.endsWith("*")) username = username + "*";
    }
}
```

Then, in the *SearchResults* page, replace the _setQueryBindings accessor with an action that performs the fetch:

```
public void fetch() {
    postsDisplayGroup.qualifyDataSource();
}
```

Lastly, and quite importantly, we must make sure that the display group doesn't use the session.defaultEditingContext. Given that the search results are being fetched as raw rows, the application.sharedEditingContext can be used instead.

The easiest way to make this change is to navigate and open the *SearchResults.wo* component in Project Builder. Select the *SearchResults.woo* file to edit it. Locate the line for the key editingContext and change it to

editingContext = **application.sharedEditingContext**;

NOTE

WebObjects components can also have a supplementary file called a WebObjects archive file. These have the .woo extension, and are normally only used by WebObjects Builder to set component settings such as Fetch On Load for display groups in a component.

Change the search links to use the direct actions from the Search action class, and then you should be ready to build and test the stateless search functionality. See Figure 12.8.

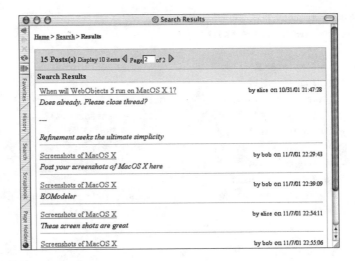

FIGURE 12.8   Search results.

Completing the Application

At last we are in a position to put the finishing touches to the online forum.

First, we'll use a template for each of the forum pages. Then, we'll add some graphics and icons to add a little frill to the user interface.

Defining a Page Template

A page template is unusual because it is treated like a normal reusable component. However, unlike all other reusable components, it is a *full document*.

Add a new component to the project ForumTemplate.

Make it a *stateless* component. However, remember to leave it as a *full* document.

Select the BODY element and make it dynamic.

Copy in a background graphic aqua_bg.gif from the file download associated with this chapter from the companion Web site (www.samspublishing.com) and set it as the *WOBody filename*. Additionally, add a new binding, *onLoad*, and hook it up to ^onLoad. This will be useful to pass page messages as JavaScript alerts if you want.

Now, place a *WOComponentContent* element in the page template. This is a special element that acts as a placeholder for where the component content should go.

Lastly, with the *WOBody* element selected, switch to the *Static Inspector*. Check the *Title is Dynamic* box and bind it to ^*title*, as in Figure 12.9.

FIGURE 12.9   Making the title dynamic.

Give the *ForumTemplate* component two API bindings *title* and *onLoad*. Make *title* a required binding.

Using a Page Template

Open the *Main* page. Convert it to a partial document. This is because the <HTML> and <BODY> elements will come from the *ForumTemplate*.

Then, choose *Edit, Select All* from the WebObjects Builder menu. Click the *Add Custom Component* button or choose Custom WebObject from the WebObjects menu to add a *ForumTemplate*.

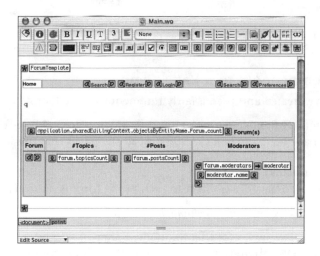

FIGURE 12.10   Using the Page Template.

Remember to set the *title* of the page template.

Repeat this process adding the *ForumTemplate* to all the *full-document* components.

Using Page Template JavaScript Alerts

On both the *UserLogin* and *Registration* pages, we use a msg to provide user feedback.

Add an onLoad key as an accessor to both pages:

```
protected String _msg;

public String onLoad() {
    String onLoad = "alert('" + _msg + "');";
    return (_msg != null) ? onLoad:null;
}
```

Then, connect it to the *ForumTemplate onLoad* binding. If your page displayed the msg in the component, you may remove it.

Now when you run the application, you will get feedback in the form of an alert panel.

FIGURE 12.11   Page template alerts.

Adding Components to a Page Template

So far we have created and used a fairly rudimentary page template.

They are extremely flexible because after they are in place, adding standard components to the page template will cascade into all the pages that use it.

Adding a ForumLinks Component

It would be nice to have links direct to each of the forums on every page.

Create a new *stateless* and *nonsynchronizing* component ForumLinks.

The bindings and variables for this component are going to be very similar to the Main page. However, there is just one point that I will highlight: Use a *WOTable* element to lay out the forum links neatly in rows. To do that, set its *maxColumns* binding. When you've completed the *ForumLinks* component, place it in the *ForumTemplate*.

Adding a Search Bar

There would also appear to be room to have a simple search bar on every page.

Create another *stateless* and *nonsynchronizing* component SearchBar.

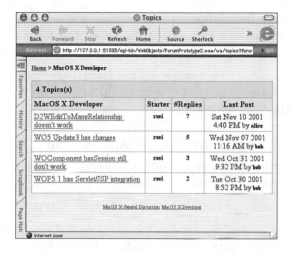

FIGURE 12.12   Forum links.

Again, this component is going to be similar to the *ForumSearch* page, but only simpler. Just have one (static) text field to search for *message*.

For aesthetics, use a *WOImageButton* instead of a static submit button. Bind its image *filename* to `arrow_button.gif` having included the image from the file download for the chapter.

Finally, position the *SearchBar* in the page template as required.

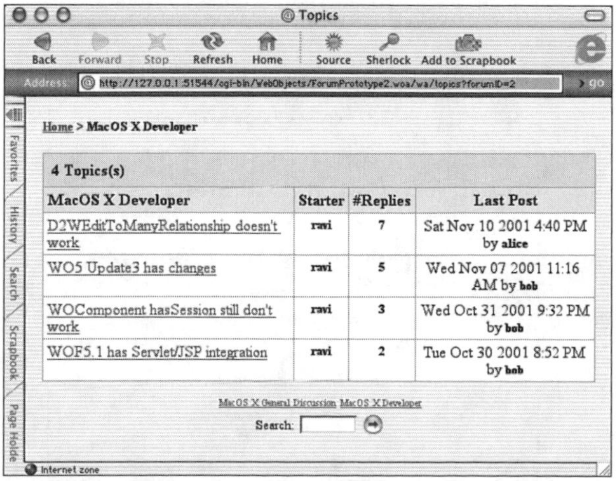

FIGURE 12.13   Add the Search Bar to the Application.

Using Multiple Page Templates

You might have noticed that although the *ForumTemplate* looks fine on most pages, it isn't particularly appropriate on the *UserLogin* and *ForumSearch* pages.

For those pages, create a simple page template, `SimpleForumTemplate`, by duplicating and adjusting the *ForumTemplate*. You might want to leave only the background image in the simple page template.

Adding Graphics and Icons to the Application

If they are not essential to the application functionality, then leave adding graphics and icons to the components until the end.

Copy the rest of the images from the file download for this chapter into the project.

You can add a little icon to represent a forum and topic if you want. However, the post useful graphics are the ones for the `reply` and `email` links on the *TopicPosts* page.

To add an email or mailto link, add a new key `mailTo` to the TopicsPost class:

```
public String mailTo() {
    String email = (String) valueForKeyPath("post.user.email");
    return "mailto:" + email;
}
```

Bind it to the *href* of a new hyperlink displaying the `email_3.gif` image. Locate it, along with the reply link, which should also be converted to display an image `reply_3.gif`.

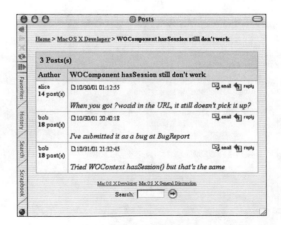

FIGURE 12.14   Add the `MailTo` link.

Additional Exercise

As an additional exercise, you might want to add a user profile page to the application, so that other registered users might look at a post's user details, and perhaps the user's other posts as well.

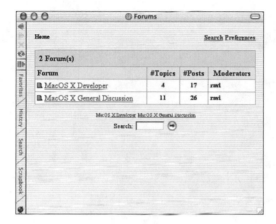

FIGURE 12.15   The Forum Home Page should look like this.

Summary

In this chapter we added the ability to upload and download files to the forum, an optimized search function, and used a page template to add the finishing touches to the application.

13

Organizing Code, Fixing Bugs, and Handling Exceptions

"Sometimes you gotta do right to be happy. Onetime you gotta believe in what you feel inside. Sometimes you gotta do right to find happiness. Sometimes, Sometimes."

—*from the song "Sometimes" by the Brand New Heavies*

This chapter is mostly an interlude, or a break from the case study.

However, there are some fairly important and useful techniques that we have yet to cover. Namely organizing project code, particularly on projects larger than the online forum; how to effectively debug and fix an application; and how to gracefully handle exceptions when they do occur.

These key techniques are essential to deliver a *deployable* system that is both robust and stable, from a final working and fully functional prototype.

Organizing Project Code

You might have noticed that the number of classes and components for the online forum started to get unwieldy. Often it is useful to organize your project files into more manageable chunks or groups.

In the next section we'll look at some simple ways of managing and sharing project code.

Using Project Code to Organize Code

Using *Project, Group* and *Project, New Group*, organize the online forum project components, classes, and model files as in Figure 13.1.

There are no hard and fast rules on how to organize your project. Although try not to use project groups excessively. As with almost any other feature, use it in moderation.

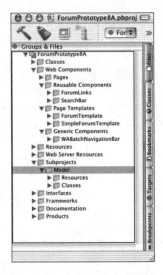

FIGURE 13.1   Grouping the online forum project files.

Sharing Code and Resources Using Frameworks

Using frameworks is another way to factor out and organize project code.

> **NOTE**
>
> A *framework* is analogous to a java package. Although in addition to class files, you can also bundle resources such as images and model files.

Note, however, that in particular the classes relating to the model along with the model files had been grouped differently. They'd been placed in a top-level Subprojects group. This is because it would have been useful to share the object model and its classes between the DirectToWeb test application and the online forum application.

Creating a Framework for the Object Model

From project builder create a new project.

1. Choose WebObjects Framework in the *New Project Assistant*, as in Figure 13.2, and then proceed to create the new project as normal. Name it Forum.

FIGURE 13.2   Creating a framework project.

1. Copy the model files into the Resources group of the framework project. Similarly, copy in the enterprise object class files into Classes.

2. Open the model files and append a suitable package name to the *Class Name* of the entities that have custom classes. In this case, try appending biz.forum.model to the classes. See Figure 13.3.

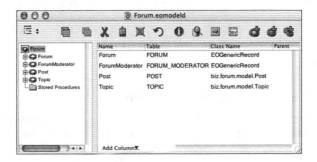

FIGURE 13.3   Appending a package name to enterprise objects.

3. Package each of the enterprise object classes by adding the line:

```
package biz.forum.model;
```

Installing a Framework

Next, install the framework from Project Builder. You do this by simply selecting *Deployment* as the Build Style from the *Targets* tab and clicking build.

By default, this will install the framework in */Library/Frameworks*.

Installing a Framework from the Command Line

Alternatively, you can install the framework, from the command line (*Terminal.app*):

```
> cd <FRAMEWORK_DIR>
> pbxbuild install
> su root
> cd /tmp/Forum.dst/
> ditto . /
```

This last step should install the framework in */Library/Frameworks*.

Using the Model Framework

Now delete the *Model* group from the Online Forum project. Then, add the *Forum* framework to the project by selecting *Project, Add Frameworks...*

Now you must import the model package into the application by adding the following line to the Application class:

```
import biz.forum.model.*;
```

Clean, build and run the application.

You can do the same with the *UserForumTest* DirectToWeb application. Remove the model and the associated classes, then add the framework to the project. Clean, build and run.

There shouldn't be any noticeable difference in the applications. However, this time, they are *sharing* the object model and classes. Updating the model will be reflected in both applications.

When to Use Frameworks: Some Model Theory

It may (or may not) be tempting to use frameworks in your projects. However, it is in your best interest to use them only if absolutely necessary. In fact, if there isn't a need at all to share the object model and classes, leave them in the application. Otherwise create a framework for the model.

Avoid excessively partitioning your object model into various frameworks. I've seen projects get stuck in a rut because the object model was over-engineered.

Often it doesn't matter how long you spend on the *requirements* gathering and *design* phases of a project, there are inevitable additions and alterations to even the most well designed object models. Sometimes these alterations might compromise a particular partition of the object model. So, it's best to avoid excessively partitioning models into frameworks. The resulting framework dependencies can become a nightmare to manage.

To illustrate these dependencies, take a look at the *Forum* and *User* models from the online forum application.

Each *Forum* has *moderators*. As a result, the *Forum* model depends on the *User* model. Also, the existence of the back relationship, *Moderator.forums,* means that the *User* model depends on the *Forum* model. As a result both models are interdependent.

However, if the back relationships *Moderator.forums* and *User.posts* were removed, the *User* model would no longer be dependent on the *Forum* model. In fact, if you did want to partition larger models, this is a way to avoid interdependent models. By removing these back relationships, the dependency between models becomes one-way, or not symmetric.

Of the two relationships, *Moderator.forums* was not used. It was part of a many-to-many relationship, which could have been removed. On the other hand, the *User.posts* relationship is used. So, removing it and replacing it with a custom accessor, for example, might be an unnecessary compromise just to force a partition of the object model.

The model dependencies should be determined by the requirements of the application.

Fixing Bugs

In this section we'll look at how to debug and bug fix an application. Often during the user testing, or *predeployment* stage, you will find bugs that have been brought to your attention. If you're lucky this will be before you launch your site or application.

So, we'll look at some techniques to isolate and fix these problems.

Tightening Validation Rules

Remember that when we developed the object model for the online forum, we relaxed the validation policy to *allow null* for most attributes.

In particular, there are some attributes that we really shouldn't *allow null*. A topic without a *name* is meaningless. Similarly, a post ought to have a *message*.

So, open the model files from the framework project and uncheck the *allows null* setting of those two attributes. Save and reinstall the framework.

NOTE

When changes are made to a framework, not only must the framework be rebuilt, but it also needs to be reinstalled. However, any application using that framework doesn't need to be rebuilt; just rerun.

However, now if a user were to post an empty reply an exception will get thrown.

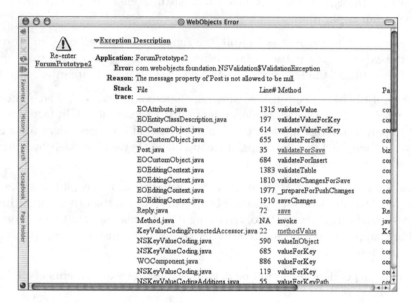

FIGURE 13.4   A validation exception being raised.

Reading Exception Pages

Follow the *Stack Trace* as listed from top to bottom.

Look at the first couple of lines that list classes from the project. In this case it'll be

```
File                    Line#   Method              Package
-----------------------------------------------------------------------------
EOAttribute.java         1315   validateValue           com.webobjects.eoaccess
EOEntityClassDescription.java197    validateValueForKey    com.webobjects.eoaccess
EOCustomObject.java       614   validateValueForKey     com.webobjects.eocontrol
EOCustomObject.java       655   validateForSave         com.webobjects.eocontrol
Post.java                  35   validateForSave         biz.forum.model
EOCustomObject.java       684   validateForInsert       com.webobjects.eocontrol
EOEditingContext.java    1383   validateTable           com.webobjects.eocontrol
EOEditingContext.java    1810   validateChangesForSavecom.webobjects.eocontrol
```

EOEditingContext.java	1977	_prepareForPushChangescom.webobjects.eocontrol
EOEditingContext.java	1910	saveChanges	com.webobjects.eocontrol
Reply.java	**72**	**save**

This might indicate where the source of the error is. In this case we know that it's a validation error as printed on the exception page because we've just tightened validation rules.

Notice that some lines are displayed as a hyperlink. Click the *save* link. This will have the effect of highlighting that line in Project Builder. In fact, the place that the exception is raised is in the save action in the *Reply* page.

```
session().defaultEditingContext().saveChanges();
```

For further reading go to the WebObjects Documentation site and look up the Advanced Topic "Understanding the Default WebObjects Error Page."

Java Exception Handling

Java has an excellent mechanism for handling exceptions, which is built into the language.

We might specifically catch the validation exception, and then pass it on as an alert to the user. Change the line to

```
try { session().defaultEditingContext().saveChanges(); }
catch (NSValidation.ValidationException exception) {
    _msg = exception.getMessage();
    return this;
}
```

Add a key _msg for the validation message. Add an onLoad accessor identical to the one in the *Login* page and bind it to the page template *onLoad* attribute.

Then, if a user will be alerted if she tries to submit a reply with no message.

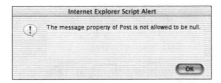

FIGURE 13.5   Alerting the user of a validation error.

Repeat the procedure for the *SubmitTopic* page.

Trapping Editing Context Exceptions

Currently a situation exists where if a user were to click a start *New Topic*, then without pressing *cancel*, were to navigate to another topic and click *reply*, an exception will be generated on submit. Try it.

In fact, it will be a validation exception saying that a post or topic has a null value. What happened was that on the *StartTopic* page a topic and a post had already been inserted. Because the changes were not reverted or saved, the edits were carried onto the *Reply* page.

We can circumvent this by reverting changes made to the `session.defaultEditingContext` in the appropriate place. In the constructors of both the *Reply* and *StartTopic* page add a statement to revert changes:

```
public Reply(WOContext context) {
    super(context);

    // revert changes
    session().defaultEditingContext().revert();
}
```

You should add the statement to the two *Preferences* components as well. Now try to replicate the error, and hopefully, it disappeared.

Using the Java Debugger

Next we'll contrive a rather obscure bug.

Launch the online forum application and navigate to any posts page. Now in your Web browser, change the *topicID* of the direct action URL (which should to look like `...wa/posts?topicID=...`) to one that doesn't exist.

Looking at the exception page WebObjects generates, it points to an exception being generated by a null pointer in the *forumID* accessor on the *TopicsPost* page.

What we will do is use the Java Debugger to follow the flow of instructions that lead to the exception.

First stop the application. Relaunch the application, but this time via the debugger. Click the debugger icon to start the Java debugger.

We will add a breakpoint to the post's direct action. In the *DirectAction* class, click the margin to the left of the line:

```
nextPage.takeValueForKeyPath(topic, "postsDisplayGroup.masterObject");
```

Then, a breakpoint should appear in the margin as in Figure 13.6.

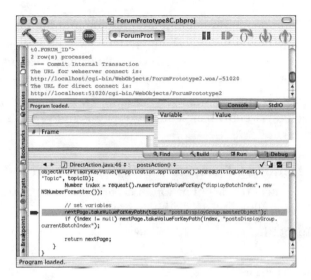

FIGURE 13.6 Setting a breakpoint.

Now navigate to a posts page in the forum application. Notice how it will stall at the point where the application executes the line where the breakpoint has been set, as shown in Figure 13.7.

In the *Debug* panel you will see a back trace, or the sequence of method calls leading up to the current point of execution. In addition you will see a list of variables used within the scope of the current method.

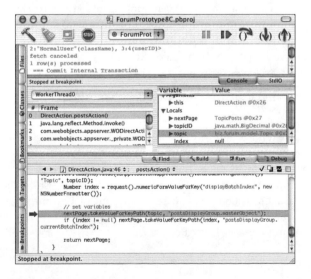

FIGURE 13.7 JDB stopped at a breakpoint.

In particular, note that a topic object has been found and returned to the next page.

Pay attention to the variable topic when navigating to a posts page. In particular, what is happening is that a value is most certainly being passed onto the next page. However, we know that a topic with such a *topicID* doesn't exist.

Given that we've contrived this unlikely scenario, I won't suggest trying to "fix" this. Instead, we should gracefully handle such exceptions and vend a simple error page when they do occur.

Gracefully Handling Exceptions with Custom Error Pages

Add a new component to the online forum ErrorPage. Give it a simple page template and place a link back to the home page.

Now in the Application class add the following exception handler:

```
/*
 * exception handling
 */
public WOResponse handleException(Exception exception, WOContext context) {
    if (!(exception instanceof NSValidation.ValidationException)) {
        WOComponent errorPage = pageWithName("ErrorPage", context);

        // log the error
        NSLog.out.appendln("Application: " + exception);

        return errorPage.generateResponse();
    } else return super.handleException(exception, context);
}
```

Here we make sure that we only handle exceptions that are not validation exceptions. The validation exceptions get handled as user feedback alert panels.

Now, if you try to replicate the contrived error you should get a page similar to Figure 13.8.

As an additional exercise you might want to similarly handle the error when a session has timed out. The method to implement is handleSessionRestorationErrorInContext() in Application. It might be helpful to set the application session timeout to a few minutes at most. Set the command-line argument -WOSessionTimeout 120 to set a timeout of two minutes. Go to WebObjects Documentation Web site for further reading on this on this Advanced Topic "Customizing Default Error Behavior."

FIGURE 13.8 A custom error page.

Summary

In this chapter we looked at how to organize project code, how to fix bugs, and handle exceptions gracefully. Essentially these are techniques required to deliver a deployable system from a fully functional application prototype.

14

Security, Logging, and Statistics

"There is no security on this earth; there is only opportunity."

—Gen. Douglas MacArthur.

In this chapter we will look at how to secure Web pages with user logins as well as how to use practical cryptography to secure sensitive data in a WebObjects application. In addition we'll look at how to log WebObjects transactions.

Securing the Application Login

In this section we'll discuss how to secure pages in a WebObjects application. In particular, we'll provide a secure login page to the online forum application.

An Introduction to Security with WebObjects

For the Web to truly become globally ubiquitous it is vital to ensure that electronic commerce is as safe as purchasing items over the counter. Electronic security has been seen as a means to this end. Hence, the need to secure sensitive data, such as passwords or credit-card details, passed over the Web.

Protecting the things that are dear to us requires attention to detail and care. Often it can be expensive, too.

Before we begin this chapter, here is a quick summary of the terms we'll be using in this acronym rich topic.

What Is HTTPS?
HTTPS or secure http is a version of the http protocol that is layered on top of *SSL*.

What Is SSL?

SSL is a transport protocol that encrypts its communication channel. The main *cryptosystem* used to encrypt the channel is the *RSA* public-key algorithm.

What Is a Cryptosystem?

A cryptosystem is a process based on algorithms to cipher and decipher information, which is used to provide a means of secret, private or secure communication between two parties.

What Is RSA?

There are several commonly used encryption algorithms that are used today. The RSA is popularly thought to be one of the strongest and most secure.

Installing or Configuring SSL on Your Web Server

Before we begin, we need to enable SSL on the Web Server.

On Mac OS X, the Apache Web Server comes installed with SSL, although it does need to be configured and activated. Configure the *mod_ssl* module on Apache by following the instructions available at
`http://developer.apple.com/internet/macosx/modssl.html`

This might be a somewhat involved task, but if you follow the steps you should have an SSL-enabled Web Server ready to develop a secure WebObjects application with.

Before you begin make sure that you enable the root user.

Testing the Secure SSL Connection to the Web Server

You are now in a position to serve secure pages from your Web Server. In fact, you might perform a simple test to see if this is the case by typing in `https:/localhost` in your Web browser.

Because we have created a developmental certificate, rather than a trusted third-party certificate, your browser might display a security warning as in Figure 14.1. Simply click continue to ignore it. This only means that a trusted authority has not validated the key. The communications will still be secure and encrypted.

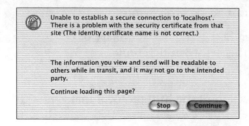

FIGURE 14.1   The Internet Explorer 5 security warning will appear.

The next most obvious step is to try to browse your WebObjects application using secure http.

Run the online forum application and try to substitute http with https in the URL. You might be disappointed to find that your browser might not be able to connect to the application. The next subsection will explain why.

Preparing to Develop a Secure WebObjects Application

Thus far in the book, we have always run our applications in what is known as *Direct Connect* mode. This is when the WebObjects server acts as a Web Server in addition to an application server. However, in a typical deployment scenario this is not normally the case. A deployed WebObjects application is run via the Web Server. The WebObjects adaptor then funnels WebObjects requests to the appropriate application.

In particular, when using SHTTP, it is no longer possible to develop an application in Direct Connect mode. We will have to switch to development via the Web Sever.

Running an Application in Non-Direct Connect Mode

Add the command-line argument -WODirectConnectEnabled NO to the application executable, as in Figure 14.2.

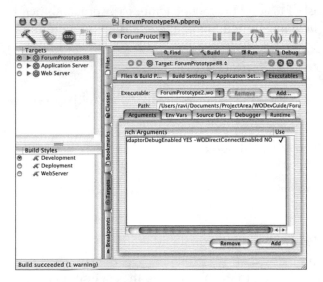

FIGURE 14.2   Connect to the Application via the Web Server.

Then, you will find that the application client launches in the browser with a URL like

```
http://localhost/cgi-bin/WebObjects/ForumPrototype2.woa/-49590
```

Where in this case, the minus number represents the port the application is running on. However, the main difference between connecting to the application instance this way is that the http requests are being made via the Web server and not directly to the WebObjects application server.

Now try substituting the http in the browser location field with https. You will now find that you are viewing the WebObjects application via a secure channel.

However, at this point there is still one caveat: The images will not display. To view the images we need to install the application resources such as images on the Web server.

Installing a WebObjects Application

From the terminal command line, type the following from the directory of the forum project:

```
> sudo pbxbuild install -buildstyle WebServer DSTROOT=/
```

You will be asked to enter the root or admin password, and then the forum application will be built and installed in two locations:

```
/Library/WebServer/Documents/WebObjects/
/Library/WebObjects/Applications/
```

The installer will place the resources needed by the Web server into the first location. This includes the images of the application. The second location is where a copy of deployed application is placed. For now the second location is not important. To develop WebObjects application via the Web server we need to have the application resources installed in the Web server document root.

Now when you run the application via the Web server, you should see the images displayed as well, as shown in Figure 14.3.

Securing WebObjects Pages

The page that needs securing is the login page. Here we want to ensure that nobody could eavesdrop and learn the password to the application.

In practice, providing a secure login to an online forum is perhaps not necessary. It is essential when building commercial applications. However, as you will see shortly, it is in fact not very difficult to do.

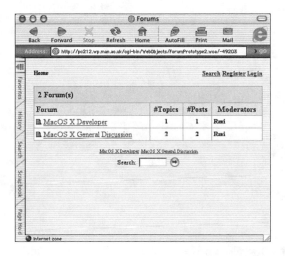

FIGURE 14.3   Running applications via the Web server requires installing the application resources.

Using a Secure WOHyperlink

To secure the login page, open the Main page in WebObjects Builder and select the WOHyperlink element for the Login action.

Open the WebObjects Inspector panel for the element. Scroll down to the binding named *secure*, and set its value to `true`, as shown in Figure 14.4.

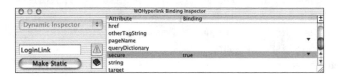

FIGURE 14.4   Making a WOHyperlink secure simply requires setting a default binding.

Now run the application again. You will notice that on clicking the login page you will be using secure http to communicate with the server. See Figure 14.5.

This is very simple indeed, but we are only half way there. Navigating the application from now on will be entirely in secure mode. What we really want is to come out of secure mode after we have logged in.

Using WORedirect to Revert to Nonsecure Mode

What we have to do to revert to nonsecure mode is redirect the browser to the return page using the standard http protocol. There is a very convenient and special component called *WORedirect* that will allow us to do just that.

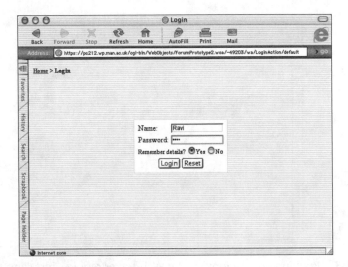

FIGURE 14.5   Login using secure http.

Alter the following fragment of the userAction from the LoginAction direct action class:

```
if (password != null && password.equals(_password)) {
    EOEnterpriseObject user = EOUtilities.objectMatchingKeyAndValue(
session().defaultEditingContext(), "User", "name", username);
    WOComponent nextPage = pageWithName("WORedirect");
    Number isPersistant = request().numericFormValueForKey("isPersistant",
new NSNumberFormatter());
    String queryString = "wosid=" + session().sessionID() + "&" +
"isPersistant=" + isPersistant;
    String url = context().completeURLWithRequestHandlerKey("wa", null,
queryString, false, 0);

    // set the session.user
    session().takeValueForKey(user, "user");

    // set the redirect URL
    nextPage.takeValueForKey(url, "url");
    return nextPage;
} else return wrongPasswordAction();
```

A WORedirect is used by simply setting its url key. We use the method completeURLWithRequestHandlerKey() on the context to generate a full URL for the direct action. Now we have completed adding a secure login page to the application.

However, because we have changed the way the Main page is vended after a successful login—by a redirect instead of returning the page directly—we must fix the default direct action to handle the isPersistant form value. You will notice that the statement that set the isPersistant value in the Main page had to be removed from the previous fragment of code. It now must be done in the direct action that vends the Main page.

Change the defaultAction of the DirectAction class:

```
public WOActionResults defaultAction() {
    WOComponent nextPage = pageWithName("Main");
    Number isPersistant = request().numericFormValueForKey("isPersistant",
new NSNumberFormatter());

    // set value
    if (isPersistant != null) nextPage.takeValueForKey(isPersistant,
"hasPersistantLogin");

    return nextPage;
}
```

Now the mechanism of storing of login values as cookies should be restored as well.

Using Basic http Authorization to Implement a WebObjects Login Panel

In this section, we'll reimplement the user login page using the browser's built-in login panel and the http basic authorization protocol.

This section is optional for those who want to look at alternative means of providing user login and client-side state storage. Implementing user login via the browser negates the need to have a custom cookie mechanism to store the user login and passwords because most browsers automatically provide this functionality.

As you will soon see, this solution is no more complex than the cookie mechanism of remembering user logins. In fact, because it doesn't have to use cookies, it could be considered the superior solution.

For the first part of the exercise, we are not going to use secure http and SSL. When we have implemented the new login mechanism, we'll make it secure afterwards.

Requesting Authorization from the Browser

First, let's open the Main component in WebObjects builder and make the login hyperlink nonsecure by setting its *secure* attribute to false.

We are going to add a key called `authorize` to the Main component. This will indicate whether to request authorization or not.

```
protected boolean authorize;
```

Now, remove the userAction in the LoginAction class. You might want to comment out the existing version because most of the functionality for checking user logins and passwords now moves into the Main component. You also might want to copy it over. Also remove the private actions we created for the userAction.

We reimplement the defaultAction in the LoginAction class:

```
public WOActionResults defaultAction() {
    WOComponent nextPage = pageWithName("Main");
    nextPage.takeValueForKey(new Integer(1), "authorize");
    return nextPage;
}
```

Notice that the cookie retrieval mechanism is no longer present. This is because in the new scheme it is redundant. The browser provides this functionality for free. You might also notice that the LoginAction class is fairly trivial now. This would be the case as the Main component is going to inherit much of the complexity.

In the Main class file, recode the appendToResponse() method.

```
public void appendToResponse(WOResponse response, WOContext context) {
    if (authorize) {
        // request authorization
        String realm = context.request().applicationName();
        response.setStatus(401);
        response.setHeader("Basic realm=\"" + realm + "\"" ,
"WWW-Authenticate");
        String encode = context.request().headerForKey("authorization");
        NSArray inputs = new NSArray();

        // decode the username/password text and validate
        if (encode != null) {
            encode = encode.substring(6);     // remove the "Basic " prefix

            // try decoding the encoded string
            try {
                BASE64Decoder decoder = new BASE64Decoder();
                InputStream inputStream = new ByteArrayInputStream(
encode.getBytes());
```

```
            String authorization = new String(decoder.decodeBuffer(
inputStream));

            // partition the username and password
            inputs = NSArray.componentsSeparatedByString(authorization,
 ":");
        } catch (IOException exception) {
            NSLog.err.appendln("Main: failed to decode authorization: "
 + encode);
        }

        // set username & password from the login
        String username = (String) inputs.objectAtIndex(0);
        EOEditingContext editingContext = new EOEditingContext();
        NSArray results = EOUtilities.rawRowsMatchingKeyAndValue(
editingContext, "User", "name", username);

        // if there are user(s) matching the username
        if (results.count() > 0) {
            NSDictionary result = (NSDictionary) results.objectAtIndex(0);
            String _password = (String) result.valueForKey("password");
            String password = (String) inputs.objectAtIndex(1);

            // check that the passwords match
            if (password.equals(_password)) {
                EOEnterpriseObject user =
EOUtilities.objectMatchingKeyAndValue(session().defaultEditingContext(),
"User", "name", username);

                // set the session.user
                session().takeValueForKey(user, "user");
            } else _msg = "Incorrect password. Try again.";
        } else _msg = "No user match. Try again.";
    }
} super.appendToResponse(response, context);
}
```

This code fragment might seem a little involved. However, only the first bit is new and might seem unfamiliar.

The request for browser authorization comes from setting the response status to 401. This will result in a second request for the page. On the second pass, when the user has entered login details, we get a chance to validate and login the user.

As part of the http basic authentication protocol, a *realm* must be passed onto the client. The user login details are then associated with this and the host name.

The other thing to note is that this scheme encodes the user login and password in BASE64. This is not an encrypted message. It is simply a non-ASCII encoding of the information. In practice this doesn't provide much security if any at all. That is achieved by SSL, which we'll add later. So next, we must decode the BASE64-encoded user string passed on by the browser. For that we use the `sun.misc.BASE64Decoder`. To make sure that the `sun.misc.*` package is imported into the class file along with `java.io.*`:

```
import sun.misc.*;
import java.io.*;
```

After that, the decoded authorization string is separated into its `username` and `password` strings. Thereafter, the user validation is pretty much the same as it was in the userAction in the LoginAction class. The principle difference is that it is more convenient to set the user feedback messages. We simply set the _msg key.

Add an `onLoad` accessor to the Main class along with the variable key _msg. Bind the `onLoad` key to the page template component as you have done in some of the other pages. The login feedback messages will then be displayed as JavaScript alerts.

```
protected String _msg;

public String onLoad() {
    String onLoad = "alert('" + _msg + "');";
    return (_msg != null) ? onLoad:null;
}
```

Now we need to tidy up and remove redundant code that was necessary to handle storing user logins as cookies. Simplify the defaultAction in the DirectAction class to return the Main page:

```
public WOActionResults defaultAction() {
    return pageWithName("Main");
}
```

Lastly, delete the Login page components and class file from the project altogether, then build and run. You should get a login panel similar to the one in Figure 14.6.

Securing the Client Login Panel

Now we can make the browser login secure. First, make the login link secure by setting its *secure* attribute to `true` again.

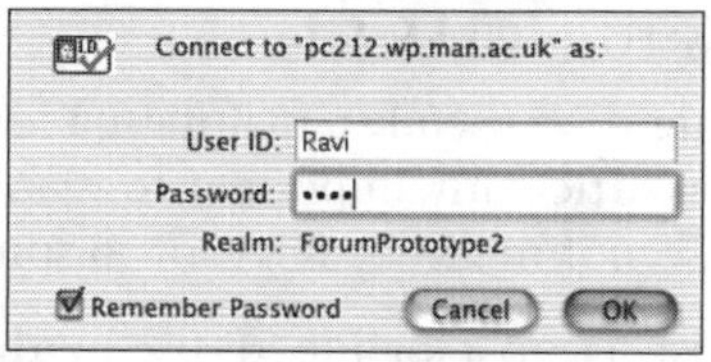

FIGURE 14.6   Using http authorization to login.

Then, in the Main class, we need to manually redirect the response on successful login. Here is the fragment of code that changes:

```
// check that the passwords match
if (password.equals(_password)) {
    EOEnterpriseObject user = EOUtilities.objectMatchingKeyAndValue(
session().defaultEditingContext(), "User", "name", username);
    String queryString = "wosid=" + session().sessionID();
    String url = context().completeURLWithRequestHandlerKey("wa", null,
queryString, false, 0);

    // set the session.user
    session().takeValueForKey(user, "user");

    // set the redirect url and headers
    response.setHeader(url, "location");
    response.setHeader("text/html", "content-type");
    response.setHeader("0", "content-length");
    response.setStatus(302);
} else _msg = "Incorrect password. Try again.";
```

Here we use the context `completeURLWithRequestHandlerKey()` to generate the full URL again. However, creating and using a WORedirect would be inappropriate here from within the `appendToResponse()` method. Instead, we manually redirect by setting the URL in the *location* http header.

Build and run to see a secure login using client-side authentication. Also note the browser handling of user logins and passwords.

Logging in WebObjects

In this section, we'll look at performing some basic logging for a WebObjects application. In particular, we'll look at logging information of user logins for the online forum application as well as at Web server logging and statistics gathering for WebObjects applications.

Logging User Logins to a CLFF File

In many applications it might be useful to maintain a log of attempted logins to an application. Again, it isn't particularly important to manage or maintain user logins to an online forum. However, it might be relevant to some.

To enable logging you must set up a log file for use by the application. The directory */Library/WebObjects/* might be a suitable place to set up a Logs directory.

From the Terminal command line enter the following to create and set permissions for a Logs directory:

```
> sudo mkdir /var/log/WebObjects/
> sudo chmod go+w /var/log/WebObjects/
```

Now in the Application class constructor, place the following line:

```
// set the log file
statisticsStore().setLogFile("/var/log/WebObjects/User.log", 10^7);
```

This lets the application statistics store where to log information. The second argument is the rotation frequency of the log file in milliseconds. The statistics store rotates or backs up the log file automatically at the given time interval.

Obtaining the Client IP Address from the http Headers

In the appendToResponse() of the Main page add the following lines to log the IP address: the username and the timestamp of the user login. The code fragment placed after the username has been parsed into the variable username.

```
// log the user and IP address
String clientIP = context.request().headerForKey("remote_addr");
NSTimestampFormatter formatter = new NSTimestampFormatter("[%d/%b/%Y:%H:%M:%S
 %z]");
application().statisticsStore().logString(clientIP + " " + username + " "
 + formatter.format(new NSTimestamp()) + "\n");
```

We also use a programmatically created timestamp formatter to log the timestamp similar to the *(Common) Log File Format* standard. This is the standard log file format used by Apache and other Web servers. If you did want to use a log file analysis tool, it is useful to log information in the same structure and standard.

After you build and run, you should find that each user login attempt is logged to the file. An example of a line printed out in the log file:

```
130.88.179.212 Ravi [03/Feb/2002:21:46:26 Etc/GMT]
```

Introduction to http Logging with WebObjects

Most Web servers maintain a log file of http requests made. On Mac OS X you will find the file located in */private/var/log/httpd/*. Here you will find the Apache log access_log, error_log, and ssl_request_log files.

Browse the contents of the access_log file. Here is a sample log file:

```
130.88.179.212 - - [02/Feb/2002:16:32:57 +0000]
➡ "GET /manual/dso.html HTTP/1.1" 200 21137
130.88.179.212 - - [02/Feb/2002:16:33:03 +0000] "GET / HTTP/1.1" 200 1456
130.88.179.212 - - [02/Feb/2002:16:33:06 +0000] "GET /manual/ HTTP/1.1" 304 -
130.88.179.212 - - [02/Feb/2002:16:33:07 +0000]
➡ "GET /manual/install.html HTTP/1.1" 200 8848
130.88.179.212 - - [02/Feb/2002:16:33:08 +0000]
➡ "GET /manual/windows.html HTTP/1.1" 200 27093
130.88.179.212 - - [03/Feb/2002:15:39:24 +0000]
➡ "GET /cgi-bin/WebObjects/ForumPrototype2.woa/-55943 HTTP/1.1" 200 3093
130.88.179.212 - - [03/Feb/2002:15:39:29 +0000] "GET /cgi-bin/WebObjects/
➡ForumPrototype2.woa/-55943/wa/topics?forumID=4 HTTP/1.1" 200 2379
130.88.179.212 - - [03/Feb/2002:15:39:32 +0000] "GET /cgi-bin/WebObjects/
➡ForumPrototype2.woa/-55943/wa/posts?topicID=1 HTTP/1.1" 200 2495
130.88.179.212 - - [03/Feb/2002:15:39:35 +0000] "GET /cgi-bin/WebObjects/
➡ForumPrototype2.woa/-55943/wa/default HTTP/1.1" 200 3093
130.88.179.212 - - [03/Feb/2002:15:39:38 +0000] "GET /cgi-bin/WebObjects/
➡ForumPrototype2.woa/-55943/wa/SearchAction HTTP/1.1" 200 1298
130.88.179.212 - - [03/Feb/2002:15:39:42 +0000] "POST /cgi-bin/WebObjects/
➡ForumPrototype2.woa/-55943/wa/SearchAction/results HTTP/1.1" 200 2430
130.88.179.212 - - [03/Feb/2002:15:39:44 +0000] "GET /cgi-bin/WebObjects/
➡ForumPrototype2.woa/-55943/wa/default HTTP/1.1" 200 3093
130.88.179.212 - - [03/Feb/2002:15:39:47 +0000] "GET /cgi-bin/WebObjects/
➡ForumPrototype2.woa/-55943/wa/Register/default HTTP/1.1" 200 2578
130.88.179.212 - - [03/Feb/2002:15:39:49 +0000] "GET /cgi-bin/WebObjects/
➡ForumPrototype2.woa/-55943/wa/default HTTP/1.1" 200 3093
130.88.179.212 - - [03/Feb/2002:15:39:51 +0000] "GET /cgi-bin/WebObjects/
➡ForumPrototype2.woa/-55943/wa/topics?forumID=3 HTTP/1.1" 200 2858
130.88.179.212 - - [03/Feb/2002:15:39:54 +0000] "GET /cgi-bin/WebObjects/
➡ForumPrototype2.woa/-55943/wa/posts?topicID=2 HTTP/1.1" 200 2427
130.88.179.212 - - [03/Feb/2002:15:39:56 +0000] "GET /cgi-bin/WebObjects/
➡ForumPrototype2.woa/-55943/wa/default HTTP/1.1" 200 3093
130.88.179.212 - - [03/Feb/2002:15:40:17 +0000] "GET /cgi-bin/WebObjects/
➡ForumPrototype2.woa/-55943/wa/default HTTP/1.1" 200 3093
130.88.179.212 - - [03/Feb/2002:15:40:31 +0000] "GET /cgi-bin/WebObjects/
➡ForumPrototype2.woa/-55943/wa/WOStats HTTP/1.1" 200 997
```

```
130.88.179.212 - - [03/Feb/2002:15:40:43 +0000] "POST /cgi-bin/WebObjects/
➥ForumPrototype2.woa/-55943/wo/J6fPMXJj9oQVx1kpr8Ya00/0.2.1 HTTP/1.1" 200 997
130.88.179.212 - - [03/Feb/2002:15:40:53 +0000] "POST /cgi-bin/WebObjects/
➥ForumPrototype2.woa/-55943/wo/J6fPMXJj9oQVx1kpr8Ya00/2.2.1 HTTP/1.1" 200 997
```

First, notice that direct actions to a WebObjects application get logged correctly.

However, look at the second highlighted entry in the previous log file: a WebObjects component action. Unlike direct actions, component actions are requests particular to a given context in a given session. As a result their URLs are active only for the duration of the session; after that they are redundant. More importantly, they do not indicate what page was accessed, for example. The point of maintaining an http log is to obtain statistics for a site. For public sites, these statistics often have huge commercial value.

Most of the time, the online forum application uses direct actions. The exception is the User Preferences, which have been implemented as component actions.

However, there are session-based direct action requests, too. The complete URLs including the sesionID are not valid after the duration of the session. So, in practice, these URLs, although more meaningful than component actions, shouldn't be logged either. So how do you manage to log data for these requests, if you're to do so at all?

Let's first address the problem of logging session-based direct action URLs.

There are two solutions to this problem. One is to configure your Web server to log the direct action without the *wosid* form key and value. The second is to store the session ID as a cookie instead of managing it in the URL.

We'll look at how to implement the second alternative first.

Storing the SessionID in Cookies

There is a certain tradeoff in storing the session ID in cookies on the client instead of in the URL. One unfortunate trade off is security, which will be demonstrated later. As a result treat this subsection as an exercise. You may or may not decide to implement this solution for one reason or another. So, make a copy of the online forum application developed so far to revert to later if need be.

To enable the storage of session IDs in cookies and to disable maintaining the session ID in URLs requires adding the following two lines to the Application createSessionForRequest() method.

```
// store sessionIDs in cookies
session.setStoresIDsInURLs(false);
session.setStoresIDsInCookies(true);
```

In addition change all occurrences of the hasSession() key to reflect the new session ID management scheme.

```
public boolean hasSession() {
    String sessionID = context().request().cookieValueForKey("wosid");
    return (super.hasSession() || sessionID != null);
}
```

Here, obtaining the session ID from the request is no longer necessary or valid. Instead we use cookieValueForKey() to obtain the session ID from the cookie.

Lastly, in the appendToResponse() of the Main component, there is no need to set a queryString, in the redirection URL. Remove the line:

```
String queryString = "wosid=" + session().sessionID();
```

Then, change the next line to:

```
String url = context().completeURLWithRequestHandlerKey("wa", null, null,
false, 0);
```

Build and run the application. This time however make sure to login and browse the User Preferences. Now take a look at the Apache access_log. You might find it convenient to type the following on the command line to do so:

```
> tail /private/var/log/httpd/access_log
```

Notice that the output is void of either any session based direct actions.

```
130.88.179.212 - - [04/Feb/2002:10:06:36 +0000] "GET /cgi-bin/WebObjects/
➡ForumPrototype2.woa/-58940/wa/topics?forumID=3 HTTP/1.1" 200 3058
130.88.179.212 - - [04/Feb/2002:10:06:39 +0000] "GET /cgi-bin/WebObjects/
➡ForumPrototype2.woa/-58940/wa/default HTTP/1.1" 200 3035
130.88.179.212 - - [04/Feb/2002:10:06:41 +0000] "GET /cgi-bin/WebObjects/
➡ForumPrototype2.woa/-58940/wo/6.0.3.1.3.3 HTTP/1.1" 200 3716
130.88.179.212 - - [04/Feb/2002:10:06:42 +0000] "GET /WebObjects/Frameworks/
➡JavaWOExtensions.framework/WebServerResources/leftTab.gif HTTP/1.1" 200 76
130.88.179.212 - - [04/Feb/2002:10:06:42 +0000] "GET /WebObjects/Frameworks/
➡JavaWOExtensions.framework/WebServerResources/rightTab.gif HTTP/1.1" 200 76
130.88.179.212 - - [04/Feb/2002:10:06:46 +0000] "GET /cgi-bin/WebObjects/
➡ForumPrototype2.woa/-58940/wa/default HTTP/1.1" 200 3035
130.88.179.212 - - [04/Feb/2002:10:06:49 +0000] "GET /cgi-bin/WebObjects/
➡ForumPrototype2.woa/-58940/wa/topics?forumID=4 HTTP/1.1" 200 2580
130.88.179.212 - - [04/Feb/2002:10:06:52 +0000] "GET /cgi-bin/WebObjects/
➡ForumPrototype2.woa/-58940/wa/posts?topicID=1 HTTP/1.1" 200 2971
```

```
130.88.179.212 - - [04/Feb/2002:10:06:54 +0000] "GET /cgi-bin/WebObjects/
➥ForumPrototype2.woa/-58940/wa/default HTTP/1.1" 200 3036
130.88.179.212 - - [04/Feb/2002:10:06:55 +0000] "GET /cgi-bin/WebObjects/
➥ForumPrototype2.woa/-58940/wo/15.0.3.1.3.3 HTTP/1.1" 200 3718
```

The Apache log is now more accurate because the direct actions are consistent regardless of whether they are stateless or not. Note, however, that it is not completely accurate though. WebObjects component actions, which are invalid, are still being logged.

Configuring Apache to Ignore WebObjects Component Actions

If your Web server is different from Apache, you will have you refer to its documentation to ignore logging all http requests that contain the string /wo/. If you wanted to make it more accurate you would ensure that /cgi-bin/WebObjects/ was also a literal in the http request string.

Here we are going to use a simple Apache technique known as *Conditional Logging* to get it to ignore WebObjects components requests. We might justify this solution given that in the online forum application typical usage would produce a very small number of component requests (made to the user preferences).

To set up the logging condition, we need to edit the httpd.conf file. On Mac OS X this is located in the /etc/httpd/ directory. In addition you will need super user permissions to save your changes to the file. So, if you are using a graphical text editor, you might have to log in as root, otherwise remember to change user before opening the file. Change the lines containing the *CustomLog* statement:

```
#
# The location and format of the access logfile (Common Logfile Format).
# If you do not define any access logfiles within a <VirtualHost>
# container, they will be logged here.  Contrariwise, if you *do*
# define per-<VirtualHost> access logfiles, transactions will be
# logged therein and *not* in this file.
#
SetEnvIf Request_URI /wo/ wo-request
CustomLog "/private/var/log/httpd/access_log" common env=!wo-request
```

Here we set up the environment variable *wo-request* if the http request contains the literal /wo/. We then log the request only if it doesn't meet the condition, that is, when the request is not a WebObjects component request.

Now stop and restart Apache:

```
> sudo apachectl stop
sudo apachectl start
```

The Web server access log will provide valid and satisfactorily accurate logging for this WebObjects application. You might then analyze the log file and statistics using any CLFF log-analyzing tool.

Note that this solution is really only suitable for logging WebObjects applications that are primarily direct action based or those that minimally use component actions.

Post Processing Web Server Logs

There are other ways to configure Apache to log http requests to a WebObjects application correctly. One is to use pipes to *post-process* the http log.

In fact this is the second solution to handle nonstateless direct actions. If you are versed in Unix or another scripting language, you might create a script to post process the access log removing any strings of the form `wosid=?xxx`. You will also have to remove any lines containing `/wo/`.

You can post process such log files at the traffic analysis stage.

Custom WebObjects CLFF Logging for Statistics

If you did want to log http requests made to a component action based WebObjects application, you can implement it as we have done the user login logs. However, it will mean that the log file you produce may still conform to the CLFF log file format and may produce meaningful statistics, there may still be some compromise.

Think for a moment about a WebObjects component request. Note that we may log the page that was requested. However, there will be a certain loss of information. Consider the User Preferences page. Do we log a request made to it or one of its subcomponent panels? On more complex component action pages, it might be harder to accurately log the information that the user has been browsing.

For further information on how to implement CLFF custom logs go to `http://developer.apple.com/techpubs/webobjects/Reference/Javadoc/com/webobjects/appserver/WOStatisticsStore.html`

In such instances it might be useful to turn to WebObjects built in statistics mechanism.

Viewing the WOStats page

Add a command-line argument to the WebObjects application target: -WOStatisticsPassword *password*.

Relaunch the application and browse several pages. Access the *WOStats* page as a direct action by typing in one of the following depending on whether you are developing in direct connect mode or not:

```
http://hostname/cgi-bin/WebObjects/ForumPrototype.woa/-port/wa/WOStats
http://hostname:port/cgi-bin/WebObjects/ForumPrototype.woa/wa/WOStats
```

Figure 14.7 shows an excerpt of a WOStats page for the online forum application. Although it might not produce as detailed reports as those produced by third-party CLFF log analyzers, it can be a valuable solution for smaller applications.

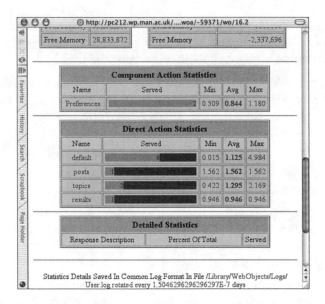

FIGURE 14.7   View statistics for a WebObjects application from the WOStats page.

Using Java Cryptography in WebObjects Applications

An often-overlooked aspect of securing applications on the Web is the *storage* of sensitive data. This could be credit-card details, account balances, or other sensitive data.

It is of utmost important that such information doesn't get into the hands of unauthorized personnel of the vender of the Web service or product.

So, in this section we'll look at encrypting sensitive data to the database. The only real sensitive data in the online forum application are the user passwords. Again, in such an application it is not critical or necessary to provide security of such sophistication. In which case treat the following section as an exercise.

Introduction to Encryption with WebObjects

Encrypting data for storage purposes is different from securing a communications channel. Trying to pass a message secretly to someone else requires more sophistication. If you have a key to secure one end of the communication, the receiving party must also have a key.

However, storing something in a safe place only requires just one person to have one key. Or, simpler yet, just the ability to hide or disguise it.

At this point it becomes necessary to explain a few new terms.

What Is the Difference Between Encoding and Encrypting?

An *encoding* is simply a representation in some language. For example the number one is represented as 1 in Hindu-Arabic numerals, or as I in Roman numerals. This if you like, is an example of an encoding of the number one.

On the other hand, aioornftinm is a jumble of the word information. Therefore, it forms a suitable *cryptogram* or *encryption* of the original message. Here the *ciphertext* is aioornftinm, and the *plaintext* is information.

As you know jumbles are easy to make, but hard to figure out, this determines the strength of the encryption or the security that it provides. In fact, the humble jumble forms the basis of what are known as hashing algorithms. One of which is SHA, a standard algorithm that is part of the Java Cryptography Architecture that ships with the Java 2 environment.

We'll use this algorithm to encrypt the passwords of the online forum application to the database.

Accommodating Ciphertexts in the Database and Object Model

Most of the changes that are required to implement password encryption are simple alterations that are going to be made to the Enterprise Object classes, the model, and the database. Open the two model files from the Forum framework project.

Setting the String Encoding of the Object Model

Open the inspector panel to examine the connection dictionary. These are the global settings the model uses to identify its data source.

Click the Add button to add a new key databaseEncoding and set its value to ISO Latin-1, as in Figure 14.8. Add this setting to the other model file as well.

Altering the Object Model

Now we also need to make a little more room for the encrypted password. Typically, ciphertexts take up more space than their plaintext counterparts.

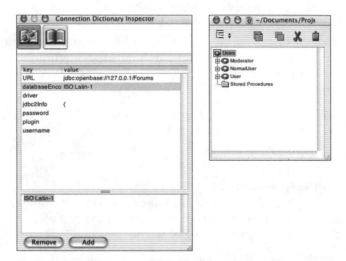

FIGURE 14.8   Set the database encoding of the Object Model File.

So, set a larger width for the User password. For example, you might set it to a width of 255 characters. Save your changes.

Altering the Database

Open OpenBase Manager and open the Schema panel for the Forum database. Change the password width of the USER table to match the model. Save the changes.

Encrypting Enterprise Object Values

We are going to use one of the algorithms that form part of the Java Cryptography Architecture to implement encryption of the User password.

Start by importing the required packages to the User enterprise object class:

```
import java.security.*;
import java.io.*;
```

Then, implement the following accessor to set the password, and the static method encrypt() to perform the encryption of the password:

```
/*
 * accessors
 */
public void setPassword(String password) {
    String encryptedPassword = encrypt(password);
    takeStoredValueForKey(encryptedPassword, "password");
}
```

```
/*
 * public static
 */
public static String encrypt(String plaintext) {
    String encoding = "ISO-8859-1";
    String ciphertext = null;

    // one-way encrption algorithm
    try {
        MessageDigest messageDigest = MessageDigest.getInstance("SHA-1");
        byte[] bytes = plaintext.getBytes(encoding);

        // encrypt
        messageDigest.reset();
        byte[] encryptedBytes = messageDigest.digest(bytes);
        ciphertext = new String(encryptedBytes, encoding);
    } catch (Exception exception) {
        NSLog.err.appendln("User: unable to encrypt plaintext: " + plaintext);
    }

    return ciphertext;
}
```

You might find that the setPassword() accessor is self-explanatory. It simply stores the result of encrypting the plaintext password.

The encryption algorithm is a little more involved. It primarily uses the *java.security.MessageDigest* class to perform the encryption. In particular, it uses the one-way encryption algorithm *SHA-1*. It is particularly suited to encrypting passwords for the reasons discussed earlier. To determine if a password is correct, you encrypt it and compare the ciphertext with that of the stored password cipher. There isn't a need to decrypt the password.

Also worth noting is that the string encoding we use is the same as the model and the database. This is vital for the encryption strategy to work correctly.

Now build and install the framework.

You will need to use your DirectToWeb test project to reset the passwords for the users currently in your system. See Figure 14.9. Otherwise clear and create a new database from scratch.

Finally, we need to change the password checking mechanism in both the user login and the user preferences, so open the forum application project again.

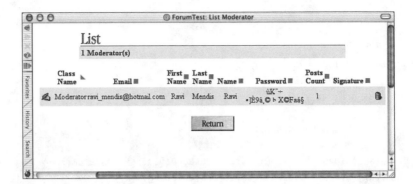

FIGURE 14.9   Use DirectToWeb to reset the user passwords. Notice the passwords display as ciphertext.

In the appendToResponse() method of the Main component navigate to the password comparison statement and change it to the following:

```
// check that the passwords match
if (_password.equals(User.encrypt(password))) {
```

Similarly, change the lines in the Password Preferences component:

```
// check the passwords match
if (_oldPassword.equals(User.encrypt(oldPassword))) {
```

Here we are using the publicly declared method encrypt() on the User class to perform the password checking. Build and run to start using the application with password encryption on.

Summary

In this chapter, we looked at implementing security and simple encryption in a WebObjects Application. In addition we examined how to log statistics and information useful to a WebObjects application.

15

SOAP and WebObjects

"What is Technology without Imagination?"

—FIAT

This chapter will examine the role SOAP can play in a modern WebObjects application. In particular, how to build SOAP services from a WebObjects application, and how to integrate a SOAP service into a WebObjects application.

Building a SOAP Service with WebObjects

To illustrate the simple techniques involved, in this section we'll build a *Topic Tracker* as a SOAP service for the online forum.

However, before that, as an introduction we'll build a simple Hello World greeting application as a WebObjects SOAP service.

Introduction to SOAP

SOAP is a simple protocol for the transfer of messages between applications. It is based on XML and lays out some conventions for communications between two applications.

The purpose of SOAP is to enable business-to-business communication; to enable a Web service provider to vend its service in an open and easily accessible manner. Thus, enabling other service providers to incorporate these services into their applications. In addition, Web services are being used to provide functionality for desktop applications. An example of this is Microsoft's .NET strategy.

A SOAP request and response is made as an XML document. The following is an example of a SOAP request:

```
<soap:Envelope>
  <soap:Body>
    <xmlns:m="http://www.stock.org/stock" />
    <m:GetStockPrice>
    <m:StockName>AAPL</m:StockName>
    </m:GetStockPrice>
  </soap:Body>
</soap:Envelope>
```

Let's take a look at this SOAP request in a little more detail. A SOAP message is composed within a SOAP *envelope*. Similar to an HTML document, a SOAP envelope consists of a SOAP *header* and a SOAP *body*. Although in this message, the optional SOAP header has not been used.

These SOAP messages rely quite substantially on XML namespaces, hence the *xmlns* declaration of the content for the body of the message.

> **NOTE**
>
> An XML namespace defines the XML tags to be used, usually in a particular fragment of an XML document.

Next, the <GetStockPrice> tag represents the method name of the SOAP message and the <StockName> contained within it is a parameter. In this example, AAPL is the stock name being requested.

When a request is made to the example SOAP service, it generates a response returning the current stock price for the symbol requested.

```
<soap:Envelope>
  <soap:Body>
    <xmlns:m="http://www.stock.org/stock" />
    <m:GetStockPriceResponse>
    <m:Price>20.5</m:Price>
    </m:GetStockPriceResponse>
  </soap:Body>
</soap:Envelope>
```

The SOAP response is very similar to the request. It is also composed of a header and a body within a SOAP envelope. The value of the stock is returned. The SOAP client must be cleaver enough to interpret the SOAP response and extract the information it needs. Now, we'll see how this works in practice.

Building a Hello World SOAP Application

We are going to create a simple SOAP service that returns a custom greeting for a requested name.

1. Create a new WebObjects Application project SOAPHelloWorld.

2. Make direct actions the default request handler. Remember that you do this by adding the following settings to the Application constructor:

   ```
   WORequestHandler directActionRequestHandler = requestHandlerForKey("wa");
   setDefaultRequestHandler(directActionRequestHandler);
   ```

3. Now change the Main component template to vend the following XML. Note that the SOAP method name we use here is getMessage. We also define a namespace wo-soap-helloworld for the example. The return tag contains the result.

   ```
   <SOAP-ENV:Envelope xmlns:SOAP ENV="http://schemas.xmlsoap.org/soap/envelope/"
                      xmlns:xsi="http://www.w3.org/1999/XMLSchema-instance"
                      xmlns:xsd="http://www.w3.org/1999/XMLSchema">
     <SOAP-ENV:Body>
       <ns1:getMessageResponse xmlns:ns1="urn:wo-soap-helloworld" SOAP-
   ENV:encodingStyle="http://schemas.xmlsoap.org/soap/encoding/">
           <return xsi:type="xsd:string">Hello World!</return>
       </ns1:getMessageResponse>
     </SOAP-ENV:Body>
   </SOAP-ENV:Envelope>
   ```

4. Build the application. Given that we have developed a SOAP service with no HTML interface, we shouldn't open up a Web client to the server application by default. Set the command-line argument -WOAutoOpenInBrowser NO to disable this default. In addition, for convenience you might want to fix the port number the application runs on by setting the command-line argument to -WOPort 10000.

Using an AppleScript as a SOAP Client

The version of AppleScript that ships with Mac OS X has SOAP connectivity features built into it. In fact, there is an example AppleScript application that ships with the AppleScript Studio on Mac OS X called SOAP Talk. We can use this AppleScript to communicate with our WebObjects SOAP service.

Locate the SOAP Talk project in /Developer/Examples/AppleScript Studio/SOAP Talk/. Make a copy of the original, then build and run it from Project Builder. You will see a screen similar to the one in Figure 15.1.

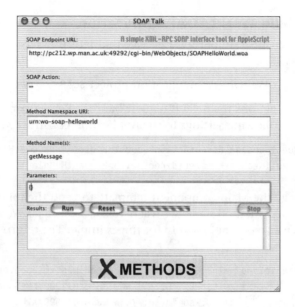

FIGURE 15.1   Using AppleScript as a SOAP client to a WebObjects SOAP server.

Enter the details into the screen as in Figure 15.1. That is copy and paste in the SOAP WebObjects application URL into the *SOAP Endpoint URL* field. Leave the SOAP Action empty as it is. Enter urn:wo-soap-helloworld as the *Method Namespace URI*. Finally, set the *Method Name* to be getMessage. Leave the *Parameters* field empty. Press Run to get the AppleScript to generate and send a SOAP request to the Hello World WebObjects application. You will see Hello World! printed out in the results scroll view of the SOAP Talk panel. Be careful to check that there are no misspelled method names and no errors in the URL, otherwise the SOAPTalk application will silently fail.

We are not quite finished yet. All we have done so far is to simply request a static greeting page from the WebObjects application. We can easily do a little more.

Parsing in SOAP Parameters

Next, let's send a request with a parameter MyName and get the WebObjects SOAP server to return a greeting with that name.

The name parameter is going to be parsed very similar to the way values are parsed in from direct action requests. The principle difference is that the parameter is stored in the contents of the request, whereas in a direct action the values are passed as form values. This enables applications to pass more sophisticated requests and responses between them.

First, import the following package into to the DirectAction class:

```
import org.w3c.dom.*;
```

Then, change the `defaultAction()` to parse in the content from the request, and then obtain the value for the tag <myname>.

```
public WOActionResults defaultAction() {
    WOComponent nextPage = pageWithName("Main");
    Document document = request().contentAsDOMDocument();
    String myName = document.getElementsByTagName("myname").item(0).
getFirstChild().getNodeValue();

    // set the name
    nextPage.takeValueForKey(myName, "myName");

    return nextPage;
}
```

Here the `contentAsDOMDocument()` parses in the SOAP request into a DOM Document. The `getElementsByTagName()` statement, obtains the value for the <myname> tag.

Add a variable key, myName, to the Main component. Add a `WOString` in place of the string World and bind its *value* to myName. It is best to edit the component template in source mode.

Then, you can pass on the name parameter from the SOAP request into the WebObjects generated SOAP response. Build and run the application. This time from the SOAP Talk panel, give the parameter MyName some value, as in Figure 15.2. When clicking Run you should get a response with the name entered as a parameter.

Examining a SOAP Request

If you want to take a closer look at the SOAP requests being made by the SOAP Talk application, add a debug line to `defaultAction()` to print out the request content as a string:

```
NSLog.debug.appendln("DirectAction: SOAP request: " + request().contentString());
```

Adding a SOAP Service to the Online Forum

To illustrate a more sophisticated use of SOAP with WebObjects, let's look at implementing a topic tracker as a SOAP service to the online forum application. The topic tracker service will return the last message posted to a topic.

FIGURE 15.2   Create a SOAP request with a Parameter.

Start by creating a new application called ForumSOAPServer and include the Forum framework into it. Create a new Direct Action class named SOAP. As you did in the previous exercise add the DOM package import statement to the class and change the defaultAction() method to the following:

```
public WOActionResults defaultAction() {
    WOComponent nextPage = pageWithName("TopicTracker");
    Document document = request().contentAsDOMDocument();
    Integer topicID = new Integer(document.getElementsByTagName("topicid").
item(0).getFirstChild().getNodeValue());

    // set the name
    nextPage.takeValueForKey(topicID, "topicID");

    return nextPage;
}
```

Here we get the topicID from the SOAP request, and we pass it onto the TopicTracker page.

Add a new page, TopicTracker, to the project and group it in a separate group titled SOAP under Web Components. This is to distinguish it from HTML components.

Make it a similar SOAP response page to the one you created for the SOAP Hello World application. We are going to keep things simple by vending the entire last post as a string. This is done so that the AppleScript client can parse it in correctly. If, on the other hand, the SOAP client is able to parse in XML-formatted data instead of a return string, we could in fact return the last post XML-encoded. So, for example, if the service was intended as a business-to-business server, you could have composed the SOAP result as an XML document.

```
<SOAP-ENV:Envelope xmlns:SOAP-ENV="http://schemas.xmlsoap.org/soap/envelope/"
                    xmlns:xsi="http://www.w3.org/1999/XMLSchema-instance"
                    xmlns:xsd="http://www.w3.org/1999/XMLSchema">
<SOAP-ENV:Body>
<ns1:getLastPostResponse xmlns:ns1="urn:forum-topic-tracker" SOAP-ENV:encod-
ingStyle="http://schemas.xmlsoap.org/soap/encoding/">
    <return xsi:type="xsd:string">Response</return>
</ns1:getLastPostResponse>
</SOAP-ENV:Body>
</SOAP-ENV:Envelope>
```

Use a different namespace for this SOAP service and a method getLastPost.

Resolving an Object from its Graph in Memory
In the class for the topic tracker response, we might obtain the last post of a given topic in two ways. One is to perform a specialized query defined as a fetch specification, as we have done before. The other simple alternative is to resolve the objects in memory. That is, in this case, to fetch the topic for the requested topicID, then fetch the post that was made at the topic.timeOfLastPost.

Before hand, add an editing context controller to the class file as a private instance:

```
private EOEditingContext editingContext = new EOEditingContext();
```

This editing context is scoped within the SOAP response. In other words, when the response has been returned to the client the page along with the editing context will be freed.

Next, add two keys for post and topic as enterprise objects. Similarly, add an accessor only key topicID.

```
/** @TypeInfo Post */
protected EOEnterpriseObject post;
/** @TypeInfo Topic */
protected EOEnterpriseObject topic;

    /*
```

```
 * accessors
 */
public void setTopicID(Number topicID) {
    topic = EOUtilities.objectWithPrimaryKeyValue(editingContext,
"Topic", topicID);
}
```

So, when the topicID is set in the topic tracker page, what we actually do is perform a fetch and set the topic. Use the EOUtilities method objectWithPrimaryKeyValue() to return the topic for the topicID.

Now we can *resolve* the last post of the topic by fetching the post that was made at topic.timeOfLastPost. Add an accessor for post, which then gets and sets the last post of the topic:

```
public EOEnterpriseObject post() {
    if (post == null) {
        NSTimestamp timestamp = (NSTimestamp) topic.valueForKey("timeOfLastPost");
        Object[] values = new Object[]{timestamp, topic};
        String[] keys = new String[]{"timestamp", "topic"};
        NSDictionary bindings = new NSDictionary(values, keys);
        post = EOUtilities.objectMatchingValues(editingContext, "Post", bindings);
    } return post;
}
```

Here again we use an EOUtilities method objectMatchingValues() to fetch the post.

Finally, add three WOStrings to represent the post.message, post.timestamp, and post.user.name, as shown in Figure 15.3.

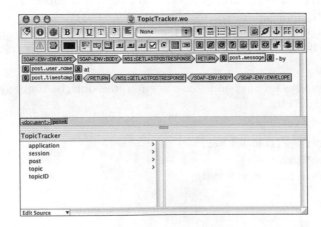

FIGURE 15.3   Format and return the topic's latest post.

Viewing XML Tags Inline in WebObjects Builder

You might be wondering how to display the SOAP-XML tags inline similar to Figure 15.3.

1. Open the Webobjects Builder Preferences panel and select the layout button.

2. Choose the *Show tags graphically inline for: all other tags* option as in Figure 15.4.

3. Click Apply.

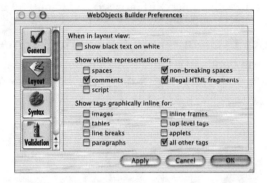

FIGURE 15.4   Set WebObjects Builder to display XML tags inline.

Finally, build and run the forum application. From the SOAP Talk application enter the details, as in Figure 15.5, remembering in particular to set the TopicID parameter.

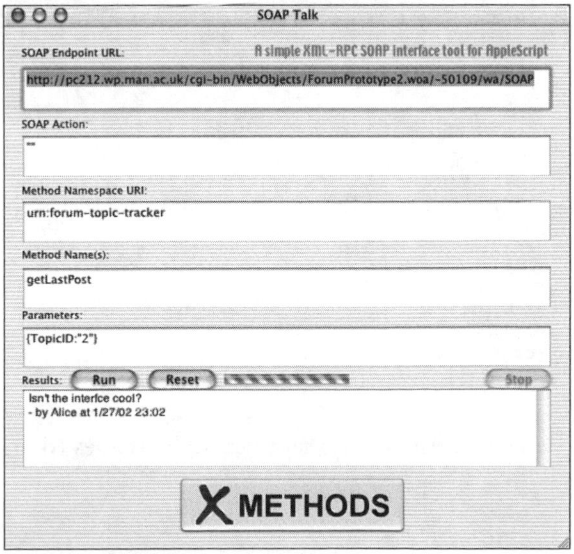

FIGURE 15.5   Track a Topic using SOAP.

Integrating a SOAP Service into a WebObjects Application

So far we have used WebObjects to develop a SOAP server; that is, an application that vends a SOAP service. It is time, however, to look at building a WebObjects application that acts as a client of an external SOAP service.

This is where SOAP services can be of great benefit. It makes it easy to integrate credit-card checking, zip-code checking, news and weather services, and many other functions into a WebObjects application. Depending on your need, you might find that one or more of these SOAP services prove to be very useful indeed.

Using a Currency Exchange Rate Calculator Service

In this section, we will build a WebObjects Application as a front end to a SOAP service that calculates and returns the exchange rate between two currencies.

Start by creating a new project for the exercise. Open the Main component and lay it out as in Figure 15.6.

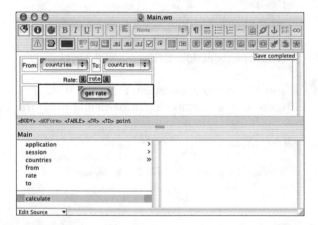

FIGURE 15.6   Use the figure as a guide for the layout of the Currency Exchange Rate Calculator.

Bind the country pop-up button, *lists*, to a variable key named countries:

```
protected NSArray countries =
new NSArray(new String[]{"us", "uk", "taiwan", "italy"});
```

Make sure their *selection* attributes are set to string variables (that is the keys) from and to.

Most of the magic for performing a SOAP request and obtaining its results go in an accessor key rate. Use a WOString to display it and set a *numberFormatter* to display it to at least three decimal places.

```java
/*
 * accessor
 */
public Float rate() {
    // Set encoding style. Use the standard SOAP encoding
    Call call = new Call();
    call.setEncodingStyleURI(Constants.NS_URI_SOAP_ENC);

    // Set service locator parameters
    call.setTargetObjectURI("urn:xmethods-CurrencyExchange");
    call.setMethodName("getRate");

    // Create the input parameter vector
    Vector parameters = new Vector();
    parameters.addElement(new Parameter("country1", String.class, from, null));
    parameters.addElement(new Parameter("country2", String.class, to, null));
    call.setParams(parameters);

    // Invoke the service ...
    try {
        URL url = new URL("http://services.xmethods.com:9090/soap");
        Response response = call.invoke(url, "");
        Parameter returnValue = response.getReturnValue();

        return (Float) returnValue.getValue();
    } catch (Exception exception) {
        NSLog.err.appendln("Main: failed to obtain a response");
    } return null;
}
```

Here we use the Apache SOAP API to perform a request to the published SOAP service. So, add the SOAP framework to the project and place the following import statements in the Main class file.

```java
import org.apache.soap.util.xml.*;
import org.apache.soap.*;
import org.apache.soap.rpc.*;
```

Note in particular the arguments required to make a SOAP request are pretty much the same as those used in the SOAP Talk application. You must give it a SOAP endpoint URL, a namespace, a SOAP method, and parameters.

Bind the submit button to a null or void action `calculate`.

Adding Third-Party Jar Files

The Apache SOAP package requires that the *JavaMail* and *Activation* packages be installed on your system.

1. Download the JavaMail package from the Sun Java site at `http://java.sun.com/products/javamail/`.

2. Copy in the `mail.jar` file into */Library/Java/Extensions/*.

3. Similarly, copy in the `activation.jar` from the Third-Party-Jars folder on your WebObjects CD.

Finally, you can build and run the application. See Figure 15.7.

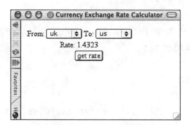

FIGURE 15.7   Running the Currency Exchange Rate Calculator.

Looking at Other Published SOAP Services

The place to look for SOAP services is at the Xmethods site located at `http://www.xmethods.com/`.

Here you will find a list of published SOAP services at your disposal. Often source code to sample client applications is provided, too. So you can use them as a guideline to build the service into your WebObjects application.

Summary

This chapter has been an introduction to building SOAP services with WebObjects and incorporating and leveraging SOAP services in WebObjects Applications.

16

Reports, Charts, and New Interfaces

"Simplicity is the Ultimate Sophistication."

—Leonardo da Vinci

Now it is time to combine some of the XML, Enterprise Objects, JavaScript Interactivity, and SVG concepts we have learned and venture into some new territory for both WebObjects and Web interfaces in general.

We'll explore building new interfaces with the technologies we have encountered in the book so far. In addition, we'll look at how to use WebObjects as a generator for print as well as the Web.

Generating Print with WebObjects

In the bold, new world of cross-media publishing, it seems that WebObjects may also have a part to play. The idea behind cross-media publishing is to develop content that is reproducible on the Web as well as in print. Ultimately, it is intended that such raw content or content that lacks presentation can be distributed to other devices and presented in other forms as well. This is the "Holy Grail" of the publishing world. However, the most important media outlets, for all intents and purposes, are print and the Web.

Dynamically generated content faces these same or similar kinds of challenges. Often many applications require the generation of PDF content, for billing or invoicing applications for example. In such cases, it makes sense to use the same foundation or even application model to do so. In reality, there isn't much difference between producing an itinerary of purchased items as an HTML page or as a PDF document. Well, there shouldn't be.

So, in this section we'll look at doing just that—producing PDF documents using the same tools and logic we used to produce applications for the Web.

Note, however, that there are several solutions for generating PDF with WebObjects, including various Java PDF-generation packages. However, what we'll look at in this first section is how to generate PDF with WebObjects in much the same way that we produce HTML pages.

Introduction to XSL Formatting Objects

Before we begin, here is a quick overview of the technologies and terms we'll encounter in the chapter.

First of all, a brief explanation of how we'll produce PDF content from WebObjects. PDF is a compact and standard format for producing professional and accurate print-quality documents. The idea behind PDF is that as electronic documents, they are self-contained and can be accurately reproduced on different devices or platforms. This makes PDF an excellent document transfer format for the Web. However, one of the disadvantages of PDF is that it is not a human-readable document format, like HTML or XML. This is important, particularly when we need to generate such documents programmatically.

SVG, or Scalable Vector Graphics, as we saw in Chapter 6, "SVG and WebObjects," is a human-readable XML grammar that is semantically equivalent to PDF, or very similar to PDF, but with one important omission. That is, SVG lacks the support for defining the structure and layout of multipage documents. This is where Formatting Objects comes in.

What Is XSL Formatting Objects?

The W3C standard, *XSL*, or eXtensible Stylesheet Language, consists of two parts: transformation and formatting objects. Here we are concerned only with the latter. Formatting Objects, in other words, is an XML vocabulary for the presentation of a document.

You can use it to describe the page size, margins, fonts, color, and textual details of a document. In fact, as a language it is so powerful that it can be daunting to manipulate let alone create by hand. In most cases, you would use a tool such as XML Spy to generate XSL-FO documents for use.

The reference for Formatting Objects can be found at http://www.w3.org/TR/xsl/.

How Can Formatting Objects Be Used to Generate PDF?

The Apache Formatting Object Processor, or FOP for short, is described as a print formatter driven by XSL. Essentially, it is a processor that converts FO documents into PDF and other raster formats.

Because FO documents are essentially XML, we already have a framework within WebObjects that can generate and vend XML quite easily, as we have seen with XHTML and SVG. Formatting Objects is just another XML and just as easy to vend using WebObjects and its tools.

However, generating an FO document alone isn't sufficient. We need to post-process the document and convert it to PDF using the Apache FO processor. There are several ways to do this. It is in fact possible to set up your Web server to post-process documents of the same MIME type as XSL FO, however, for simplicity we'll perform the post-processing from within WebObjects.

More details on the Apache FOP can be found at `http://xml.apache.org/fop/`.

Installing Apache FOP

You can download the latest distribution of FOP from the Apache FOP site at `http://xml.apache.org/fop/download.html`.

Copy the `fop.jar` from the build directory into the standard location for Java extensions. On Mac OS X that is */Library/Java/Extensions*.

In addition, copy the auxiliary packages `batik.jar`, `avalon-framework*.jar`, and `logkit*.jar` from the lib folder into the Java extensions directory as well. You might have to download `mail.jar` from the Sun Java site. Copy it into the Java Extensions directory. Of these packages that are used by the FOP, Batik is of some significance. The FOP uses Batik to process or transform mixed FO and SVG XML documents into PDF.

Generating XSL FO with WebObjects

First of all let's generate a Formatting Object application. After that is completed we can look at transforming the FO into PDF.

Instead of adding this functionality into the forum application directly, we'll start by developing the code and components in isolation. Subsequently, we can incorporate them back into the main application if we want.

Create a new WebObjects Application project titled `ForumReports`. What we are going to create, however, are not really reports, but simple listings of an entire topic as a PDF document. The motivation for this is that for some forums, developer forums for example, it might be useful to have a downloadable listing of the entire discussion or thread. This could be refined further to produce PDF documents of search results, for reference.

Begin by including the Forum framework as you did for the ForumSOAPServer application. Again we are taking advantage of the fact that the forum model was built separately as a framework to share its model between these separate applications.

We'll keep things simple for this first iteration and vend a Formatting Object document without performing the PDF transformation. This is so that we can develop the FO document and components correctly.

Creating a XSL FO WebObjects Component

Create and add a second-page component named TopicArchive. You might want to group the HTML components into a separate group than the FO components. Use the menu item *New Group* from the Project menu to create a project group folder.

Copy the Formatting Objects elements from the TopicArchive.fo from the file download associated with the chapter from the Sams companion Web site (www.samspublishing.com) into the TopicArchive.html template. You will then have to mark up the document to generate a list of posts for a topic.

```
<?xml version="1.0" encoding="utf-8"?>

<fo:root xmlns:fo="http://www.w3.org/1999/XSL/Format">

    <!-- defines the layout master -->
    <fo:layout-master-set>
      <fo:simple-page-master master-name="first"
                             page-height="29.7cm"
                             page-width="21cm"
                             margin-top="1cm"
                             margin-bottom="2cm"
                             margin-left="2.5cm"
                             margin-right="2.5cm">
        <fo:region-body margin-top="3cm"/>
        <fo:region-before extent="3cm"/>
        <fo:region-after extent="1.5cm"/>
      </fo:simple-page-master>
    </fo:layout-master-set>

    <!-- starts actual layout -->
    <fo:page-sequence master-reference="first">

    <fo:flow flow-name="xsl-region-body">

        <!-- this defines a title level 1-->
      <fo:block id="sec0"
```

```
                text-align="left"
                font-family="Helvetica"
                font-weight="bold"
                font-size="18pt"
                color="#0050B2" space-after.optimum="6pt">
          Topic: <webobject name=TopicName></webobject>
      </fo:block>

<webobject name=PostRepetition>
    <!-- post made by, date, etc...-->
    <fo:block font-family="Helvetica"
              font-weight="bold"
              space-after.optimum="6pt"
              space-before.optimum="11pt" >
      <webobject name=Username></webobject> @ <webobject name=Timestamp></webobject>
    </fo:block>

    <!-- post text -->
    <fo:block space-after.optimum="6pt">
      <webobject name=Message></webobject>
    </fo:block>

</webobject>

    </fo:flow>
  </fo:page-sequence>
</fo:root>
```

Add a topic key and a post key as EOEnterpriseObject variables.

Set up the WebObjects definitions as follows:

```
Timestamp: WOString {
    value = post.timestamp;
    dateformat = "%X %x";
}

Message: WOString {
    escapeHTML = false;
    value = message;
}
```

```
PostRepetition: WORepetition {
    item = post;
    list = topic.posts;
}

TopicName: WOString {
    value = topic.name;
}

Username: WOString {
    value = post.user.name;
}
```

Note that this time we are not using a display group as a controller. This is because the Archive is a complete listing of a `topic.posts`; therefore, a display group becomes unnecessary.

Finally, set the response content type header to `text/xml` so that we can use the browser's native XML viewer. Internet Explorer 5, for example, has an XML viewer that will display the XML source in the browser. This will be useful to check that we are generating correct XSL FO documents.

```
/*
 * request/response
 */
public void appendToResponse(WOResponse response, WOContext context) {
    response.setHeader("text/xml", "Content-Type");

    // generate PDF response
    super.appendToResponse(response, context);
}
```

In the Main page, add a hyperlink bound to a direct action called posts. This is very similar to the `postsAction` we created for the online forum.

```
public WOActionResults postsAction() {
    WOComponent nextPage = pageWithName("TopicArchive");
    Number topicID = request().numericFormValueForKey("topicID",
new NSNumberFormatter());
    EOEditingContext editingContext = new EOEditingContext();
    EOEnterpriseObject topic = EOUtilities.objectWithPrimaryKeyValue(
editingContext, "Topic", topicID);
```

```
    // set variables
    nextPage.takeValueForKeyPath(topic, "topic");

    return nextPage;
}
```

This application is really to develop the TopicArchive document component and test PDF generation. So, add a form value binding to the link ?topicID and set it to any primary key of a topic that exists in your Forums database.

Build and run, and you should be able to view the FO XML in Internet Explorer 5, as shown in Figure 16.1.

FIGURE 16.1   Viewing a Formatting Object document archive of a Topic in Internet Explorer.

Vending PDF with WebObjects

As you've seen, vending FO documents is pretty straightforward from WebObjects. It is just like vending HTML, XHTML, or SVG.

To turn that FO document into PDF, we need to transform or *serialize* it.

Having installed fop.jar and its auxiliary packages, we can add a FO2PDFSerializer class to the project.

```java
import java.io.*;
import org.apache.fop.apps.*;
import org.w3c.dom.*;
import org.apache.log.*;

public class FO2PDFSerializer extends WOComponent {

    /*
     * constructor
     */
    public FO2PDFSerializer(WOContext context) {
        super(context);
    }

    /*
     * request/response
     */
    public void appendToResponse(WOResponse response, WOContext context) {
        super.appendToResponse(response, context);

        // parse FO tree
        Document document = response.contentAsDOMDocument();
        ByteArrayOutputStream out = new ByteArrayOutputStream();
        Logger log = Hierarchy.getDefaultHierarchy().getLoggerFor("fop");
        Driver driver = new Driver();

        driver.setRenderer(Driver.RENDER_PDF);
        driver.setOutputStream(out);
        driver.setLogger(log);

        // render to PDF
        try { driver.render(document); }
        catch (Exception exception) {
            NSLog.err.appendln("PDF: render: " + exception);
        }

        // set the PDF content and header
        response.setContent(new NSData(out.toByteArray()));
        response.setHeader("application/pdf", "Content-Type");
    }
}
```

First, we generate the FO document by calling `appendToResponse()` on super. Then, it is parsed into a DOM document using the response `contentAsDOMDocument()` method. The resulting DOM document is then rendered into a PDF using the FOP driver method, `render()`. Finally, the PDF content type is set in the header so that the document is identified as having PDF content.

To use the `FO2PDFSerializer`, you will need to change the superclass of the `TopicArchive` component to that of `FO2PDFSerializer`. That's all. Build and run again to churn out your first PDF document from XSL FO components in WebObjects. (See Figure 16.2.)

If you want to set the filename of the PDF document add the following line to the `appendToResponse()` of the `TopicArchive` class:

```
response.setHeader("attachment;filename=\"" + "Archive.pdf" + "\"",
"Content-Disposition");
```

FIGURE 16.2 A sample PDF topic archive viewed in Acrobat Reader.

Incorporating PDF Functions into a WebObjects Application

Next, we'll incorporate the topic archive as a PDF function into the forum application.

Start by copying into the forum application the `FO2PDFSerializer` class and the `TopicArchive` component and associated files. When copying the WebObjects component, recall that you must select Create Folder References to add it correctly into the project.

Separate the direct action logic for the topic archiving by creating a new direct action class named Archive. Copy the code for the postsAction from the ForumReports project into the Archive class, renaming it as the defaultAction.

Now add a direct action link to the Archive/default direct action from the TopicPosts page so that you get a result similar to Figure 16.3. You will have to bind the hyperlink *queryDictionary* to the topicKey to generate the correct direct action URL for the topicID form value.

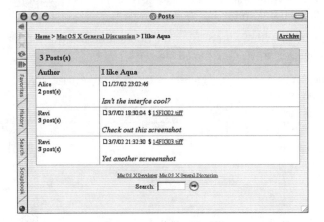

FIGURE 16.3   Incorporate PDF archiving into the forum application.

Build and run the application. You have now successfully incorporated a simple WebObjects PDF function into your application.

Data Visualization with WebObjects

In this section, we'll look at producing nonstandard or new ways of presenting data and information.

With the tools that we have at our disposal, that is, SVG, JavaScript, WebObjects, and even HTML we are in a position to present data in ways other than as a bar, pie, or scatter graph.

Furthermore, the focus of this section is on exploring new ways of presenting data, not a discussion of performance or applicability to any particular Web application be it the online forum or otherwise.

Creating DHTML Charts with WebObjects

The first and simplest method we'll explore is vending HTML graphs of data.

Start by creating a new development project titled ForumCharts. Include the Forum framework so that we can use the forum data source.

Include the link.gif and user.gif from the images directory of the file download associated with the chapter (www.samspublishing.com). As usual for images, copy them into the Web Server Resources group of the project Web Server target.

Open the Main page component and set up a topic display group by dragging in the Topic entity from an open forum model in EOModeler. Layout a table and components as in Figure 16.4 with the two table rows bound in a WORepetition. You will need to add a topic key for the topic repetition. You might want to set the batch limit of the display group to say, 10, if your forum database has quite a few topics. Also set it to fetch on load.

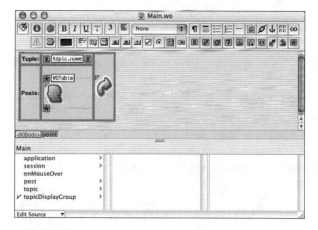

FIGURE 16.4   Layout the HTML Topic Chart as in the figure.

In the second row, place a WOTable. What we want to do here is to display the number of posts graphically. So bind the WOTable *list* to topic.posts and the item to a new variable key you create called post. Inside it, place an image for user.gif. The point of using a WOTable is that a *maxColumns* can be set to wrap the images onto a new row.

In the second column place an image of the link.gif. For now don't bind these to any actions, simply build and run to see the results of generating a simple HTML graph. Figure 16.5 is a sample graph.

Using JavaScript To Add Interactivity

We won't implement anything sophisticated or complex, but instead use an old, but simple, JavaScript trick to indicate which user made a post and when. All we'll do is display the username and timestamp of the post in the browser status bar.

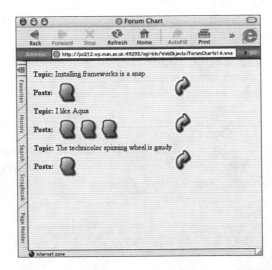

FIGURE 16.5   A Graph of topic posts can be produced with just HTML.

Add a key, onMouseOver, as an accessor to the Main component.

```
public String onMouseOver() {
    String username = (String) post.valueForKeyPath("user.name");
    NSTimestamp timestamp = (NSTimestamp) post.valueForKey("timestamp");
    return "javascript: window.status = '" + username + " @ " + timestamp + "';";
}
```

Add a new binding to the user image *onMouseOver* and bind it to the key of the same name. Add another binding to the image, *onMouseOut*, and make it revert the window status bar message.

```
UserPostImage: WOImage {
    filename = "post.gif";
    onmouseout = "javascript:window.status = '';";
    onmouseover = onMouseOver;
}
```

Now, if you roll your mouse over one of the user images when you build and run the application , the status bar will display the name of the user and the time the post was made.

Graphically Highlighting Moderator Posts
One potentially useful avenue to explore is to differentiate moderator posts from user posts. This is fairly simple to implement.

Add the `moderator.gif` from the images folder of the file download associated with the chapter (available at www.samspublishing.com). Copy the resource into the Web Server Resources group as normal.

Wrap the WebObjects image representing `user.gif` within a WOConditional bound to `post.user.isModerator`. This conditional must be negated (that is, have its *negate* attribute set to `true`) because we display the image for a user post only if a normal user made the post. Set up a similar conditionally bound image representing `moderator.gif` without the conditional negation. Compare your results with Figure 16.6.

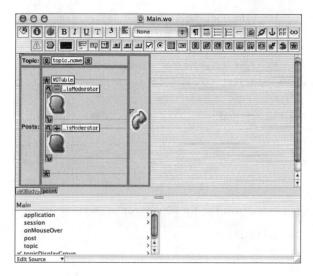

FIGURE 16.6   Use WOConditionals to display the respective image for a Moderator and a User.

Building a HTML Bar Graph Component

Our intentions for this section are not so much at looking how to produce traditional graphs such as bar graphs, pie charts, and so on, but looking at producing nonstandard presentation of data like we did for topics versus posts. Sometimes, subtle customizations can help to present data in more meaningful ways than with traditional techniques. However, we'll make one exception here. That is, we'll look at producing an HTML bar graph more or less as an exercise. This might prove to be useful later.

Essentially, we'll construct a bar graph from tables. Each bar can be composed of a table of two cells: one representing the bar and the other white space. All of the bars are formatted and wrapped as table rows.

Start by creating a test or development project `WOHorizontalBarGraphTest`. Add a new component to the project to represent the bar graph `WOHorizontalBarGraph` layout as demonstrated in the HTML template as follows:

```
<table border=0 cellspacing=1 cellpadding=1>
    <webobject name=BarRepetition>
      <tr>
        <td><font size=2><webobject name=LabelString></webobject></font></td>
        <td>
          <table border=0 cellpadding=0 cellspacing=0>
            <tr>
              <td><webobject name=bargraph_left></webobject></td>
              <td><webobject name=bargraph_bar></webobject></td>
              <td><webobject name=bargraph_right></webobject></td>
              <td><font size=2> <webobject
name=ValueString></webobject></font></td>
            </tr>
          </table>
        </td>
      </tr>
    </webobject>
</table>
```

The WebObjects Declaration file for `WOHorizontalBarGraph`:

```
BarRepetition: WORepetition {
    item = item;
    list = ^list;
}

LabelString: WOString {
    value = label;
}

ValueString: WOString {
    value = value;
}

bargraph_bar: WOImage {
    filename = "bargraph_bar.gif";
    height = 14;
    width = width;
}
```

```
bargraph_left: WOImage {
    filename = "bargraph_left.gif";
}

bargraph_right: WOImage {
    filename = "bargraph_right.gif";
}
```

Note that you will need to copy into the project the three images bargraph.gif, bargraph_left.gif, bargraph_right.gif from the file download associated with the chapter.

The WOHorizontalBarGraph has been designed specifically with enterprise objects in mind, therefore we'll take advantage of key value coding to set the graph labels and values. Use the API Editor to give the component an API: *list* (required), *valueKey* (required), *labelKey*, and *max, min*. Although not essential, the last two keys are needed to display well-proportioned graphs.

Make the component stateless and define the following keys as accessors: width, value, label, labelKey, valueKey, max, min.

```
/*
 * accessors
 */
public int width() {
    return (value()/(max() - min()))*100;
}

public int value() {
    Number value = (Number) item.valueForKey(valueKey());
    return value.intValue();
}

    public String label() {
        return (labelKey() != null) ? (String) item.valueForKey(labelKey()): null;
    }

    public String labelKey() {
        return (String) valueForBinding("labelKey");
    }

    public String valueKey() {
        return (String) valueForBinding("valueKey");
    }
```

```
public int max() {
    Number max = (Number) valueForBinding("max");
    return (max != null) ? max.intValue(): 100;
}

public int min() {
    Number min = (Number) valueForBinding("min");
    return (min != null) ? min.intValue(): 0;
}
```

Now, to test the component in action, we will use the Forum model again for data, so add the framework to the project. Set up a `topicsDisplayGroup` again to fetch on load. Then, add a WOHorizontalBarGraph component to the Main page.

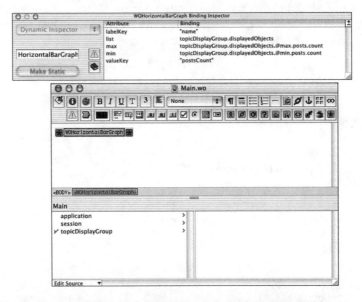

FIGURE 16.7   Bind the WOHorizontalBarGraph in WebObjects Builder.

Build and run the application. You should get a graph display similar to Figure 16.8.

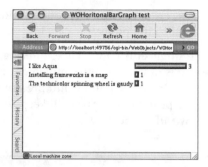

FIGURE 16.8   Vend a simple HTML graph.

Developing New Interfaces with WebObjects: The PopIdol App

Finally, we come to the crux of this chapter: Developing new interfaces with WebObjects.

With the advent of Internet-inspired television programs such as Big Brother, the melding of media began to take on a new shape. Television was beginning to draw a different audience to the Web. Along with them came the desire and the need to present interfaces in new ways, or in ways more familiar to them. Interactivity, simplicity, visually rich are qualities becoming necessary for graphic interfaces on the Web.

Hot on the heels of the very popular Big Brother Internet-TV series in Europe and the United States, came the Pop Idol show. Here a few contestants are selected to live and work together to become pop stars. Every week one contested would be voted off, and in the end the remaining contestant is crowned Pop Idol.

Several million viewers in the UK called in to place their votes. As these television programs inspired by the Internet become more popular, Web developers are challenged to produce a compelling Internet experience to complement the TV show. However, disappointingly there was no online voting.

What we are going to do in this section is build a simple voting/polling app for Pop Idol.

Building the PopIdol App

Let's start by creating a simple database for Pop Idol, so we can keep track of votes. Open OpenBase Manager and create a new database called PopIdol, and start it.

Create a new project called `PopIdol`. Open EOModeler and create a new model to the `PopIdol` database and save it to the project.

The model consists of the single entity Idol. Give it a `name`, `votes`, and a `primary` key. The purpose of the exercise is not so much to implement a proper fully functional voting application, but to develop the polling and presentation interface with WebObjects, SVG, and enterprise objects. So, we'll keep things simple and model votes as a number, as shown in Figure 16.9.

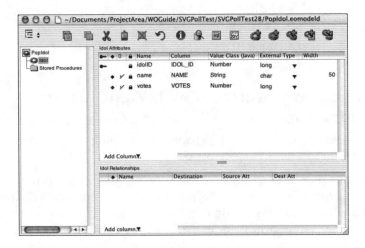

FIGURE 16.9   Model the Pop Idol.

From OpenBase Manager add two rows for the two final Pop Idol contestants. See Figure 16.10.

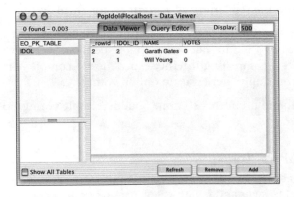

FIGURE 16.10   Add two idols to the database.

Include the SVGObjects framework in the project. We'll be using SVG for the main interface. Copy in the `popidol_title.gif` into the project from the file download associated with the chapter. Open the Main page and place the image center. Then, place a WOSVG element with width and height of 500. Set its *pageName* to `PopIdol`.

Next, we'll create an SVG page called `PopIdol`. Add the component to the project and copy the SVG from the file `PopIdol.svg` into the HTML template. The graphic was created and saved to the Web with Adobe Illustrator 10.

```
<?xml version="1.0" encoding="utf-8"?>
<!-- Generator: Adobe Illustrator 10, SVG Export Plug-In .
SVG Version: 3.0.0 Build 76)-->
<!DOCTYPE svg PUBLIC "-//W3C//DTD SVG 1.0//EN"
    "http://www.w3.org/TR/2001/REC-SVG-20010904/DTD/svg10.dtd" [
    <!ENTITY ns_flows "http://ns.adobe.com/Flows/1.0/">
    <!ENTITY ns_extend "http://ns.adobe.com/Extensibility/1.0/">
    <!ENTITY ns_ai "http://ns.adobe.com/AdobeIllustrator/10.0/">
    <!ENTITY ns_svg "http://www.w3.org/2000/svg">
    <!ENTITY ns_xlink "http://www.w3.org/1999/xlink">
]>
<svg  xmlns:x="&ns_extend;" xmlns:i="&ns_ai;" xmlns:graph="&ns_graphs;"
    xmlns="&ns_svg;" xmlns:xlink="&ns_xlink;"
  xmlns:a="http://ns.adobe.com/AdobeSVGViewerExtensions/3.0/"
  width="624" height="574"
    viewBox="-0.207 -0.078 624 574" overflow="visible"
  enable-background="new -0.207 -0.078 624 574" xml:space="preserve">
  <g id="Layer_1_2_" transform="scale(1.6)">
      <g>
          <defs>
              <path id="XMLID_2_" d="M312.304,359.0291-87.
➡311-71.6511-105.388,39.76137.548-114.9431-64.389-96.4621110.512,0.616
➡165.594-99.376130.755,115.3241104.923,35.042191.503,70.659L312.304,359.029z"/>
          </defs>
          <clipPath id="XMLID_4_">
              <use xlink:href="#XMLID_2_" />
          </clipPath>
          <g>
              <g>
                  <defs>
                      <path id="XMLID_6_"
d="M21.8,356.418L31.425,01382.499,10.361L404.3,366.78L21.8,356.418z"/>
                  </defs>
                  <clipPath id="XMLID_8_" clip-path="url(#XMLID_4_)">
```

```
                        <use xlink:href="#XMLID_6_" />
                    </clipPath>
                    <g transform="matrix(1 1.513335e-09 2.298206e-09 1
➥-3.814697e-06 -6.911989e-08)" clip-path="url(#XMLID_8_)">

                            <image width="462" height="400"
                            id="XMLID_10_" xlink:href="4DCEDA6.jpg"
                            transform="matrix(0.8279 0.0224 -0.0241 0.891 31.4253
0)"/>
                    </g>
                </g>
            </g>
        </g>
        <g>
            <path d="M623.438,440.373l-114.242,25.283l-44.711,108.125l-58.
➥453-100.469l-116.446-8.168l78.114-87.377l-27.252-113.173
➥l106.729,46.468l99.604-61.776l-12.152,116.095L623.438,440.373z"/>
            <g>
                <defs>
                    <path id="XMLID_9_" d="M623.495,440.451l-
➥114.242,25.285L464.54,573.859l-58.454-100.469l-116.444-
➥8.168l78.114-87.375l-27.254-113.174l106.731,46.468l99.602-
➥61.777l-12.152,116.096L623.495,440.451z"/>
                </defs>
                <clipPath id="XMLID_12_">
                    <use xlink:href="#XMLID_9_" />
                </clipPath>
                <g>
                    <g>
                        <defs>
                            <path id="XMLID_11_"
d="M0,517.021l116.048-330.636l533.57,25.897l-16.049,330.635L0,517.021z"/>
                        </defs>
                        <clipPath id="XMLID_13_" clip-path="url(#XMLID_12_)">
                            <use xlink:href="#XMLID_11_" />
                        </clipPath>
                        <g transform="matrix(1 -2.799101e-09
➥-3.035266e-09 1 1.907349e-06 0)" clip-path="url(#XMLID_13_)">

                                <image width="540" height="346"
id="XMLID_14_" xlink:href="4DCEDA7.jpg"
transform="matrix(0.9881 0.048 -0.0464 0.9556 16.0479 186.3857)"/>
```

```
                    </g>
                </g>
            </g>
        </g>
    </g>
</g>
</svg>
```

The first thing you must do is copy the pictures for the two Pop Idols into the Web Server Resources of the project. They are gareth.jpg and will.jpg, which can also be found in the file download associated with the chapter (available at www. samspublishing.com). Then, use SOImage to display the images. That is, make the two <image> elements dynamic. This might involve performing this task by hand, copying the individual attributes manually into a dynamic equivalent.

Remember to add the image/svg-xml header to the response in the PopIdol SVG component:

```
public void appendToResponse(WOResponse response, WOContext context) {
    super.appendToResponse(response, context);

    // set the header
    response.setHeader("image/svg-xml", "Content-Type");
}
```

At this point it would be useful to build and run the application to test that the images display correctly.

Next, we'll add two actions to the PopIdol component so that a user can click their favorite idol to vote for him. For now add the two actions voteGarath and voteWill by simply returning the Main page. We need to add the two XLINK hyperlinks to the SVG component. Locate the <g> element, which is highlighted in the previous PopIdol template listing. Wrap each group around two WXHyperlink elements. Set the actions to voteGarath and voteWill, respectively.

Now build and run again to check that the actions on the SVG image are working correctly. Let's implement the logic to increment the vote of the idol back to the database.

```
/*
 * actions
 */
public WOComponent voteGarath() {
    int votes = ((Number) valueForKeyPath("session.garath.votes")).intValue();
```

```
        // increment the votes
        takeValueForKeyPath(new Integer(++votes), "session.garath.votes");

        // save to database
        session().defaultEditingContext().saveChanges();

        // debug
        NSLog.debug.appendln("PopIdol: vote cast: garath");

        return pageWithName("Main");
    }

    public WOComponent voteWill() {
        int votes = ((Number) valueForKeyPath("session.will.votes")).intValue();

        // increment the votes
        takeValueForKeyPath(new Integer(++votes), "session.will.votes");

        // save to database
        session().defaultEditingContext().saveChanges();

        // debug
        NSLog.debug.appendln("PopIdol: vote cast: will");

        return pageWithName("Main");
    }
```

We manage the voting in the session. Add the two variable keys garath and will to Session as EOEnterpriseObjects. In the session constructor, fetch the two objects:

```
garath = EOUtilities.objectMatchingKeyAndValue(defaultEditingContext(),
"Idol", "name", "Garath Gates");
will = EOUtilities.objectMatchingKeyAndValue(defaultEditingContext(),
"Idol", "name", "Will Young");
```

Again, it would be useful to check that the two actions increment the votes of the two idols before proceeding to the next step.

Now, what we have implemented so far could have been done without SVG. The aim of using SVG was so that we could use the same single page or interface to perform the voting as well as presenting the results as a chart. In other words, we will create a truly interactive chart.

Add `totalVotes`, an accessor to Session:

```
public int totalVotes() {
    int votes_garath = ((Number) will.valueForKey("votes")).intValue();
    int votes_will = ((Number) will.valueForKey("votes")).intValue();

    return votes_garath + votes_will;
}
```

Then, make the two highlighted <g> tags dynamic, that is, convert them to SOGroup elements. Add the two accessors `transform_will` and `transform_garath` to the PopIdol component.

```
public String transform_will() {
        float total = ((Number) valueForKeyPath("session.totalVotes")).float-
Value();
        float votes = ((Number) valueForKeyPath("session.will.votes")).float-
Value();
        float scale = votes/total;

        return "scale(" + scale + ")";
    }

    public String transform_garath() {
        float total = ((Number) valueForKeyPath("session.totalVotes")).float-
Value();
        float votes = ((Number) valueForKeyPath("sesssion.garath.votes")).float-
Value();
        float scale = votes/total;

        return "scale(" + scale + ")";
    }
```

Change the transform attribute of the two SOGroups to use the two keys `transform_will` and `transform_garath`. Now the two Pop Idols will be displayed proportionally. The one with more votes will appear larger than the other, in real time. That is, each time you click a Pop Idol to vote, the resulting chart is displayed instantaneously. See Figure 16.11 for the application in action.

FIGURE 16.11   Vote for your favorite idol.

Summary

In this chapter we have looked at producing alternative media with WebObjects, be it PDF for print or interactive SVG interfaces with WebObjects for new media applications.

17

Stress Testing and Deploying Applications

"If at first you don't succeed, then dust yourself off and try again."

—from the song "Try Again" by Aaliya.

To wrap up the book, I'll present some practical and useful techniques that are often necessary to test and deploy an application.

Testing Deployment

This book would be incomplete without some description of deploying an application with WebObjects. So, in this section we'll learn how to use the WebObjects monitor to deploy applications. In fact, it will be necessary when we stress test an application.

Introduction to Deploying Applications

For a thorough description and overview of deploying WebObjects applications refer the *Deploying WebObjects Application* reference, which can be found online from the WebObjects Documentation site:

```
http://developer.apple.com/techpubs/webobjects/
DeployingWebObjects/index.html
```

Here we'll take a brief look at what is involved in deploying an application such as the online forum. Let's jump right in.

Starting Up and Configuring WebObjects Monitor

Locate the WebObjects Monitor at */System/Library/ WebObjects/JavaApplications/JavaMoitor.woa* and double click it to launch it. This assumes that you do not have the

WebObjects deployment package installed and have Monitor auto-configured to start. In addition, the Apache Web Server should be running.

First, we need to set up your machine as a WebObjects host.

1. Click the Hosts tab in the WebObjects Monitor window.

2. Type localhost or the network name of your machine and click Add Hosts to submit. Then, Monitor will add localhost to the host's list, as shown in Figure 17.1.

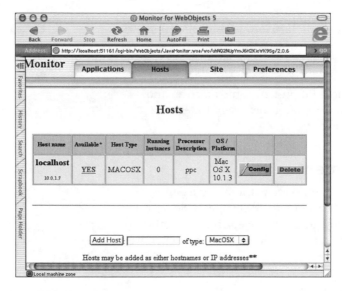

FIGURE 17.1   Add a host to Monitor.

Adding an Application to Monitor

Now we can add the Forum application to Monitor. First, install the Forum application if you haven't already done so. Refer back to the "Installing WebObjects Applications" section in Chapter 14, "Security, Logging, and Statistics."

1. Click the Applications tab to open the Applications panel.

2. Type Forum in the Add Application Named text field, then click the Add Application submit button. This will take you to the Application Configuration page.

3. Under the New Instance Defaults set the Path by clicking the Path Wizard button. Click a machine/host name and proceed to the path wizard screen.

Navigate to the location of the application. If it is already installed, it will be found in */Library/WebObjects/Applications*. See Figure 17.2. When you select the application executable, make sure that you choose the executable inside the woa application wrapper directory. For example: */Library/WebObjects/Applications/ForumPrototype2.woa/ForumPrototype2*.

4. Finally, click the Push All button to submit the values.

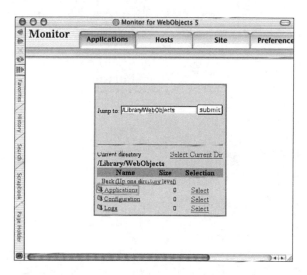

FIGURE 17.2   Set the application path using the Path Wizard.

5. For now we won't look at any of the other application configuration settings. Click the Detail View to proceed and add an application instance to Monitor.

6. Click the Add button. You should see an instance added to the Application Detail Page, as in Figure 17.3.

Starting Application Instances

Starting and stopping an application is pretty straightforward. Click the green button in the start/stop column. Then, wait a few minutes before refreshing the browser window.

After the application has been successfully started, the status toggle icon will change to on. You should then be able to click the Forum link to open a browser to the deployed Forum application.

Fault Tolerance and Load-Balancing in WebObjects

The WebObjects application architecture is such that you can deploy several more instances of an application if you want to. In fact, you could deploy application servers on more than one machine. This leaves the Web server acting as a funnel, channeling requests to the WebObjects application to the various instances of an application on separate machines as required.

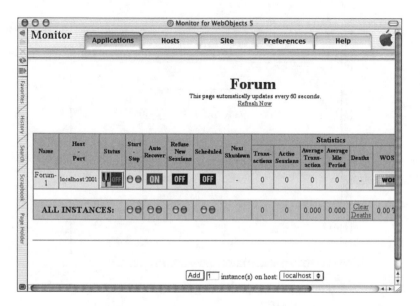

FIGURE 17.3   Add an application instance from the Detail View.

Adding a Second Instance

Adding a second instance is just as simple as adding the first. Navigate to the Detail View of the application in Monitor. Click the Add button to add a second instance of the Forum application.

See Figure 17.4, and notice that the second instance is given a different port number. Each application instance communicates with the Web Server and its WebObjects adaptor via these unique port numbers.

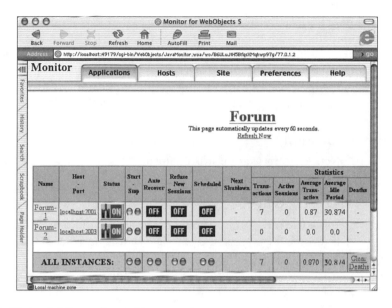

FIGURE 17.4 Adding a Second Instance is a snap.

Stress Testing Applications

Now we'll take a look at a very important part of deployment testing. If you are uncertain how your application will fair live, it can be comforting to perform what is known as stress testing or load testing.

Introduction to Stress Testing in WebObjects

We attempt to simulate a live application deployment in a stress test. You will have to make an estimate of how many users that you might experience on average. In particular, it is helpful to make an estimate of the load the application server might experience at launch because this is likely to be several times greater than average. Also, it is perhaps better to prepare for an application launch because first impressions are very important. You probably don't want to give your users the idea that the site or service is sluggish.

The way we stress test an application is by first making a *recording* of a typical user interacting with the site. Then, a simulated Web client plays back this recording.

You can then simulate several users accessing the site by running multiple playback clients. We'll look at both tests.

There are, however, some limitations of the tools used to stress test an application. That is, the simulated sessions are usually just one or one set of recorded sessions being played back. It doesn't mimic the sometimes random and spurious usage that some users can put your site through. Nevertheless, don't let this stop you from trying out some of these tests with your application. If for nothing else do it for peace of mind and a good night's sleep before you go live; if that is indeed possible.

Recording a Session

Launch WebObjects Monitor again if it isn't already.

1. From the Applications panel click the Forum application's Config button to go to the application configuration screen.

2. Under the New Instance Defaults scroll down to the Additional Arguments and enter `-WORecordingPath`, `/tmp`, and `WOConcurrentRequestHandling false`, as in Figure 17.5. Press Push to submit the defaults.

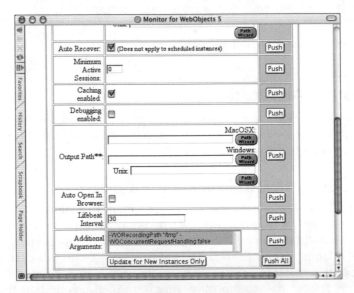

FIGURE 17.5   Set the application to record a user session.

3. Click Details View button to be taken back to the list of application instances set up for Forum. Start up just one application instance by clicking on the green button in the start/stop column. You might need to restart the application instance if it was running already.

4. After the application has been started open a browser window to the Forum application by clicking on the Forum link.

5. From now on every request made is being recorded as a session. So, emulate the average user performing some tasks. Try a search, and click a few forum topics and posts. Keep your first recording simple. After you are done, close the browser window and stop the instance.

6. Finally, return to the Forum configuration screen and remove the additional arguments. Then, restart both application instances.

Playing a Recording

Now that we've recorded a session, we can play it back to the Forum application. For this we use the Playback Manager client application.

1. From the command line (that is, Terminal.app) navigate to the client side package directory of Playback Manager:

   ```
   > cd /System/Library/WebObjects/JavaApplications/JavaPlaybackManager.woa/
   Contents/Resources/ClientSideJava.framework/Resources/Java
   ```

2. To startup the Playback session, type:

   ```
   > java -classpath clientsidejava.jar com.apple.client.playback.Playback
   -r /tmp/Forum.rec/
   ```

3. The Playback client will then produce some output like the following:

   ```
   ========= STARTING PLAYBACK TOOL ========
   URL base is http://localhost:80/cgi-bin/WebObjects
   Playing recording indefinitely.
   Playing without sleeping.
   Diff'ing received and recorded responses to a + or - 5% match.
   Will not save failures.
   Loaded 0000-request(645)
   Loaded 0000-response(3054)
   Loaded 0001-request(731)
   Loaded 0001-response(2406)
   Loaded 0002-request(803)
   Loaded 0002-response(2522)
   Loaded 0003-request(746)
   Loaded 0003-response(3054)
   Loaded 0004-request(796)
   Loaded 0004-response(2406)
   Loaded 0005-request(797)
   Loaded 0005-response(3054)
   Loaded 0006-request(748)
   ```

```
Loaded 0006-response(1449)
Loaded 0007-request(893)
Loaded 0007-response(2455)
Loaded 0008-request(801)
Loaded 0008-response(3054)

---- Beginning New Playback (Mon Mar 25 20:50:37 GMT 2002) ----
0: Request 0 - 4.916 sec. Average 0.0 Bytes 3069 / 3069 . PASSED.
1: Request 1 - 5.08 sec. Average 4.916 Bytes 2378 / 2378 . PASSED.
2: Request 2 - 1.222 sec. Average 4.998 Bytes 2494 / 2494 . PASSED.
3: Request 3 - 0.261 sec. Average 3.739 Bytes 3069 / 3069 . PASSED.
4: Request 4 - 0.533 sec. Average 2.869 Bytes 2378 / 2378 . PASSED.
5: Request 5 - 0.07 sec. Average 2.402 Bytes 3069 / 3069 . PASSED.
6: Request 6 - 0.266 sec. Average 2.013 Bytes 1292 / 1292 . PASSED.
7: Request 7 - 0.406 sec. Average 1.764 Bytes 2384 / 2384 . PASSED.
8: Request 8 - 0.084 sec. Average 1.594 Bytes 3069 / 3069 . PASSED.
9: Request 0 - 0.022 sec. Average 1.426 Bytes 3069 / 3069 . PASSED.
10: Request 1 - 0.085 sec. Average 1.286 Bytes 2378 / 2378 . PASSED.
11: Request 2 - 0.607 sec. Average 1.176 Bytes 2494 / 2494 . PASSED.
12: Request 3 - 0.021 sec. Average 1.129 Bytes 3069 / 3069 . PASSED.
13: Request 4 - 0.097 sec. Average 1.044 Bytes 2378 / 2378 . PASSED.
14: Request 5 - 0.084 sec. Average 0.976 Bytes 3069 / 3069 . PASSED.
15: Request 6 - 0.253 sec. Average 0.916 Bytes 1292 / 1292 . PASSED.
16: Request 7 - 0.315 sec. Average 0.875 Bytes 2384 / 2384 . PASSED.
17: Request 8 - 0.022 sec. Average 0.842 Bytes 3069 / 3069 . PASSED.
18: Request 0 - 0.069 sec. Average 0.796 Bytes 3069 / 3069 . PASSED.
19: Request 1 - 0.101 sec. Average 0.758 Bytes 2378 / 2378 . PASSED.
20: Request 2 - 0.118 sec. Average 0.725 Bytes 2494 / 2494 . PASSED.
21: Request 3 - 0.022 sec. Average 0.696 Bytes 3069 / 3069 . PASSED.
22: Request 4 - 0.068 sec. Average 0.666 Bytes 2378 / 2378 . PASSED.
23: Request 5 - 0.018 sec. Average 0.64 Bytes 3069 / 3069 . PASSED.
24: Request 6 - 0.076 sec. Average 0.614 Bytes 1292 / 1292 . PASSED.
25: Request 7 - 0.134 sec. Average 0.592 Bytes 2384 / 2384 . PASSED.
```

4. Press Ctrl-C to terminate the Playback session whenever you want to stop the client application.

Starting Up a Second Playback Client

It is simple enough to set up two or more clients by opening a new Terminal window and starting up a client as you did before. So, start up a second Playback client as described previously.

Now return to the WebObjects Monitor screen for the Forum application, as in Figure 17.6. Notice how the number of transactions is logged as roughly even. This is a result of the load balancing in WebObjects.

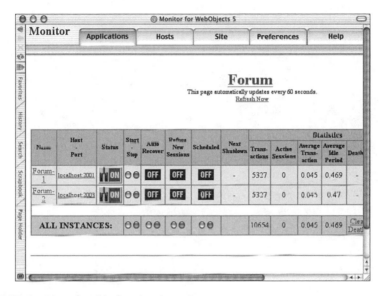

FIGURE 17.6   Note load balancing in action.

Summary

In this chapter we have looked at basic application deployment using WebObjects Monitor and how to stress test an application.

Conclusion

Now in its fifth revision, WebObjects as we have demonstrated, has much to offer in the brave new world of XML, cross-media publishing, and Web services by integrating with technologies such as SOAP, XHTML, SVG, and SMIL.

Having come to the end of the book, I hope that you have started to develop an appreciation for WebObjects and its technologies. This is just as important as learning the concepts and paradigms of WebObjects and as mastering its principles. In addition, I hope that Enterprise Objects has proved to be a compelling solution for modeling sophisticated, but simple applications for the Web.

Further Reading

For further assistance start with Appendix B, "Developer Resources," where you will find a slew of Web sites and pointers to documentation as well as articles to guide and assist you further.

A

Troubleshooting Guide

Here is a compilation of solutions to problems you might encounter when working through the book. In addition, please check the WebObjects 5 release notes for bugs and possible workarounds.

Building Applications

If your project fails to build for some reason, try the following solutions.

Problem: Build Silently Fails

Stop the application, and then build and run again. If the problem still persists, you might want to clean the index. Select the project in the Files tab, and choose Show Info from the Project menu. Click the Rebuild Index button.

Error: Build Fails

Projects will not build if any folder it is in contains a space. For example, a project in *~/Project Folder/WOGuide/Forum* will not build.

Build Warning: Deprecated API

There can be several places where deprecated API is used. Try the following:

1. If the class is a *WOComponent*, make sure that the (*WOContext*) single argument default constructor is defined.

2. Use `stringFormValueflorKey`, `numberFormValueforKey` instead of the depreciated `formValueforKey`.

3. Try using `NSLog.out.appendln` instead of `logString` and
`NSLog.debug.appendln` in place of `debugString`.

Exception: java.lang.NumberFormatException

It might be that a form value in a direct action hasn't been bound properly or parsed correctly. Check that form values bound in the WebObjects components have the ? prefix if appropriate.

Note/Warning: Do Not Use name as a WOComponent Key

The key `name` is already defined as a method on *WOComponent*. It returns the name or class of the component.

Running Applications

Here is a list of problems you might encounter when running applications:

- **Problem: Pages are not updated in a Web browser**—You might need to refresh/reload the page. Otherwise, flush the browser cache as it could cache an older version of a page.

- **Problem/Limitation: Cookie mechanism not working**—The Cookie storage mechanism might not work if network configuration changes. For example, if you were to use your laptop from home, and then on your office network, cookie details will have to be captured twice.

Using EOModeler

Here are some issues you might encounter with EOModeler:

- **Problem: EOModeler fails to see a back-relationship when using multiple model files**—When manually adding a JOIN table to a many-to-many relationship between entities in separate model files, add the JOIN table to one model file before opening the second model file.

- **Note: When using derived attributes**—Remember to include the surrounding () in the SQL for the subselect statements.

B

Developer Resources and Tools for WebObjects

Here is a list of resources for learning more about WebObjects.

Developer Documentation

WebObjects comes with both softcopy and hardcopy documentation. However, the most important and up-to-date version is the online documentation:

```
http://developer.apple.com/techpubs/webobjects/
webobjects.html
```

API Reference

You will find the reference for the WebObjects API here:

```
http://developer.apple.com/techpubs/webobjects/
Reference/Javadoc/index.html
```

```
http://developer.apple.com/techpubs/webobjects/
Reference/DynamicElements/index.html
```

Online Books and Manuals

For a thorough discussion of deploying WebObjects applications, look at the manual "Deploying WebObjects Applications:"

```
http://developer.apple.com/techpubs/webobjects/
DeployingWebObjects/index.html
```

Developer Help Center

Choose Developer Help Center from the Help menu in Project Builder. This will bring up the Developer Help Center application.

Release Notes

These can be very helpful if you encounter a problem. The release notes indicate if what you are experiencing is in fact a known bug or not and can give you information on workarounds or solutions to the problems.

```
http://developer.apple.com/techpubs/webobjects/ReleaseNotes/ReleaseNotes.
html
```

Current Patch List

```
http://docs.info.apple.com/article.html?artnum=70037
```

Apple KnowledgeBase

Apple frequently posts bug reports, updates, and commonly asked questions relating WebObjects here. It is the place to look if you cannot find what you are looking for in the release notes.

```
http://kbase.info.apple.com/cgi-bin/WebObjects/kbase.woa
```

Mailing Lists and Discussions

The most informative mailing list is `webobjects-dev@omnigroup.com`. You can subscribe or view the list archives online at

```
http://www.omnigroup.com/developer/mailinglists/webobjects-dev/
```

There is a very helpful WebObjects developer community that might be able to assist with a question. So feel free to post a question to the mailing list if all else fails.

WebObjects Newbies Yahoo! Group

If you are starting out with WebObjects and have a question, this might be the more appropriate place to post rather than the webobjects-dev mailing list, which is intended for more advanced developers.

```
http://groups.yahoo.com/group/webobjects-newbies/
```

Apple WebObjects Discussion Forum

Another place to post messages is the Apple WebObjects Discussion.

```
http://discussions.info.apple.com/
```

Third-Party Developer Web Sites

There are a host of third-party developer sites that have a wealth of expertise and information that might be useful.

Stepwise

Your first port of call should be Stepwise, which has a history of providing WebObjects developer tutorials and articles in a timely manner.

```
http://www.stepwise.com
```

Apple Developer Connection

Apple's ADC Web site provides sample code, news, and updates on WebObjects:

```
http://developer.apple.com/webobjects/
```

Other Sites

Here are some other sites that also provide more specific expertise:

SVGObjects
Tutorials and articles on developing SVG/FO in WebObjects applications:

```
http://www.svgobjects.com
```

WODev
```
http://www.wodev.com/
```

WOCode
```
http://www.wocode.com
```

Project Wonder
```
http://sourceforge.net/projects/wonder
```

Tales of WO
```
http://www.talesofwo.com/
```

Missing Link
```
http://www.darwinlinux.com/
```

Examples and Source Code

In */Developer/Examples/JavaWebObjects/* you will find a host of example WebObjects applications, frameworks, and components. These are an excellent source for developers. Use these examples as a guide on how to develop with particular technologies of WebObjects. Also pay attention to style and approach.

Object Modeling

Look at the JavaBusinessLogic framework example for basic object modeling. For more advanced modeling examples look at WOInheritanceExample and SophisticatedDatabaseExample.

Handling Long Responses

Use the LongRequest example as a guide to set up and use your own long response page.

Localization

The HelloWorld application is an example of a standard (nondirect action) localized application.

WebObjects Components

The JavaWOExtensions framework under the Source directory is the source to several standard WebObjects components. Use them as a guide to develop your own if and when you need to.

Index

Symbols

A

cross-media publishing, 283

cross model relationships

defining, 165

testing, 166

cryptograms, encoding, 267

cryptography, Java, 266

ciphertext accommodations, 267-268

Cryptography Architecture, 267-268

databases, altering, 268

encoding and encrypting, comparing, 267

Enterprise Object values, encrypting, 268-270

object models, 267

cryptosystems, application logins, 250

curly braces ({ }), 47

currency exchange rate calculator service (SOAP), 280-282

custom classes

Enterprise Objects

creating, 154

when not to use, 157-158

names in EOModeler, 154

custom error pages, exception handling, 246

custom logs, CLFF Web site, 265

custom WebObject elements, adding to components, 106

customizing

applications with DirectToWeb Assistant, 149-151

DirectToWeb, 149-152

CustomLog statement, changing lines, 264

D

D2WcustomComponent, password fields, 164

da Vinci, Leonardo, 283

data

data, raw rows, 198

blob attribute, 217

visualization

DHTML (Dynamic HTML) charts, 292-295

HTML (Hypertext Markup Language) bar graphs, building, 295-298

Database menu commands, New, 111

databaseEncoding key, 267

databases

altering, 268

ciphertexts, accommodating, 267-268

connecting to from JDBC panel, 112

Crazy Eights

creating, 111-112

populating, 119-120

creating, 111

designing, 133

DirectToWeb, changing, 153

encoding, localizing direct-action applications, 70

EOEditingContext controller, 122

object model

files, encoding, 267-268

synchronizing, 153

objects, fetching, 121-122

online forums, setting up, 134

OpenBase Manager, 111, 268

pointers, foreign keys, 136

PopIdol application, 299-305

populated, restoring, 119

relational, 132-133

schemas, OpenBase Manager, 210

SQL (Structured Query Language) naming conventions, 113

tables, creating from EOModeler, 116

Debug icon, 6

files. *See also* PDF

access_log, contents, 261-262

Application.java, 48

archive, 229

attachments, 217-222

CLFF, 260, 265-266

Common Log File Format, 260

declaration, WOHorizontalBarGraph, 296

DirectAction.java, 61, 179

fop.jar, copying, 285, 289

Form model, 168

gareth.jpg, downloading, 303

ImageMap.plist, 47

jar (third party), SOAP (Simple Object Access Protocol) services, 282

link.gif, downloading, 293

locales, examining in Project Builder Inspector, 67

Main class, appendToResponse( ) method (recoding), 256-257

Main.html, editing templates, 6

Main.wo, opening, 21

Main.wod, 6

model, EOModeler fails to see back-relationships, 318

moderator.gif, downloading, 295

moving to Group folder, 36

object models, setting database encoding, 267-268

online forum project, grouping, 238

ProjectBuilder.app, 3

Stripes.svg, downloading, 90

user.gif, downloading, 293

will.jpg, downloading, 303

.woo extension, 229

Find and Replace (Project Builder), 19-20

Flash and SVG (Scalable Vector Graphic), comparing, 89

Flatten Property command (Property menu), 175

flattened relationships in many-to-many relationships, 175-177

FO XML, viewing, 289

FO2PDFSerializer class (PDF documents), 289-290

folders, Group, moving files to, 36

fonts, perfecting Web page presentations, 211

FOP (Apache Formatting Object Processor), 285

fop.jar files, copying, 285, 289

Ford, Henry, 217

foreign keys, 136

formats

Common Log File Format, 260

HTML (Hypertext Markup Language), reformatting, 74

formatters (DirectToWeb), setting, 151-152

formatting topic posts, 278

Formatting Object Processor (FOP), 285

Formatting Objects (XSL), 285-290

forms

dynamic elements, marking up, 11

elements (XHTML), prototyping, 78-79

Feedback, 64-65

Registration form action, binding to Register userAction, 214

values, 95-100, 318

WOForm, adding actions, 12

WOPopupButton, adding, 93

Forms menu commands (WOForm, WOSubmmitButton, WOTextField), 11

Forum

application, adding to WebObjects Monitor, 308-309

deleted objects, testing, 145

Edit Page for Forum, opening, 150

home page, 212, 235

DHTML (Dynamic HTML) charts, 292-295

displaying in Project Builder, 22

moderators, displaying, 295

online forums, 234

in tables, aligning, 38

urlForResourceNamed( ) method, 31

users, displaying, 295

in WebObjects, vending, 30

WOImage, embedded in WOHyperlink, 27

WOMappedRolloverTest project, downloading, 41

graphs

HTML (Hypertext Markup Language), 293-298

objects, resolving in memory, 277-278

greetingAction, 61

Group folder, moving files to, 36

grouping

direct actions, 83

online forum project files, 238

groups

detail display, 169-171

discussion, online documentation, 320

display, configuring for SearchResults page, 225

DisplayGroup applications, creating, 116-119

master-detail display, configuration, 170

queryBindings display, SearchResults page, 226

Groups & Files panel, 5

guidelines for Enterprise Objects, 166

H

handleSessionRestorationErrorInContext( ) method, 246

handling multiple submit with direct actions, 97-98

handling exceptions, 243-246

hasBinding( ) method, 77

hasSession( ) key, 263

headers, SOAP (Simple Object Access Protocol), 272

Hello World application

actions, adding, 12-13

applications, 17-18

background images, setting, 22

component state (memory), 13-17

components, adding keys, 9-10

creating, 4-5

dynamic form elements, 11

elements, binding values, 10-11

Find and Replace (Project Builder), 19-20

frameworks, adding, 21

French version, running, 68

images, adding, 20-21

inputs, 11

Japanese version, running, 69-70

key value coding, 15-16

localized, 322

pages, 12-15

projects, duplicating, 19

renaming, 25

Session variables, moving component states, 17-18

SOAP (Simple Object Access Protocol) applications, building, 273

SVG (Scalable Vector Graphic), 90-91

WOString, 7-9

HelloDirect, 60-62

help

API Web site, 319

Deploying WebObjects Applications Web site, 307

/Developer/Examples/JavaWebObjects/ directory, 321-322

J

Jackson, Janet, 89

Japanese language

Hello World, running, 69-70

strings, adding in WebObjects Builder, 69

support, direct-action applications, 68-69

jar files (third party), SOAP (Simple Object Access Protocol) services, 282

Java

Application.java file, 48

cryptography, 266-270

Cryptography Architecture, 267-268

Debugger, 244-246

exception handling, 243

Sun Java Web site, downloading JavaMail package (SOAP), 282

java.security.MessageDigest class, encryption, 269

JavaBusinessLogic framework (basic object modeling), 322

JavaMail package (SOAP), downloading and installing, 282

JavaScript

alerts, 26-27, 231-232

DHTML (Dynamic HTML) charts, adding interactivity, 293-294

DynamicHello application, 25-27

search (reserved word), 38

WOJavaSript, optimizing DHTML (Dynamic HTML), 35-36

JavaWOExtensions framework, 322

JDBC panel, connecting to databases, 112

Join in Many-to-Many command (Property menu), 177

JOIN tables, creating for many-to-many relationships, 174

jumbles of words, 267

K

key hasSession (Main pages), 199

key value coding, 15-16

keyboard shortcuts

Command+R, 11

Shift+Space, 28

keys

components, adding to, 9-10

databaseEncoding, 267

displaying with WebObjects Builder, 226

foreign, Web site, 136

hasSession( ), 263

mutually exclusive, 77-78

onLoad, binding, 26

onMouseOut, 294

onMouseOver, 294

primary, 174, 179

Propagate Primary Key (Advanced Relationship Inspector), 175

Session variables, 18

src accessor, altering, 77

underscore (_), 226

url (WORedirect), 254

keywords, name (not using as WOComponent key), 318

L

languages. *See also* HTML; XML

French, 66-68

Japanese, 68-70

locales, choosing, 67

preferences, explicitly setting, 70

N

O

project files, grouping, 238

relationships (among Forum, Post, Topic)

to-many relationships, 138-139

to-one relationships, 136-138

Search pages, 222-229

SOAP (Simple Object Access Protocol) services, 275-279

Topic, modeling, 135

Topic Tracker, 271

user profile pages, 235

online resources, SVG (Scalable Vector Graphic), 89

onLoad

key, binding, 26

scripts (JavaScript alerts), 26-27

onMouseOut, 51, 294

onMouseOver, 51, 294

OpenBase Manager, 111, 268

database schema, 210

Pop Idol contestants, 300

opening

Edit Page for Forum, 150

Main.wo file, 21

Search fetch specification in EOModeler, 227

optimizing

components, 41

DHTML (Dynamic HTML), 34-36

fetches with raw rows, 227

object model performance for application prototypes, 180-186

optionality

Mandatory (relationships), 144

setting with Advanced Relationship Inspector, 138

ordering, sort (master-detail configuration), 172

organizing project code, 237-240

outlining

Crazy Eights object model, 110-111

WOCollapsibleListContent, 55

Owns Destination property (relationships), setting, 146

P

<p> tag, 73

Package Definition Files. *See* PDF

packages

Activation or JavaMail (SOAP), downloading and installing, 282

names, appending to Enterprise Objects, 239

page templates, 230-233

pageName binding, deleting, 30

pages. *See* Web pages

pageWithName( ) method, 82

palettes, Premade Elements, 168

panels

client login, securing, 258-259

Groups & Files, 5

Inspector, WOHyperlink, 253

JDBC, connecting to databases, 112

login, 255-259

Run, SQL output, 127

parameters

name, parsing, 274

SOAP (Simple Object Access Protocol), 274-275

parent entities, qualifiers, 161

parentheses ( ), derived attributes, 318

scripts

    AppleScript, SOAP (Simple Object Access Protocol), 273-274

    JavaScript, DHTML charts (adding interactivity), 293-294

    onLoad, JavaScript alerts, 26-27

    WOJavaSript, optimizing DHTML (Dynamic HTML), 35-36

search bars, page templates, 232-233

Search fetch specification, opening and editing in EOModeler, 227

Search pages

    developing, 222

    fetches

        optimizing with raw rows, 227

        specifications, 222-223

    ForumSearch page, 224-229

    SearchResults page, stateless direct actions, 227-229

search (reserved word), 38

SearchBar component, 232

searching documentation, 32

SearchResults page, 225-229

secure http

    applications, 249-251

    logins, 253

secure sockets layer (SSL), 250-251

security

    application logins, 249-255

    BASE64 encoding, 258

    client login panels, 258-259

    developmental certificates, 250

    Java cryptography, 266-270

    Java Cryptography Architecture, algorithms, 268

    java.security.MessageDigest class, encryption, 269

    logins, 253, 258-259

passwords, 268-270

warnings on Internet Explorer 5, 250

WOHyperlink, 253

WORedirect, reverting to nonsecure mode, 253-255

Select Make Localized command (Localization & Platforms), 66

senderEmail method, 101

SenderEmail project, 100

sending

    attachment filenames, 221

    HTML (Hypertext Markup Language) e-mail, 100-102

sentAction method, 101

serializing FO (Formatting Objects) documents, 289-290

servers, SOAP (Simple Object Access Protocol), AppleScript, 273. *See* also Web servers

services, SOAP (Simple Object Access Protocol)

    Activation package, installing, 282

    adding to online forums, 275-279

    currency exchange rate calculations, 280-282

    integrating into applications, 280-282

    jar files (third-party), adding, 282

    JavaMail package, downloading and installing, 282

    objects, resolving in memory, 277-278

    published, 282

    Xmethods Web site, 282

    XML (eXtensible Markup Language) tags inline, viewing in Builder, 279

Session

    creation behavior, 201

    defaultEditingContext, 198, 201

    state, storing on browsers, 203-204

    variables, 17-18

session.languages( ) method, 70

SessionID, storing in cookies, 262-264

X-Y-Z

Hey, you've got enough worries.

Don't let IT training be one of them.

Get on the fast track to IT training at InformIT,
your total Information Technology training network.

 | www.informit.com | S∧MS

■ Hundreds of timely articles on dozens of topics ■ Discounts on IT books from all our publishing partners, including Sams Publishing ■ Free, unabridged books from the InformIT Free Library ■ "Expert Q&A"—our live, online chat with IT experts ■ Faster, easier certification and training from our Web- or classroom-based training programs ■ Current IT news ■ Software downloads ■ Career-enhancing resources

InformIT is a registered trademark of Pearson. Copyright ©2001 by Pearson.
Copyright ©2001 by Sams Publishing.

SAMS DEVELOPER'S LIBRARY

Cookbook   Handbook   Dictionary

PHP
DEVELOPER'S COOKBOOK

Sterling Hughes and
Andrei Zmievski

ISBN: 0-672-32325-7
$39.99 US/$59.95 CAN

PostgreSQL
DEVELOPER'S HANDBOOK

Ewald Geschwinde and
Hans–Jürgen Schönig

ISBN: 0-672-32260-9
$44.99 US/$67.95 CAN

Perl
DEVELOPER'S DICTIONARY

Clinton Pierce

ISBN: 0-672-32067-3
$39.99 US/$59.95 CAN

OTHER DEVELOPER'S LIBRARY TITLES

PHP
DEVELOPER'S DICTIONARY

Allen Wyke,
Michael J. Walker,
and Robert M. Cox

ISBN: 0-672-32029-0
$39.99 US/$59.95 CAN

mod_perl
DEVELOPER'S COOKBOOK

Geoffrey Young,
Paul Linder, and
Randy Kobes

ISBN: 0-672-32240-4
$39.99 US/$62.95 CAN

JavaScript
DEVELOPER'S DICTIONARY

Alexander Vincent

ISBN: 0-672-32201-3
$39.99 US/$59.95 CAN

Python
DEVELOPER'S HANDBOOK

André Lessa

ISBN: 0-672-31994-2
$44.99 US/$67.95 CAN

ALL PRICES ARE SUBJECT TO CHANGE

www.samspublishing.com